Tyson Kopczynski

Windows®
PowerShell

UNLEASHED

 800 East 96th Street, Indianapolis, Indiana 46240 USA

Windows® PowerShell Unleashed

International Standard Book Number: 0-672-32953-0

Library of Congress Cataloging-in-Publication Data

Kopczynski, Tyson.
  Microsoft PowerShell unleashed / Tyson Kopczynski.
        p. cm.
  ISBN 0-672-32953-0
  1. Microsoft Windows (Computer file) 2. Operating systems (Computers) I. Title.

QA76.76.063K66 2007
005.4'46—dc22

2007008894
Printed in the United States of America
First Printing:
10   09   08   07   4   3   2   1

Trademarks

All terms mentioned in this book that are known to be trademarks or service marks have been appropriately capitalized. Sams Publishing cannot attest to the accuracy of this information. Use of a term in this book should not be regarded as affecting the validity of any trademark or service mark.

Warning and Disclaimer

Every effort has been made to make this book as complete and as accurate as possible, but no warranty or fitness is implied. The information provided is on an "as is" basis. The authors and the publisher shall have neither liability nor responsibility to any person or entity with respect to any loss or damages arising from the information contained in this book.

Bulk Sales

Sams Publishing offers excellent discounts on this book when ordered in quantity for bulk purchases or special sales. For more information, please contact

U.S. Corporate and Government Sales
1-800-382-3419
corpsales@pearsontechgroup.com

For sales outside of the U.S., please contact

International Sales
international@pearsoned.com

Editor-in-Chief
Karen Gettman

Senior Acquisitions Editor
Neil Rowe

Development Editor
Mark Renfrow

Managing Editor
Gina Kanouse

Project Editor
George E. Nedeff

Copy Editor
Lisa M. Lord

Senior Indexer
Cheryl Lenser

Proofreader
Water Crest Publishing

Contributing Authors
Pete Handley, Mark Weinhardt, and Josh Tolle

Technical Editor
Pawam Bhardwaj

Publishing Coordinator
Cindy Teeters

Book Designer
Gary Adair

Page Layout
Jake McFarland
Nonie Ratcliff

Contents at a Glance

Table of Contents

About the Author

With more than nine years of experience in the information technology sector, **Tyson Kopczynski** has become a specialist in Active Directory, Group Policy, Windows scripting, Windows Rights Management Services, PKI, and information technology security practices. Tyson has been a contributing author for such books as *Microsoft Internet Security and Acceleration (ISA) Server 2004 Unleashed* and *Microsoft Windows Server 2003 Unleashed (R2 Edition)*. In addition, he has written detailed technical papers and guides covering the various in-the-field technologies he works with extensively. As a consultant at Convergent Computing (CCO), Tyson has been able to work with the next generation of Microsoft technologies since their inception and played a key role in expanding scripting and development practices at CCO. Tyson also holds the SANS Security Essentials Certification (GSEC), Microsoft Certified Systems Engineer (MCSE) Security certification, CompTIA Security+ certification, and SANS Certified Incident Handler (GCIH) certification.

Dedication

I dedicate this book to the love of my life and very understanding wife (Maiko). Without her support, my continuing pursuit of the perfect script surely would have ended in disaster by now.

Acknowledgments

The first of many acknowledgments I would like to make starts with Rand Morimoto. Without his support and guidance, this book would never have gotten off the ground. In addition, I would like to thank Neil Rowe for giving me a chance to do this book and overseeing it to fruition. I'm also grateful to my contributing authors, Pete Handley, Mark Weinhardt, and Josh Tolle, for assisting me with putting the technical aspects of this book together. To the editing team, Pawam Bhardwaj, George Nedeff, Mark Renfrow, and Lisa Lord, I'm deeply indebted to you for the fantastic suggestions and your meticulous work in editing this book. Also, to all my family, friends, and coworkers who have been wondering if I still exist, I was working on a book, not ignoring you!

Last, but not least, I would like to give a huge thanks to the little turtle (PowerShell) that lives in the eBay koi pond. During a project there, I spent many lunch hours watching that little guy and his antics. Although his world was small in size, he obsessively attempted to explore and understand every micron of it. Keep learning, little guy, as will I!

We Want to Hear from You!

As the reader of this book, *you* are our most important critic and commentator. We value your opinion and want to know what we're doing right, what we could do better, what areas you'd like to see us publish in, and any other words of wisdom you're willing to pass our way.

As a senior acquisitions editor for Sams Publishing, I welcome your comments. You can e-mail or write me directly to let me know what you did or didn't like about this book—as well as what we can do to make our books better.

Please note that I cannot help you with technical problems related to the topic of this book. We do have a User Services group, however, where I will forward specific technical questions related to the book.

When you write, please be sure to include this book's title and author as well as your name, e-mail address, and phone number. I will carefully review your comments and share them with the author and editors who worked on the book.

E-mail: feedback@samspublishing.com

Mail: Neil Rowe
            Senior Acquisitions Editor
            Sams Publishing
            800 East 96th Street
            Indianapolis, IN 46240 USA

For more information about this book or another Sams Publishing title, visit our Web site at www.samspublishing.com. Type the ISBN (excluding hyphens) or the title of a book in the Search field to find the page you're looking for.

Introduction

When I first started working on the *PowerShell Unleashed* book, I happened to be reading a book on public key infrastructure (PKI). Although the materials in the book gave good background and reference information about PKI, they lacked details on how to apply PKI in an environment. Applied presentation is a component I have often wished was included in many technical books. With this realization, I decided I would try to approach the subject matter in the PowerShell book in a way different from most other technical books.

The outcome of this realization is the book you're now reading. Although this book contains detailed reference information about what PowerShell is, I made an effort to show readers how PowerShell can be applied to meet their specialized needs. This approach might not be new or groundbreaking, but I hope it helps you gain a unique perspective on one of the most impressive Microsoft products to be recently released.

That last statement is by no means free marketing for Microsoft. The PowerShell team has truly created a shell that's enjoyable, easy, fun, and, yes, powerful. I can't wait to see what's in store for the future of PowerShell and what products will embrace its use.

Who Is This Book's Intended Audience?

This *Unleashed* book is intended for an intermediate level of systems administrators who have invested time and energy in learning Windows scripting and want to translate those skills into PowerShell skills while learning how it can meet their real-world needs. This book has been written so that anyone with a scripting background can understand what PowerShell is and how to use it, but by no means is it meant to be a complete PowerShell reference. Instead, think of it as a resource for learning how PowerShell can be applied in your own environment. Therefore, the structure of this book reflects that focus by including numerous command examples and working scripts.

How This Book Is Organized

The book is divided into the following three parts:

- *Part I, "Introduction to PowerShell"*—This part introduces you to what PowerShell is and how to use it. Topics covered include why PowerShell came into existence, general use of PowerShell, an in-depth review of code signing, and PowerShell best practices.

- *Part II, "Translating Your Existing Knowledge into PowerShell"*—This part dives into a point-by-point comparison of how existing Windows scripting knowledge can be translated to learning PowerShell scripting. Topics covered include working with the Windows file system, Registry, Windows Management Instrumentation (WMI), and Active Directory Services Interfaces (ADSI). To assist you, examples of performing automation tasks and working scripts in both VBScript and PowerShell are included.

- *Part III, "Using PowerShell to Meet Your Automation Needs"*—The goal of this part is to expand on how PowerShell can be used to manage systems. Topics covered include using PowerShell to meet security needs, automating changes across numerous systems, and managing Exchange Server 2007 with PowerShell.

Conventions Used in This Book

Commands, scripts, and anything related to code are presented in a special `monospace` computer typeface. Bolding indicates key terms being defined, and italics are used to indicate variables and sometimes for emphasis. Great care has been taken to be consistent in letter case, naming, and structure, with the goal of making command and script examples more readable. In addition, you might find instances in which commands or scripts haven't been fully optimized. This lack of optimization is for your benefit, as it makes those code samples more intelligible and follows the practice of writing code for others to read. For more details about the layout, conventions, and practices used for commands and scripts in this book, see Chapter 5, "PowerShell Scripting Best Practices."

Other standards used throughout this book are as follows:

Black Code Boxes

```
These code boxes contain commands that run in a PowerShell or Bash
shell session.
```

Gray Code Boxes

```
These code boxes contain source code from scripts, configuration files, or
other items that aren't run directly in a shell session.
```

CAUTION

Cautions alert you to actions that should be avoided.

NOTE

Notes give you additional background information about a topic being discussed.

PART I

Introduction to PowerShell

IN THIS PART

Introduction to Shells and PowerShell

Shells are a necessity when using operating systems because they make it possible to perform arbitrary actions such as traversing the file system, running commands, or using applications. As such, every computer user has dealt with a shell by typing commands at a prompt or by clicking an icon to start an application. Shells are inescapable when you're working on a computer system.

In this chapter, you take a look at what a shell is and see the power that can be harnessed by interacting with one. To do this, you walk through some basic shell commands, and then build a shell script from those basic commands to see how they can become more powerful via scripting. Next, you take a brief tour of how shells have evolved over the past 35 years. Finally, you learn why there was a need for PowerShell and what its inception means to scripters and system administrators.

What Is a Shell?

A **shell** is an interface that allows users to interact with the operating system. A shell isn't considered an application because of its inescapable nature, but it's the same as any other process running on a system. The difference between a shell and an application is that a shell's purpose is to allow users to run other applications. In some operating systems (such as UNIX, Linux, and VMS), the shell is a command-line interface (CLI); in other operating systems (such as Windows and Mac OS X), the shell is a graphical user interface (GUI).

In addition, two types of systems in wide use are often neglected in discussions of shells: networking equipment and kiosks. Networking equipment usually has a GUI shell (mostly a Web interface on consumer-grade equipment) or a CLI shell (in commercial-grade equipment). Kiosks are a whole other animal; because many kiosks are built from applications running atop a more robust operating system, often kiosk interfaces aren't shells. However, if the kiosk is built with an operating system that serves only to run the kiosk, the interface is accurately described as a shell. Unfortunately, kiosk interfaces continue to be referred to generically as shells because of the difficulty in explaining the difference to nontechnical users (which is a virtue that results in the automation of tasks, thereby increasing the efficiency with which tasks are accomplished as well as the accuracy and consistency with which tasks are performed).

Both CLI and GUI shells have benefits and drawbacks. For example, most CLI shells allow powerful command chaining (using commands that feed their output into other commands for further processing; this is commonly referred to as the **pipeline**). GUI shells, however, require commands to be completely self-contained. Furthermore, most GUI shells are easy to navigate, whereas CLI shells require a preexisting knowledge of the system to avoid attempting several commands to discern the location and direction to head in completing an automation task. Your choice of shell depends on what you're comfortable with and what's best suited to perform the task at hand.

Even though GUI shells exist, the term "shell" is used almost exclusively to describe a command-line environment, not a task you perform with a GUI application, such as Windows Explorer. Likewise, shell scripting refers to collecting commands normally entered on the command line or into an executable file.

Basic Shell Use

Many shell commands, such as listing the contents of the current working directory, are simple. However, shells can quickly become complex when more powerful results are required.

The following example lists the contents of the current working directory.

```
$ ls
apache2 bin     etc     include lib     libexec man    sbin    share   var
```

However, often seeing just filenames isn't enough and so a command-line argument needs to be passed to the command to get more details about the files.

> **NOTE**
>
> If these commands are unfamiliar, don't worry. They're here for the sake of illustration, not to teach you the intricacies of the Bash shell.

The following command gives you more detailed information about each file using a
command-line argument.

```
$ ls -l
total 8
drwxr-xr-x    13 root    admin     442 Sep 18 20:50 apache2
drwxrwxr-x    57 root    admin    1938 Sep 19 22:35 bin
drwxrwxr-x     5 root    admin     170 Sep 18 20:50 etc
drwxrwxr-x    30 root    admin    1020 Sep 19 22:30 include
drwxrwxr-x   102 root    admin    3468 Sep 19 22:30 lib
drwxrwxr-x     3 root    admin     102 Sep 18 20:11 libexec
lrwxr-xr-x     1 root    admin       9 Sep 18 20:12 man -> share/man
drwxrwxr-x     3 root    admin     102 Sep 18 20:11 sbin
drwxrwxr-x    13 root    admin     442 Sep 19 22:35 share
drwxrwxr-x     3 root    admin     102 Jul 30 21:05 var
```

Now you need to decide what to do with this information. As you can see, directories are
interspersed with files, making it difficult to tell them apart. If you want to view only
directories, you have to pare down the output by piping the ls command output into the
grep command. In the following example, the output has been filtered to display only
lines starting with the letter *d*, which signifies that the file is a directory.

```
          | grep '^d'
drwxr-xr-x    13 root    admin     442 Sep 18 20:50 apache2
drwxrwxr-x    57 root    admin    1938 Sep 19 22:35 bin
drwxrwxr-x     5 root    admin     170 Sep 18 20:50 etc
drwxrwxr-x    30 root    admin    1020 Sep 19 22:30 include
drwxrwxr-x   102 root    admin    3468 Sep 19 22:30 lib
drwxrwxr-x     3 root    admin     102 Sep 18 20:11 libexec
drwxrwxr-x     3 root    admin     102 Sep 18 20:11 sbin
drwxrwxr-x    13 root    admin     442 Sep 19 22:35 share
drwxrwxr-x     3 root    admin     102 Jul 30 21:05 var
```

However, now that you have only directories listed, the other information like date,
permissions, sized, etc. is superfluous because only the directory names are needed. So in
this next example, you use the awk command to print only the last column of output
shown in the previous example.

```
          | grep '^d' | awk '{ print $NF }'
apache2
bin
etc
include
lib
libexec
sbin
share
var
```

The result is a simple list of directories in the current working directory. This command is fairly straightforward, but it's not something you want to type every time you want to see a list of directories. Instead, we can create an alias or command shortcut for the command that we just executed.

```
$ alias lsd="ls -l | grep '^d' | awk '{ print \$NF }'"
```

Then, by using the lsd alias, you can get a list of directories in the current working directory without having to retype the command from the previous examples.

```
$ lsd
apache2
bin
etc
include
lib
libexec
sbin
share
var
```

As you can see, using a CLI shell offers the potential for serious power when you're automating simple repetitive tasks.

Basic Shell Scripts

Working in a shell typically consists of typing each command, interpreting the output, deciding how to put that data to work, and then combining the commands into a single streamlined process. Anyone who has gone through dozens of files, manually adding a single line at the end of each one, will agree that scripting makes as much sense as breathing.

You've seen how commands can be chained together in a pipeline to manipulate output from the preceding command and how a command can be aliased to minimize typing. Command aliasing is the younger sibling of shell scripting and gives the command line some of the power of shell scripts. However, shell scripts can harness even more power than aliases.

Collecting single-line commands and pipelines into files for later execution is a powerful technique. Putting output into variables for reference later in the script and further manipulation takes the power to the next level. Wrapping any combination of commands into recursive loops and flow control constructs in a sense makes scripting a form of programming.

Some say that scripting isn't programming, but that's not true, especially with the variety and power of scripting languages these days. Shell scripting is no different in that respect, as compiling code doesn't necessarily mean you're programming. With this in mind, try developing your one-line command from the previous section into something more useful.

You have a listing of each directory in the current working directory. Suppose you want a utility to show how much space each directory uses on the disk. The utility you use to show disk usage in Bash does so on a specified directory's entire contents or a directory's overall disk usage in a summary; it also gives use amounts in bytes by default. With all that in mind, if you want to know each directory's disk usage as a freestanding entity, you need to get and display information for each directory, one by one. The following examples show what this process would look like as a script.

Notice the command you worked on in the previous section. The for loop goes through the directory list the command returns, assigning each line to the DIR variable and executing the code between the do and done keywords.

```
#!/bin/bash

for DIR in $(ls -l ¦ grep '^d' ¦ awk '{ print $NF }'); do
    du -sk ${DIR}
done
```

Saving the above code as directory.sh script file and then running the script within a Bash session produces the following output.

```
$ big_directory.sh
17988     apache2
5900      bin
72        etc
2652      include
82264     lib
0         libexec
0         sbin
35648     share
166768    var
```

This output doesn't seem especially helpful. With a few additions, you could get something more useful considering you want to know the names of all directories using more than a certain amount of disk space. To achieve this requirement, modify the directory.sh script file as shown in this next example.

```
#!/bin/bash

PRINT_DIR_MIN=35000

for DIR in $(ls -l | grep '^d' | awk '{ print $NF }'); do
    DIR_SIZE=$(du -sk ${DIR} | cut -f 1)
    if [ ${DIR_SIZE} -ge ${PRINT_DIR_MIN} ];then
        echo ${DIR}
    fi
done
```

Now, you've started adding variables; `PRINT_DIR_MIN` is the minimum number of kilobytes a directory uses to meet the printing criteria. This value could change fairly regularly, so you want to keep it as easily editable as possible. Also, you could reuse this value elsewhere in the script so that you don't have to change the amount in multiple places when the number of kilobytes changes.

You might be thinking the `find` command would be easier to use. However, the reason the convoluted `ls` command is used is that `find` is terrific for browsing through directory structures but too cumbersome for simply viewing the current directory. If you're looking for files in the hierarchy, the `find` command is highly recommended. However, you're simply looking for directories in the current directory because only those directories are relevant in this example.

The following is an example of the output rendered by the script so far.

```
$ big_directory.sh
lib
share
var
```

This output could be used in a number of ways. For example, systems administrators might use this script to watch user directories for disk usage thresholds if they want to notify users when they have reached a certain level of disk space. For this purpose, knowing when a certain percentage of users reaches or crosses the threshold would be useful.

> **NOTE**
>
> Keep in mind that plenty of commercial products on the market notify administrators of overall disk thresholds being met, so although some money could be saved by writing a shell script to monitor overall disk use, it's not necessary. The task of finding how many users have reached a certain use threshold is different, as it involves proactive measures to prevent disk use problems before they get out of control. The solution is notifying the administrator that certain users should be offloaded to new disks

because of growth on the current disk. This approach isn't foolproof but is an easy way to add a layer of proactive monitoring to ensure that users don't encounter problems when using their systems. Systems administrators could get creative and modify this script with command-line parameters to serve several functions, such as listing the top disk space users and indicating when a certain percentage of users have reached the disk threshold. That kind of complexity, however, is beyond the scope of this chapter.

Next, the script is modified to display a message when a certain percentage of directories are a specified size.

```
#!/bin/bash

DIR_MIN_SIZE=35000
DIR_PERCENT_BIG_MAX=23

DIR_COUNTER=0
BIG_DIR_COUNTER=0

for DIR in $(ls -l ¦ grep '^d' ¦ awk '{ print $NF }'); do
    DIR_COUNTER=$(expr ${DIR_COUNTER} + 1)
    DIR_SIZE=$(du -sk ${DIR} ¦ cut -f 1)
    if [ ${DIR_SIZE} -ge ${DIR_MIN_SIZE} ];then
        BIG_DIR_COUNTER=$(expr ${BIG_DIR_COUNTER} + 1)
    fi
done

if [ ${BIG_DIR_COUNTER} -gt 0 ]; then
    DIR_PERCENT_BIG=$(expr $(expr ${BIG_DIR_COUNTER} \* 100) / ${DIR_COUNTER})
    if [ ${DIR_PERCENT_BIG} -gt ${DIR_PERCENT_BIG_MAX} ]; then
        echo "${DIR_PERCENT_BIG} percent of the directories are larger than
${DIR_MIN_SIZE} kilobytes."
    fi
fi
```

Now, the preceding example barely looks like what you started with. The variable name PRINT_DIR_MIN has been changed to DIR_MIN_SIZE because you're not printing anything as a direct result of meeting the minimum size. The DIR_PERCENT_BIG_MAX variable has been added to indicate the maximum allowable percentage of directories at or above the minimum size. Also, two counters have been added: one (DIR_COUNTER) to count the directories and one (BIG_DIR_COUNTER) to count the directories exceeding the minimum size.

Inside the for loop, DIR_COUNTER is incremented, and the if statement in the for loop now simply increments BIG_DIR_COUNTER instead of printing the directory's name. An if statement has been added after the for loop to do additional processing, figure out the percentage of directories exceeding the minimum size, and then print the message if necessary. With these changes, the script now produces the following output:

```
$ big_directory.sh
33 percent of the directories are larger than 35000 kilobytes.
```

The output shows that 33% of the directories are 35MB or more. By modifying the echo line in the script to feed a pipeline into a mail delivery command and tweaking the size and percentage thresholds for the environment, systems administrators could schedule this shell script to run at specified intervals and produce directory size reports easily. If administrators want to get fancy, they could make the size and percentage thresholds configurable via command-line parameters.

As you can see, even a basic shell script can be powerful. With a mere 22 lines of code, you have a useful shell script. Some quirks of the script might seem inconvenient (using the expr command for simple math can be tedious, for example), but every programming language has its strengths and weaknesses. As a rule, some tasks you need to do are convoluted to perform, no matter what language you're using.

The moral is that shell scripting, or scripting in general, can make your life easier. For example, say your company merges with another company. As part of that merger, you have to create 1,000 user accounts in Active Directory or another authentication system. Usually, a systems administrator grabs the list, sits down with a cup of coffee, and starts clicking or typing away. If an administrator manages to get a migration budget, he or she could hire an intern or consultants to do the work or purchase migration software. But why bother performing repetitive tasks or spending money that could be put to better use (such as a bigger salary)?

Instead, the answer should be automating those tasks by using scripting. Automation is the purpose of scripting. As a systems administrator, you should take advantage of scripting with CLI shells or command interpreters to have access to the same functionality developers have when coding the systems you manage. However, scripting is within a platter that tends to be more open, flexible, and focused on the tasks that you as an IT professional need to perform.

A Shell History

The first shell in wide use was the Bourne shell, the standard user interface for the UNIX operating system, and UNIX systems still require it for booting. This robust shell provided pipelines and conditional and recursive command execution. It was developed by C programmers for C programmers.

Oddly, however, despite being written by and for C programmers, the Bourne shell didn't have a C-like coding style. This lack of a similarity to the C language drove the invention of the C shell, which introduced more C-like programming structures. While the C shell inventors were building a better mousetrap, they decided to add command-line editing and command aliasing (defining command shortcuts), which eased the bane of every UNIX user's existence: typing. The less a UNIX user has to type to get results, the better.

Although most UNIX users liked the C shell, learning a completely new shell was a challenge for some. So the Korn shell was invented, which added a number of the C shell features to the Bourne shell. Because the Korn shell is a commercially licensed product, the open-source software movement needed a shell for Linux and FreeBSD. The collaborative result was the Bourne Again Shell, or Bash, invented by the Free Software Foundation.

Throughout the evolution of UNIX and the birth of Linux and FreeBSD, other operating systems were introduced along with their own shells. Digital Equipment Corporation (DEC) introduced Virtual Memory System (VMS) to compete with UNIX on its VAX systems. VMS had a shell called Digital Command Language (DCL) with a verbose syntax, unlike that of its UNIX counterparts. Also, unlike its UNIX counterparts, it wasn't case sensitive nor did it provide pipelines.

Somewhere along the line, the PC was born. IBM took the PC to the business market, and Apple rebranded roughly the same hardware technology and focused on consumers. Microsoft made DOS run on the IBM PC, acting as both kernel and shell and including some features of other shells. (The pipeline syntax was inspired by UNIX shells.)

Following DOS was Windows, which went from application to operating system quickly. Windows introduced a GUI shell, which has become the basis for Microsoft shells ever since. Unfortunately, GUI shells are notoriously difficult to script, so Windows provided a DOSShell-like environment. It was improved with a new executable, `cmd.exe` instead of command.com, and a more robust set of command-line editing features. Regrettably, this change also meant that shell scripts in Windows had to be written in the DOSShell syntax for collecting and executing command groupings.

Over time, Microsoft realized its folly and decided systems administrators should have better ways to manage Windows systems. Windows Script Host (WSH) was introduced in Windows 98, providing a native scripting solution with access to the underpinnings of Windows. It was a library that allowed scripting languages to use Windows in a powerful and efficient manner. WSH is not its own language, however, so a WSH-compliant scripting language was required to take advantage of it, such as JScript, VBScript, Perl, Python, Kixstart, or Object REXX. Some of these languages are quite powerful in performing complex processing, so WSH seemed like a blessing to Windows systems administrators.

However, the rejoicing was short lived because there was no guarantee that the WSH-compliant scripting language you chose would be readily available or a viable option for everyone. The lack of a standard language and environment for writing scripts made it difficult for users and administrators to incorporate automation by using WSH. The only way to be sure the scripting language or WSH version would be compatible on the system being managed was to use a native scripting language, which meant using DOSShell and enduring the problems that accompanied it. In addition, WSH opened a large attack vector for malicious code to run on Windows systems. This vulnerability gave rise to a stream of viruses, worms, and other malicious programs that have wreaked havoc on computer systems, thanks to WSH's focus on automation without user intervention.

The end result was that systems administrators viewed WSH as both a blessing and a curse. Although WSH presented a good object model and access to a number of automation interfaces, it wasn't a shell. It required using `Wscript.exe` and `Cscript.exe`, scripts had to be written in a compatible scripting language, and its attack vulnerabilities posed a security challenge. Clearly, a different approach was needed for systems management; over time, Microsoft reached the same conclusion.

Enter PowerShell

Microsoft didn't put a lot of effort into a CLI shell; instead, it concentrated on a GUI shell, which is more compatible with its GUI-based operating systems. (Mac OS X didn't put any effort into a CLI shell, either; it used the Bash shell.) However, the resulting DOSShell had a variety of limitations, such as conditional and recursive programming structures not being well documented and heavy reliance on `goto` statements. These drawbacks hampered shell scripters for years, and they had to use other scripting languages or write compiled programs to solve common problems.

The introduction of WSH as a standard in the Windows operating system offered a robust alternative to DOSShell scripting. Unfortunately, WSH presented a number of challenges, discussed in the preceding section. Furthermore, WSH didn't offer the CLI shell experience that UNIX and Linux administrators had enjoyed for years, thus resulting in Windows administrators being made fun of by the other chaps for the lack of a CLI shell and its benefits.

Luckily, Jeffrey Snover (the architect of PowerShell) and others on the PowerShell team realized that Windows needed a strong, secure, and robust CLI shell for systems management. Enter PowerShell. PowerShell was designed as a shell with full access to the underpinnings of Windows via the .NET Framework, Component Object Model (COM) objects, and other methods. It also provided an execution environment that's familiar, easy, and secure. PowerShell is aptly named, as it puts the power into the Windows shell. For users wanting to automate their Windows systems, the introduction of PowerShell was exciting because it combined "the power of WSH with the warm-fuzzy familiarity of a shell."

PowerShell provides a powerful native scripting language, so scripts can be ported to all Windows systems without worrying about whether a particular language interpreter is installed. You might have gone through the rigmarole of scripting a solution with WSH in Perl, Python, VBScript, JScript, or another language, only to find that the next system you worked on didn't have that interpreter installed. At home, users can put whatever they want on their systems and maintain them however they see fit, but in a workplace, that option isn't always viable. PowerShell solves that problem by removing the need for non-native interpreters. It also solves the problem of wading through Web sites to find command-line equivalents for simple GUI shell operations and coding them into `.cmd` files. Last, PowerShell addresses the WSH security problem by providing a platform for secure Windows scripting. It focuses on security features such as script signing, lack of executable extensions, and execution policies (which are restricted by default).

For anyone who needs to automate administration tasks on a Windows system, PowerShell provides a much-needed injection of power. Its object-oriented nature boosts the power available to you, too. If you're a Windows systems administrator or scripter, becoming a PowerShell expert is highly recommended.

PowerShell is not just a fluke or a side project at Microsoft. The PowerShell team succeeded at creating an amazing shell and winning support within Microsoft for its creation. For example, the Exchange product team adopted PowerShell as the backbone of the management interface in Exchange Server 2007. That was just the start. Other product groups at Microsoft, such as System Center Operations Manager 2007, System Center Data Protection Manager V2, and System Center Virtual Machine Manager, are being won over by what PowerShell can do for their products.

In fact, PowerShell is the approach Microsoft has been seeking for a general management interface to Windows-based systems. Over time, PowerShell could replace current management interfaces, such as cmd.exe, WSH, CLI tools, and so on, and become integrated into the Windows operating system as its backbone management interface. With the introduction of PowerShell, Microsoft has addressed a need for a strong Windows CLI shell. The sky is the limit for what Windows systems administrators and scripters can achieve with it.

Summary

In summary, this chapter has served as an introduction to what a shell is, where shells came from, how to use a shell, and how to create a basic shell script. While learning these aspects about shells, you have also learned why scripting is so important to systems administrators. As you have come to discover, scripting allows systems administrators to automate repetitive tasks. In doing so, task automation allows systems administrators to perform their jobs more effectively, thus freeing them up to perform more important business enhancing tasks.

In addition, to learning about shells, you have also been introduced to what PowerShell is, and why PowerShell was needed. As explained, PowerShell is the replacement to WSH, which, while powerful, had a number of shortcomings (security and interoperability being the most noteworthy). PowerShell was also needed because Windows lacked a viable CLI that could be used to easily complete complex automation tasks. The end result, for replacing WSH and improving on the Windows CLI, is PowerShell, which is built on the .NET Framework and brings a much-needed injection of backbone to the world of Windows scripting and automation.

CHAPTER 2

PowerShell Basics

Introduction

This chapter brings you up to speed on the technical basics of PowerShell and how to use it. You learn how to download and install PowerShell, work with the PowerShell command-line interface (CLI), use cmdlets, use variables, use aliases, understand scopes, and write a basic script. This chapter isn't intended to be a complete getting-started guide; instead, it covers the important concepts you need to understand for later chapters.

Getting Started

The best way to get started with PowerShell is to visit the Windows PowerShell home page at www.microsoft.com/windowsserver2003/technologies/management/powershell/default.mspx (see Figure 2.1).

This site is a great resource for information about PowerShell, download documentation, tools, and provides access to the latest news, and the latest versions of PowerShell. Your next step is downloading and installing PowerShell, but first, you need to make sure your system meets the following PowerShell installation requirements:

- Windows XP Service Pack 2, Windows 2003 Service Pack 1, or later versions of Windows

- Microsoft .NET Framework 2.0

If .NET Framework 2.0 is not installed on your machine, you can download its installation package from the Microsoft Download Center at www.microsoft.com/downloads/ (see Figure 2.2).

FIGURE 2.1   The Microsoft Windows PowerShell home page

FIGURE 2.2   The Microsoft Download Center

After installing .NET Framework 2.0, your next step is downloading the PowerShell instal-lation package from www.microsoft.com/windowsserver2003/technologies/management/powershell/download.mspx (see Figure 2.3).

To install PowerShell, on the download page, find the correct PowerShell installation package for your x86 or x64 version of Windows. Then download the PowerShell installation package by clicking the appropriate download link. Next, start the

PowerShell installation by clicking Open in the download box or double-clicking the installation file. (The filename differs depending on the platform, Windows version, and language pack.) After the installer has started, follow the installation instructions.

FIGURE 2.3   Download Windows PowerShell 1.0

Another installation method is a silent installation at the command line, using the /quiet switch with the PowerShell installation filename. This installation method can be useful if you plan to install PowerShell on many different systems and want to distribute the installation via a logon script, Systems Management Server (SMS), or another software management method. To perform a silent installation, follow these steps:

1. Click **Start** > **Run**.

2. Type **cmd** and click **OK** to open a cmd command prompt.

3. Type ***PowerShell-exe-filename*_/quiet** (replacing the italicized text with the PowerShell installation filename) and press **Enter**.

Accessing PowerShell

After installing PowerShell, you can access it with three methods. To use the first method of accessing it from the Start menu, follow these steps:

1. Click **Start** > **All Programs** > **Windows PowerShell 1.0**.

2. Click **Windows PowerShell**.

To use the second method, follow these steps:

1. Click **Start** > **Run**.

2. Type **PowerShell** in the Run dialog box and click **OK**.

Both these methods open the PowerShell console, shown in Figure 2.4.

FIGURE 2.4   The PowerShell console

Follow these steps to use the third method from a cmd command prompt:

1. Click **Start** > **Run**.

2. Type **cmd** and click **OK** to open a cmd command prompt.

3. At the command prompt, type **powershell**, as shown in Figure 2.5, and press **Enter**.

FIGURE 2.5   The PowerShell console launched through the cmd command prompt

Understanding the Command-Line Interface (CLI)

The syntax for using PowerShell from the CLI is similar to the syntax for other CLI shells. The fundamental component of a PowerShell command is, of course, the name of the command to be executed. In addition, the command can be made more specific by using parameters and arguments for parameters. Therefore, a PowerShell command can have the following formats:

```
[command name]
[command name] -[parameter]
[command name] -[parameter] -[parameter] [argument1]
[command name] -[parameter] -[parameter] [argument1],[argument2]
```

> **NOTE**
>
> In PowerShell, a **parameter** is a variable that can be accepted by a command, script, or function. An **argument** is a value assigned to a parameter. Although these terms are often used interchangeably, remembering these definitions is helpful when discussing their use in PowerShell.

You can see an example of using a command, a parameter, and an argument by running the dir command with the /w parameter (which displays the output of dir in a wide format) and an argument of C:\temp*.txt, as shown here:

```
C:\>dir /w C:\temp*.txt
 Volume in drive C is OS
 Volume Serial Number is 1784-ADF9

 Directory of C:\temp

Bad Stuff.txt    mediapc.txt        note.txt          Progress.txt
                 4 File(s)            953 bytes
                 0 Dir(s)  16,789,958,656 bytes free

C:\>
```

The result of this command is a wide-format directory listing of all the .txt files in C:\temp. If you use the dir command without any parameters or arguments, the outcome would be entirely different. The same result happens with PowerShell. For example, here is a basic PowerShell command that gets process information about explorer.exe:

```
PS C:\> get-process -Name explorer

Handles  NPM(K)    PM(K)      WS(K) VM(M)   CPU(s)     Id ProcessName
-------  ------    -----      ----- -----   ------     -- -----------
    807      20    31672      14068   149    62.95   1280 explorer

PS C:\>
```

In this example, Get-Process is the command, -Name is the parameter, and explorer is the argument. The result of this command is process information about explorer.exe. If no parameters or arguments are used, the Get-Process command just lists process information about all currently running processes, not information about a specific process. To have control over what a command does or have it perform more than its default action, you need to understand the command's syntax. To use commands effectively in the CLI, use the Get-Help command, discussed later in "Useful cmdlets," to get detailed information about what a command does and its use requirements.

Navigating the CLI

As with all CLI-based shells, you need to understand how to navigate the PowerShell CLI to use it effectively. Table 2.1 lists the editing operations associated with various keys when using the PowerShell console.

TABLE 2.1   PowerShell Console Editing Features

Keys	Editing Operation
Left and right arrows	Moves the cursor left and right through the current command line.
Up and down arrows	Move up and down through the list of recently typed commands.
Insert	Switches between insert and overstrike text-entry modes.
Delete	Deletes the character at the current cursor position.
Backspace	Deletes the character immediately preceding the current cursor position.
F7	Displays a list of recently typed commands in a pop-up window in the command shell. Use the up and down arrows to select a previously typed command, and then press Enter to execute the selected command.
Tab	Auto-completes command-line sequences. Use the Shift+Tab sequence to move backward through a list of potential matches.

Luckily, most of the features in Table 2.1 are native to the cmd command prompt, which makes PowerShell adoption easier for administrators already familiar with the Windows command line. The only major difference is that the Tab key auto-completion is enhanced in PowerShell beyond what's available with the cmd command prompt.

As with the cmd command prompt, PowerShell performs auto-completion for file and directory names. So if you enter a partial file or directory name and press Tab, PowerShell returns the first matching file or directory name in the current directory. Pressing Tab again returns a second possible match and allows you to cycle through the list of results. Like the cmd command prompt, PowerShell's Tab key auto-completion can also auto-complete with wild cards, as shown in this example:

```
PS C:\< cd C:\Doc*
<tab>
PS C:\> cd 'C:\Documents and Settings'
PS C:\Documents and Settings>
```

The difference between Tab key auto-completion in cmd and PowerShell is that PowerShell can auto-complete commands. For example, you can enter a partial command name and press the Tab key, and PowerShell steps through a list of possible command matches, as shown here:

```
PS C:\> get-pro
<tab>
PS C:\> get-process
```

PowerShell can also auto-complete parameter names associated with a particular command. Simply enter a command and partial parameter name and press the Tab key, and PowerShell cycles through the parameters for the command you have specified. This method also works for variables associated with a command. In addition, PowerShell performs auto-completion for methods and properties of variables and objects. Take a look at an example using a variable named $Z set to the value "Variable":

```
PS C:\> $Z = "Variable"
PS C:\> $Z.<tab>
```

After you type $Z and press the Tab key, PowerShell cycles through the possible operations that can be performed against the $Z variable. For example, if you select the $Z.Length property and press Enter, PowerShell returns the length of the string in the $Z variable, as shown here:

```
PS C:\> $Z = "Variable"
PS C:\> $Z.
<tab>
PS C:\> $Z.Length
8
PS C:\
```

The auto-complete function for variables distinguishes between **properties** and **methods**. Properties are listed without an open parenthesis (as in the preceding $Z.Length example), and methods are listed with an open parenthesis, as shown in this example:

```
PS C:\> $Z = "Variable"
PS C:\> $Z.con
<tab>
PS C:\> $Z.Contains(
```

When the $Z.Contains(prompt appears, you can use this method to query whether the $Z variable contains the character V by entering the following command:

```
PS C:\> $Z = "Variable"
PS C:\> $Z.Contains("V")
True
PS C:\
```

PowerShell corrects capitalization for the method or property name to match its definition. For the most part, this functionality is cosmetic because by default, PowerShell is not case sensitive.

PowerShell Command Types

When you execute a command in PowerShell, the command interpreter looks at the command name to figure out what task to perform. This process includes determining the type of command and how to process that command. There are four types of PowerShell commands: cmdlets, shell function commands, script commands, and native commands.

cmdlet

The first command type is a **cmdlet** (pronounced "command-let"), which is similar to the built-in commands in other CLI-based shells. The difference is that cmdlets are implemented by using .NET classes compiled into a dynamic link library (DLL) and loaded into PowerShell at runtime. This difference means there's no fixed class of built-in cmdlets; anyone can use the PowerShell Software Developers Kit (SDK) to write a custom cmdlet, thus extending PowerShell's functionality.

A cmdlet is always named as a verb and noun pair separated by a - (hyphen). The verb specifies the action the cmdlet performs, and the noun specifies the object being operated on. More details on cmdlets and cmdlet syntax are covered later in "Understanding cmdlets."

Shell Function Commands

The next type of command is a **shell function command**. Shell function commands provide a way to assign a name to a list of commands. Functions are similar to subroutines and procedures in other programming languages. The main difference between a script and a function is that a new instance of the shell is started for each shell script, and functions run in the current instance of the same shell. Here's an example of defining a simple function in PowerShell:

```
PS C:\> function my-dir-function {get-childitem | ft Mode,Name}
```

After my-dir-function has been defined, it yields a formatted listing for the current directory, as shown in this example:

```
PS C:\Stuff> my-dir-function

Mode                              Name
----                              ----
d----                             Books
d----                             Dev
d----                             Tools
d----                             VMs
-a---                             Bad Stuff.txt
-a---                             Configuring Credential Roaming.doc
-a---                             mediapc.txt


PS C:\Stuff>
```

You can see how PowerShell is executing an existing function in the current console session by enabling debug logging. To do this, use the following command:

```
PS C:\Stuff> set-psdebug -trace 2
```

Next, execute the function:

```
PS D:\Stuff> my-dir-function
DEBUG:      1+ my-dir-function
DEBUG:       ! CALL function 'my-dir-function'
DEBUG:      1+ function my-dir-function {get-childitem | ft Mode,Name}
...
```

When the my-dir-function function is pushed onto the stack, PowerShell runs the Get-ChildItem cmdlet as specified in the function. To turn off PowerShell debugging, enter the Set-PSDebug -trace 0 command.

NOTE

Functions defined at the command line (as with my-dir-function) remain in effect only during the current PowerShell session. They are also local in scope and don't apply to new PowerShell sessions. For more information, see "Understanding Scopes" later in this chapter.

Although a function defined at the command line is a useful way to create a series of commands dynamically in the PowerShell environment, these functions reside only in memory and are erased when PowerShell is closed and restarted. Therefore, although creating complex functions dynamically is possible, writing these functions as a set of script commands might be more practical.

Script Commands

Script commands, the third command type, are PowerShell commands stored in a .ps1 file. The main difference from shell function commands is that script commands are stored on disk and can be accessed any time, unlike shell function commands that don't persist across PowerShell sessions.

Script commands can be run in a PowerShell session or at the cmd command prompt. To run a script in a PowerShell session, type the script name without the extension. The script name can be followed by any parameters. The shell then executes the first .ps1 file matching the typed name in any of the paths located in the PowerShell $ENV:PATH variable.

```
PS C:\> myscript arg1 arg2
```

The preceding command runs the myscript.ps1 script using the arg1 and arg2 arguments if the script is located in any of the paths located in the PowerShell $ENV:PATH variable. If not, you must specify where the script is by using one of these two methods:

```
PS C:\> & 'C:\My Scripts\myscript.ps1' arg1 arg2
PS C:\Scripts> .\myscript.ps1 arg1 arg2
```

NOTE

The & call operator is used in the preceding example because the script path has spaces that requires the script name to be encapsulated in quotes. This operator instructs the shell to evaluate the string as a command. If the path doesn't have spaces, you can omit the & call operator and the quotes from the script name.

To run a PowerShell script from a cmd command prompt, first use the cd command to change to the directory where the script is located. Then run the PowerShell executable with the -command parameter and specify which script to be run, as shown here:

```
C:\Scripts>powershell -command .\myscript.ps1
```

If you don't want to change to the script's directory with the cd command, you can also
run it by using an absolute path, as shown in this example:

```
C:\>powershell -command C:\Scripts\myscript.ps1
```

An important detail about script commands in PowerShell concerns their default security
restrictions. By default, scripts are not enabled to run as a method of protection against
malicious scripts. You can control this policy with the Set-ExecutionPolicy cmdlet,
which is explained in Chapter 3, "PowerShell: A More In-Depth Look."

Native Commands

The last type of command, a **native command**, consists of external programs that the
operating system can run. Because a new process must be created to run native
commands, they are less efficient than other types of PowerShell commands. Native
commands also have their own parameters for processing commands, which are usually
different from PowerShell parameters.

One serious usability concern is the way PowerShell handles the focus for native
commands. When a native command runs, PowerShell might wait for the command to
finish or continue processing. Take a look at this example:

```
PS C:\> .\myfile.txt
PS C:\>
```

The PowerShell prompt returns almost immediately, and the default editor for files with
the .txt extension starts and displays C:\myfile.txt. In this case, notepad.exe starts and
opens the C:\myfile.txt file if you haven't changed the default text editor.

> **NOTE**
>
> PowerShell has a unique security feature. To run or open a file from the current direc-
> tory, you must prefix the command with .\ or ./. This security feature prevents
> PowerShell users from accidentally running a native command or script without specify-
> ing its execution explicitly.

The same behavior occurs when specifying native commands explicitly, as in the following command:

```
PS C:\> notepad C:\myfile.txt
PS C:\>
```

In this example, the `C:\myfile.txt` file is opened in Notepad, and the PowerShell prompt is returned immediately. However, when you run a native command in the middle of a pipeline (described in Chapter 1, "Introduction to Shells and PowerShell"), PowerShell waits for the external process to stop before returning control to the console, as in this example:

```
PS C:\> ping myserver | findstr "TTL"
Reply from 10.0.0.2: bytes=32 time<1ms TTL=126
Reply from 10.0.0.2: bytes=32 time<1ms TTL=126
Reply from 10.0.0.2: bytes=32 time<1ms TTL=126
Reply from 10.0.0.2: bytes=32 time<1ms TTL=126
PS C:\>
```

PowerShell waits for the `ping` process to stop before returning control to the console and finishing the pipeline. When this command is entered (replacing `myserver` with a valid host on your local network), the PowerShell prompt briefly disappears as the output of the `ping` command is piped to the `findstr` command to look for the string `"TTL"`. The PowerShell prompt is returned only when the native command has stopped processing.

Calling PowerShell from Other Shells

In addition to the command-line functionality of PowerShell you've been exploring, you can call PowerShell from other shells, such as the cmd command prompt. When you call PowerShell as an external application, you can make use of a wide variety of supported commands, parameters, and arguments. The following command example lists all of the commands, parameters, and arguments when PowerShell is used from the cmd command prompt:

```
C:\>powershell -?

powershell[.exe] [-PSConsoleFile <file> | -Version <version>]
    [-NoLogo] [-NoExit] [-NoProfile] [-NonInteractive]
    [-OutputFormat {Text | XML}] [-InputFormat {Text | XML}]
    [-Command { - | <script-block> [-args <arg-array>]
                  | <string> [<CommandParameters>] } ]

powershell[.exe] -Help | -? | /?


-PSConsoleFile
    Loads the specified Windows PowerShell console file. To create a console
    file, use Export-Console in Windows PowerShell.

-Version
    Starts the specified version of Windows PowerShell.

-NoLogo
    Hides the copyright banner at startup.
```

2

```
-NoExit
    Does not exit after running startup commands.

-NoProfile
    Does not use the user profile.

-Noninteractive
    Does not present an interactive prompt to the user.

-OutputFormat
    Determines how output from Windows PowerShell is formatted. Valid values
    are "Text" (text strings) or "XML" (serialized CLIXML format).

-InputFormat
    Describes the format of data sent to Windows PowerShell. Valid values are
    "Text" (text strings) or "XML" (serialized CLIXML format).

-Command
    Executes the specified commands (and any parameters) as though they were
    typed at the Windows PowerShell command prompt, and then exits, unless
    NoExit is specified. The value of Command can be "-", a string. or a
    script block.

    If the value of Command is "-", the command text is read from standard
    input.

    Script blocks must be enclosed in braces ({}). You can specify a script
    block only when running PowerShell.exe in Windows PowerShell. The results
    of the script are returned to the parent shell as deserialized XML objects,
    not live objects.

    If the value of Command is a string, Command must be the last parameter
    in the command , because any characters typed after the command are
    interpreted as the command arguments.
        To write a string that runs a Windows PowerShell command, use the format:

        "& {<command>}"
    where the quotation marks indicate a string and the invoke operator (&)
    causes the command to be executed.

-Help, -?, /?
    Shows this message. If you are typing a powershell.exe command in Windows
    PowerShell, prepend the command parameters with a hyphen (-), not a forward
    slash (/). You can use either a hyphen or forward slash in Cmd.exe.


EXAMPLES
    powershell -psconsolefile sqlsnapin.psc1
    powershell -version 1.0 -nologo -inputformat text -outputformat XML
    powershell -command {get-eventlog -logname security}
    powershell -command "& {get-eventlog -logname security}"


C:\>
```

One useful way to take advantage of this capability is to run PowerShell commands from a cmd command prompt. When PowerShell is called with the `-command` parameter, PowerShell scripts or other cmdlets and commands can be used as arguments to the `-command` parameter. The following example shows PowerShell being called from a cmd command prompt, executing a `Get-Service` cmdlet, selecting the services currently in the `Running` state, and then sorting the results by the service's `DisplayName`. The entire command string is enclosed in quotation marks to prevent cmd from attempting to handle the pipeline.

```
C:\>powershell.exe -command "get-service | where-object {$_.Status -eq
'Running'} | sort DisplayName"

Status   Name                DisplayName
------   ----                -----------
Running  ALG                 Application Layer Gateway Service
Running  wuauserv            Automatic Updates
Running  EventSystem         COM+ Event System
Running  CryptSvc            Cryptographic Services
Running  DcomLaunch          DCOM Server Process Launcher
Running  Dhcp                DHCP Client
Running  Dnscache            DNS Client
Running  ERSvc               Error Reporting Service
Running  Eventlog            Event Log
Running  helpsvc             Help and Support
Running  IISADMIN            IIS Admin
Running  PolicyAgent         IPSEC Services
Running  dmserver            Logical Disk Manager
Running  MDM                 Machine Debug Manager
Running  McAfeeFramework     McAfee Framework Service
Running  Messenger           Messenger
Running  MSExchangeMGMT      Microsoft Exchange Management
Running  Netlogon            Net Logon
Running  McShield            Network Associates McShield
Running  McTaskManager       Network Associates Task Manager
Running  Netman              Network Connections
Running  Nla                 Network Location Awareness (NLA)
Running  OracleMTSRecove...  OracleMTSRecoveryService
Running  PlugPlay            Plug and Play
Running  Spooler             Print Spooler
Running  ProtectedStorage    Protected Storage
Running  RasMan              Remote Access Connection Manager
Running  RpcSs               Remote Procedure Call (RPC)
Running  RemoteRegistry      Remote Registry
Running  seclogon            Secondary Logon
Running  SamSs               Security Accounts Manager
Running  lanmanserver        Server
Running  ShellHWDetection    Shell Hardware Detection
Running  SMTPSVC             Simple Mail Transfer Protocol (SMTP)
Running  SSDPSRV             SSDP Discovery Service
Running  SENS                System Event Notification
Running  srservice           System Restore Service
Running  Schedule            Task Scheduler
```

```
Running  LmHosts             TCP/IP NetBIOS Helper
Running  TapiSrv             Telephony
Running  TermService         Terminal Services
Running  Themes              Themes
Running  WebClient           WebClient
Running  AudioSrv            Windows Audio
Running  SharedAccess        Windows Firewall/Internet Connectio...
Running  winmgmt             Windows Management Instrumentation
Running  W32Time             Windows Time
Running  WZCSVC              Wireless Zero Configuration
Running  lanmanworkstation   Workstation
Running  W3SVC               World Wide Web Publishing
```

Understanding cmdlets

cmdlets are a fundamental part of PowerShell's functionality. They are implemented as managed classes (built on the .NET Framework) that include a well-defined set of methods to process data. A cmdlet developer writes the code that runs when the cmdlet is called and compiles the code into a DLL that's loaded into a PowerShell instance when the shell is started.

cmdlets are always named with the format Verb-Noun where the verb specifies the action and the noun specifies the object to operate on. As you might have noticed, most PowerShell names are singular, not plural, to make PowerShell more universally usable. This is done because a command might provide a value or a set of values, and there's no way to know ahead of time whether a cmdlet name should be plural. Also, the English language is inconsistent in dealing with plurals. For example, the word *fish* can be singular or plural, depending on the context. If English isn't your first language, figuring out what's supposed to be plural or the correct plural form could be daunting.

NOTE

The default PowerShell verb is Get, which is assumed if no other verb is given. The effect of this default setting is that the Process command produces the same results as Get-Process.

To determine the parameters a cmdlet supports, you can review the help information for the cmdlet by using either of the following commands:

```
PS C:\> cmdletName -?
PS C:\> get-help cmdletName
```

Furthermore, you can use the Get-Command cmdlet to determine what parameters are available and how they are used. Here's an example of the syntax:

```
PS C:\> get-command cmdletName
```

When working with the Get-Command cmdlet, piping its output to the Format-List cmdlet produces a more concise list of the cmdlet's use. For example, to display just the definition information for Get-Process, use the following command:

```
PS C:\> get-command get-process | format-list Definition

Definition : Get-Process [[-Name] <String[]>] [-Verbose] [-Debug]
[-ErrorAction
               <ActionPreference>] [-ErrorVariable <String>]
[-OutVariable <String>] [-OutBuffer <Int32>]
            Get-Process -Id <Int32[]> [-Verbose] [-Debug]
[-ErrorAction <ActionPreference>] [-ErrorVariable <String>]
[-OutVariable <String>] [-OutBuffer <Int32>]
            Get-Process -InputObject <Process[]> [-Verbose] [-Debug]
[-ErrorAction <ActionPreference>] [-ErrorVariable <String>]
[-OutVariable <String>] [-OutBuffer <Int32>]


PS C:\>
```

Common Parameters

Because cmdlets derive from a base class, a number of **common parameters**, which are available to all cmdlets, can be used to help provide a more consistent interface for PowerShell cmdlets. These common parameters are described in Table 2.2.

TABLE 2.2   PowerShell Common Parameters

Parameter	Data Type	Description
Verbose	Boolean	Generates detailed information about the operation, much like tracing or a transaction log. This parameter is effective only in cmdlets that generate verbose data.
Debug	Boolean	Generates programmer-level detail about the operation. The cmdlet must support the generation of debug data for this parameter to be effective.
ErrorAction	Enum	Determines how the cmdlet responds when an error occurs. Values are Continue (the default), Stop, SilentlyContinue, and Inquire.

Parameter	Data Type	Description
ErrorVariable	String	Specifies a variable that stores errors from the command during processing. This variable is populated in addition to $error.
OutVariable	String	Specifies a variable that stores output from the command during processing.
OutBuffer	Int32	Determines the number of objects to buffer before calling the next cmdlet in the pipeline.
WhatIf	Boolean	Explains what happens if the command is executed but doesn't actually execute the command.
Confirm	Boolean	Prompts the user for permission before performing any action that modifies the system.

NOTE

The last two parameters in Table 2.2, WhatIf and Confirm, are special, in that they require a cmdlet to support the .NET method ShouldProcess, which might not be true for all cmdlets. The ShouldProcess method confirms the operation with the user, sending the name of the resource to be changed for confirmation before performing the operation.

Useful cmdlets

When you're getting started with PowerShell, the Get-Help and Get-Command cmdlets are extremely useful. These two cmdlets, described in the following sections, help you explore what PowerShell does and learn more about the commands you can run.

Get-Help

As you might expect, you use the Get-Help cmdlet to retrieve help information about cmdlets and other topics. To display a list of all help topics, enter Get-Help * at the PowerShell command prompt, as shown here:

```
PS C:\> get-help *

Name                    Category                Synopsis
----                    --------                --------
ac                      Alias                   Add-Content
asnp                    Alias                   Add-PSSnapin
clc                     Alias                   Clear-Content
cli                     Alias                   Clear-Item
clp                     Alias                   Clear-ItemProperty
clv                     Alias                   Clear-Variable
cpi                     Alias                   Copy-Item
cpp                     Alias                   Copy-ItemProperty
cvpa                    Alias                   Convert-Path
```

```
diff                Alias           Compare-Object
epal                Alias           Export-Alias
epcsv               Alias           Export-Csv
fc                  Alias           Format-Custom
fl                  Alias           Format-List
foreach             Alias           ForEach-Object
...
Get-Command         Cmdlet          Gets basic information...
Get-Help            Cmdlet          Displays information a...
Get-History         Cmdlet          Gets a list of the com...
Invoke-History      Cmdlet          Runs commands from the...
Add-History         Cmdlet          Appends entries to the...
ForEach-Object      Cmdlet          Performs an operation ...
Where-Object        Cmdlet          Creates a filter that ...
Set-PSDebug         Cmdlet          Turns script debugging...
Add-PSSnapin        Cmdlet          Adds one or more Windo...
Remove-PSSnapin     Cmdlet          Removes Windows PowerS...
Get-PSSnapin        Cmdlet          Gets the Windows Power...
Export-Console      Cmdlet          Exports the configurat...
Start-Transcript    Cmdlet          Creates a record of al...
Stop-Transcript     Cmdlet          Stops a transcript.
Add-Content         Cmdlet          Adds content to the sp...
Clear-Content       Cmdlet          Deletes the contents o...
Clear-ItemProperty  Cmdlet          Deletes the value of a...
Join-Path           Cmdlet          Combines a path and ch...
Convert-Path        Cmdlet          Converts a path from a...
Copy-ItemProperty   Cmdlet          Copies a property and ...
Get-EventLog        Cmdlet          Gets information about...
Get-ChildItem       Cmdlet          Gets the items and chi...
Get-Content         Cmdlet          Gets the content of th...
Get-ItemProperty    Cmdlet          Retrieves the properti...
Get-WmiObject       Cmdlet          Gets instances of WMI ...
Move-ItemProperty   Cmdlet          Moves a property from ...
Get-Location        Cmdlet          Gets information about...
Set-Location        Cmdlet          Sets the current worki...
Push-Location       Cmdlet          Pushes the current loc...
Pop-Location        Cmdlet          Changes the current lo...
New-PSDrive         Cmdlet          Installs a new Windows...
Remove-PSDrive      Cmdlet          Removes a Windows Powe...
Get-PSDrive         Cmdlet          Gets information about...
...
Alias               Provider        Provides access to the...
Environment         Provider        Provides access to the...
FileSystem          Provider        The PowerShell Provide...
Function            Provider        Provides access to the...
Registry            Provider        Provides access to the...
Variable            Provider        Provides access to the...
Certificate         Provider        Provides access to X50...
about_alias         HelpFile        Using alternate names ...
```

```
about_arithmetic_operators     HelpFile     Operators that can be ...
about_array                    HelpFile     A compact data structu...
about_assignment_operators     HelpFile     Operators that can be ...
about_associative_array        HelpFile     A compact data structu...
about_automatic_variables      HelpFile     Variables automaticall...
about_break                    HelpFile     A statement for immedi...
about_command_search           HelpFile     How the Windows PowerS...
about_command_syntax           HelpFile     Command format in the ...
about_commonparameters         HelpFile     Parameters that every ...
about_comparison_operators     HelpFile     Operators that can be ...
about_continue                 HelpFile     Immediately return to ...
about_core_commands            HelpFile     Windows PowerShell cor...
about_display.xml              HelpFile     Controlling how object...
about_environment_variable     HelpFile     How to access Windows ...
...

PS C:\>
```

If that list seems too large to work with, you can shorten it by filtering on topic name and category. For example, to get a list of all cmdlets starting with the verb Get, try the command shown in the following example:

```
PS C:\> get-help -Name get-* -Category cmdlet

Name                 Category          Synopsis
----                 --------          --------
Get-Command          Cmdlet            Gets basic information...
Get-Help             Cmdlet            Displays information a...
Get-History          Cmdlet            Gets a list of the com...
Get-PSSnapin         Cmdlet            Gets the Windows Power...
Get-EventLog         Cmdlet            Gets information about...
Get-ChildItem        Cmdlet            Gets the items and chi...
Get-Content          Cmdlet            Gets the content of th...
...

PS C:\>
```

After you have selected a help topic, you can retrieve the help information by using the topic name as the parameter to the Get-Help cmdlet. For example, to retrieve help for the Get-Content cmdlet, enter the following command:

```
PS C:\> get-help get-content
```

> **NOTE**
>
> In Windows PowerShell RC2, two parameters were added for the `get-help` cmdlet: `-detailed` and `-full`. The `-detailed` parameter displays additional information about a cmdlet, including descriptions of parameters and examples of using the cmdlet. The `-full` parameter displays the entire help file for a cmdlet, including technical information about parameters.

cmdlet Help Topics

PowerShell help is divided into sections for each cmdlet. Table 2.3 describes the help details for each cmdlet.

TABLE 2.3   PowerShell Help Sections

Help Section	Description
Name	The name of the cmdlet
Synopsis	A brief description of what the cmdlet does
Detailed Description	A detailed description of the cmdlet's behavior, usually including usage examples
Syntax	Specific usage details for entering commands with the cmdlet
Parameters	Valid parameters that can be used with this cmdlet
Input Type	The type of input this cmdlet accepts
Return Type	The type of data that the cmdlet returns
Terminating Errors	If present, identifies any errors that result in the cmdlet terminating prematurely
Non-Terminating Errors	Identifies noncritical errors that might occur while the cmdlet is running but don't cause the cmdlet to terminate its operation.
Notes	Additional detailed information on using the cmdlet, including specific scenarios and possible limitations or idiosyncrasies
Examples	Common usage examples for the cmdlet
Related Links	References other cmdlets that perform similar tasks

Get-Command

Another helpful cmdlet is `Get-Command`, used to list all available cmdlets in a PowerShell session:

```
PS C:\> get-command

CommandType       Name                    Definition
-----------       ----                    ----------
Cmdlet            Add-Content             Add-Content [-Path] <String[...
Cmdlet            Add-History            Add-History [[-InputObject] ...
Cmdlet            Add-Member             Add-Member [-MemberType] <PS...
Cmdlet            Add-PSSnapin           Add-PSSnapin [-Name] <String...
Cmdlet            Clear-Content          Clear-Content [-Path] <Strin...
```

```
Cmdlet              Clear-Item              Clear-Item [-Path] <String[]...
Cmdlet              Clear-ItemProperty      Clear-ItemProperty [-Path] <...
Cmdlet              Clear-Variable          Clear-Variable [-Name] <Stri...
Cmdlet              Compare-Object          Compare-Object [-ReferenceOb...
...

PS C:\>
```

The Get-Command cmdlet is more powerful than Get-Help because it lists all available commands (cmdlets, scripts, aliases, functions, and native applications) in a PowerShell session, as shown in this example:

```
PS C:\ get-command note*

CommandType     Name            Definition
-----------     ----            ----------
Application     NOTEPAD.EXE     C:\WINDOWS\NOTEPAD.EXE
Application     notepad.exe     C:\WINDOWS\system32\notepad.exe


PS C:\>
```

When using Get-Command with elements other than cmdlets, the information returned is a little different from information you see for a cmdlet. For example, with an existing application, the value of the Definition property is the path to the application. However, other information about the application is also available, as shown here:

```
PS C:\> get-command ipconfig | format-list *
FileVersionInfo : File:            C:\WINDOWS\system32\ipconfig.exe
                  InternalName:    ipconfig.exe
                  OriginalFilename: ipconfig.exe
                  FileVersion:     5.1.2600.2180
                                   (xpsp_sp2_rtm.040803-2158)
                  FileDescription: IP Configuration Utility
                  Product:         Microsoft© Windows© Operating
                                   System
                  ProductVersion:  5.1.2600.2180
                  Debug:           False
                  Patched:         False
                  PreRelease:      False
                  PrivateBuild:    False
                  SpecialBuild:    False
                  Language:        English (United States)

Path            : C:\WINDOWS\system32\ipconfig.exe
Extension       : .exe
Definition      : C:\WINDOWS\system32\ipconfig.exe
Name            : ipconfig.exe
CommandType     : Application
```

With a function, the `Definition` property is the body of the function:

```
PS C:\> get-command Prompt

CommandType     Name                      Definition
-----------     ----                      ----------
Function        prompt                    Write-Host ("PS " + $(Get-Lo...


PS C:\>
```

With an alias, the `Definition` property is the aliased command:

```
PS C:\> get-command write

CommandType     Name                           Definition
-----------     ----                           ----------
Alias           write                          Write-Output


PS C:\>
```

With a script file, the `Definition` property is the path to the script. With a non-PowerShell script (such as a `.bat` or `.vbs` file), the information returned is the same as other existing applications.

Expressions

An additional capability of PowerShell is evaluating expressions. In the following example, PowerShell returns a result for a simple mathematical expression:

```
PS C:\> (100 / 2) * 3
150
PS C:\>
```

NOTE

What's important to notice in this example is that PowerShell calculates and outputs the result of the expression immediately. This approach is different from other shells and scripting languages, where the result of this expression would need to be assigned to a variable or printed before it could be displayed.

Although PowerShell displays the results of expressions immediately, you can also store the output of expressions in variables or text files for later use. The following example stores the output of the expression in the $Calc variable:

```
PS C:\> $Calc = (100 / 2) * 3
PS C:\> $Calc
150
PS C:\>
```

This technique can also be extended to PowerShell cmdlets. In the following example, the $Procinfo variable is set to contain the results of the Get-Process cmdlet by using the -Name parameter:

```
PS C:\> $Procinfo = get-process -Name explorer
PS C:\> $Procinfo

Handles   NPM(K)    PM(K)     WS(K) VM(M)   CPU(s)    Id    ProcessName
-------   ------    -----     ----- -----   ------    --    -----------
    494       12    14248     24804    83   107.45    2964  explorer


PS C:\> $Procinfo

Handles   NPM(K)    PM(K)     WS(K) VM(M)   CPU(s)    Id    ProcessName
-------   ------    -----     ----- -----   ------    --    -----------
    494       12    14248     24804    83   107.51    2964  explorer


PS C:\>
```

In this example, the $Procinfo variable is set to contain the results of the get-process -Name explorer command. The value of $Procinfo is then queried, which returns the results for the explorer process. When $Procinfo is queried a second time, the value for CPU(s) is different from the first query. This example demonstrates that the contents of the $Procinfo variable are dynamic, meaning you get real-time information on the explorer process.

Understanding Variables

A **variable** is a storage place for data. In most shells, the only data that can be stored in a variable is text data. In advanced shells and programming languages, data stored in variables can be almost anything, from strings to sequences to objects. Similarly, PowerShell variables can be just about anything.

To define a PowerShell variable, you must name it with the $ prefix, which helps delineate variables from aliases, cmdlets, filenames, and other items a shell operator might want to use. A variable name is case sensitive and can contain any combination of alphanumeric characters (A–Z and 0–9) and the underscore (_) character. Although PowerShell variables have no set naming convention, using a name that reflects the type of data the variable contains is recommended, as shown in this example:

```
PS C:\> $MSProcesses = get-process | where {$_.company -match
".*Microsoft*"}
PS C:\> $MSProcesses

Handles  NPM(K)    PM(K)     WS(K) VM(M)   CPU(s)     Id ProcessName
-------  ------    -----     ----- -----   ------     -- -----------
     68       4     1712      6496    30     0.19   2420 ctfmon
    715      21    27024     40180   126    58.03   3620 explorer
    647      19    23160     36924   109    18.69   1508 iexplore
    522      11    31364     30876   151     6.59   3268 powershell
    354      17    28172     47612   482    36.22   2464 WINWORD


PS C:\>
```

As you can see from the previous example, the information that is contained within the $MSProcesses variable is a collection of Microsoft processes that are currently running on the system.

> **NOTE**
>
> A variable name can consist of any characters, including spaces, provided the name is enclosed by braces ({ and } symbols). However, if you use a nonstandard variable name, PowerShell warns you this practice is not recommended.

Built-in Variables

When a PowerShell session is started, a number of variables are defined automatically, as shown in this example:

```
PS C:\> set-location variable:
PS Variable:\> get-childitem

Name                    Value
----                    -----
Error                   {CommandNotFoundException}
DebugPreference         SilentlyContinue
PROFILE                 \\bob'shosting.com\homes\tyson\My Documents\P...
HOME                             U:\
Host
System.Management.Automation.Internal.Host.In...
MaximumHistoryCount     64
MaximumAliasCount       4096
```

```
input                            System.Array+SZArrayEnumerator
StackTrace                           at System.Management.Automation.
                                     CommandDis...
ReportErrorShowSource            1
ExecutionContext                 System.Management.Automation.
                                 EngineIntrinsics
true                             True
VerbosePreference                SilentlyContinue
ShellId                          Microsoft.PowerShell
false                            False
null
MaximumFunctionCount             4096
ConsoleFileName
ReportErrorShowStackTrace        0
FormatEnumerationLimit           4
?                                True
PSHOME                           C:\Program Files\Windows
                                 PowerShell\v1.0
MyInvocation                     System.Management.Automation.
                                 InvocationInfo
PWD                              Variable:\
^                                set-location

_
ReportErrorShowExceptionClass    0
ProgressPreference               Continue
ErrorActionPreference            Continue
args                             {}
MaximumErrorCount                256
NestedPromptLevel                0
WhatIfPreference                 0
$                                variable:
ReportErrorShowInnerException    0
ErrorView                        NormalView
WarningPreference                Continue
PID                              3124
ConfirmPreference                High
MaximumDriveCount                4096
MaximumVariableCount             4096


PS C:\>
```

These built-in shell variables are divided into two types. The first type has a special
meaning in PowerShell because it stores configuration information for the current
PowerShell session. Of these special variables, the following should be considered noteworthy because they're used often throughout this book:

- $_   Contains the current pipeline object

- $Error   Contains error objects for the current PowerShell session

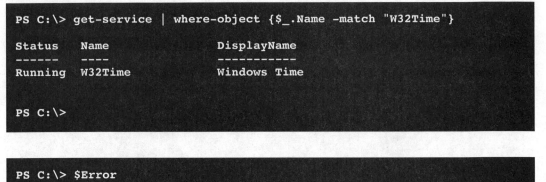

```
PS C:\> get-service | where-object {$_.Name -match "W32Time"}

Status     Name                DisplayName
------     ----                -----------
Running    W32Time             Windows Time


PS C:\>
```

```
PS C:\> $Error
Unexpected token 'Name' in expression or statement.
PS C:\>
```

The second type of built-in variable consists of preference settings used to control the behavior of PowerShell. Table 2.4 describes these variables, based on the PowerShell User Guide.

> **NOTE**
>
> A command policy can be one of the following strings: SilentlyContinue, NotifyContinue, NotifyStop, or Inquire.

TABLE 2.4   PowerShell Preference Settings

Name	Allowed Values	Description
$DebugPreference	Command policy	Action to take when data is written via Write-Debug in a script or WriteDebug() in a cmdlet or provider
$ErrorActionPreference	Command policy	Action to take when data is written via Write-Error in a script or WriteError() in a cmdlet or provider
$MaximumAliasCount	Int	Maximum number of aliases
$MaximumDriveCount	Int	Maximum number of allowed drives
$MaximumErrorCount	Int	Maximum number of errors held by $Error
$MaximumFunctionCount	Int	Maximum number of functions that can be created
$MaximumVariableCount	Int	Maximum number of variables that can be created
$MaximumHistoryCount	Int	Maximum number of entries saved in the command history
$ShouldProcessPreference	Command policy	Action to take when ShouldProcess is used in a cmdlet

Name	Allowed Values	Description
$ProcessReturnPreference	Boolean	ShouldProcess returns this setting
$ProgressPreference	Command policy	Action to take when data is written via Write-Progress in a script or WriteProgress() in a cmdlet or provider
$VerbosePreference	Command policy	Action to take when data is written via Write-Verbose in a script or WriteVerbose() in a cmdlet or provider

Understanding Aliases

Unfortunately, using PowerShell requires a lot of typing unless you're running a script. For example, open a PowerShell console and try typing the following command:

```
PS C:\> get-process | where-object {$_.Company -match ".*Microsoft*"}
| format-table Name, ID, Path —Autosize
```

That's a long command to type. Luckily, like most shells, PowerShell supports aliases for cmdlets and executables. So if you want to cut down on the typing in this command, you can use PowerShell's default aliases. Using these aliases, the Get-Process example looks like this:

```
PS C:\> gps | ? {$_.Company -match ".*Microsoft*"} | ft Name, ID, Path
—Autosize
```

This example isn't a major reduction in the amount of typing, but aliases can save you some time and prevent typos. To get a list of the current PowerShell aliases supported in your session, use the Get-Alias cmdlet, as shown here:

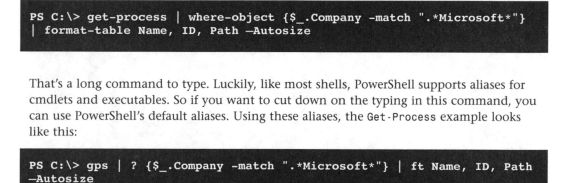

```
PS C:\> get-alias

CommandType        Name                               Definition
-----------        ----                               ----------
Alias              ac                                 Add-Content
Alias              asnp                               Add-PSSnapin
Alias              clc                                Clear-Content
Alias              cli                                Clear-Item
Alias              clp                                Clear-ItemProperty
Alias              clv                                Clear-Variable
Alias              cpi                                Copy-Item
Alias              cpp                                Copy-ItemProperty
Alias              cvpa                               Convert-Path
```

Alias	diff	Compare-Object
Alias	epal	Export-Alias
Alias	epcsv	Export-Csv
Alias	fc	Format-Custom
Alias	fl	Format-List
Alias	foreach	ForEach-Object
Alias	%	ForEach-Object
Alias	ft	Format-Table
Alias	fw	Format-Wide
Alias	gal	Get-Alias
Alias	gc	Get-Content
Alias	gci	Get-ChildItem
Alias	gcm	Get-Command
Alias	gdr	Get-PSDrive
Alias	ghy	Get-History
Alias	gi	Get-Item
Alias	gl	Get-Location
Alias	gm	Get-Member
Alias	gp	Get-ItemProperty
Alias	gps	Get-Process
Alias	group	Group-Object
Alias	gsv	Get-Service
Alias	gsnp	Get-PSSnapin
Alias	gu	Get-Unique
Alias	gv	Get-Variable
Alias	gwmi	Get-WmiObject
Alias	iex	Invoke-Expression
Alias	ihy	Invoke-History
Alias	ii	Invoke-Item
Alias	ipal	Import-Alias
Alias	ipcsv	Import-Csv
Alias	mi	Move-Item
Alias	mp	Move-ItemProperty
Alias	nal	New-Alias
Alias	ndr	New-PSDrive
Alias	ni	New-Item
Alias	nv	New-Variable
Alias	oh	Out-Host
Alias	rdr	Remove-PSDrive
Alias	ri	Remove-Item
Alias	rni	Rename-Item
Alias	rnp	Rename-ItemProperty
Alias	rp	Remove-ItemProperty
Alias	rsnp	Remove-PSSnapin
Alias	rv	Remove-Variable
Alias	rvpa	Resolve-Path
Alias	sal	Set-Alias
Alias	sasv	Start-Service
Alias	sc	Set-Content
Alias	select	Select-Object
Alias	si	Set-Item
Alias	sl	Set-Location

```
Alias           sleep               Start-Sleep
Alias           sort                Sort-Object
lias            sp                  Set-ItemProperty
lias            spps                Stop-Process
Alias           spsv                Stop-Service
Alias           sv                  Set-Variable
Alias           tee                 Tee-Object
Alias           where               Where-Object
lias            ?                   Where-Object
lias            write               Write-Output
lias            cat                 Get-Content
lias            cd                  Set-Location
Alias           clear               Clear-Host
Alias           cp                  Copy-Item
lias            h                   Get-History
lias            history             Get-History
Alias           kill                Stop-Process
Alias           lp                  Out-Printer
lias            ls                  Get-ChildItem
Alias           mount               New-PSDrive
lias            mv                  Move-Item
Alias           popd                Pop-Location
Alias           ps                  Get-Process
lias            pushd               Push-Location
Alias           pwd                 Get-Location
lias            r                   Invoke-History
Alias           rm                  Remove-Item
lias            rmdir               Remove-Item
Alias           echo                Write-Output
Alias           cls                 Clear-Host
Alias           chdir               Set-Location
Alias           copy                Copy-Item
lias            del                 Remove-Item
Alias           dir                 Get-ChildItem
Alias           erase               Remove-Item
lias            move                Move-Item
Alias           rd                  Remove-Item
Alias           ren                 Rename-Item
Alias           set                 Set-Variable
lias            type                Get-Content

PS C:\>
```

Discovering Alias cmdlets

Several alias cmdlets enable you to define new aliases, export aliases, import aliases, and display existing aliases. By using the following command, you can get a list of all related alias cmdlets:

```
PS C:\> get-command *-Alias

CommandType       Name              Definition
-----------       ----              ----------
Cmdlet            Export-Alias      Export-Alias [-Path] <String...
Cmdlet            Get-Alias         Get-Alias [[-Name] <String[]...
Cmdlet            Import-Alias      Import-Alias [-Path] <String...
Cmdlet            New-Alias         New-Alias [-Name] <String> [...
Cmdlet            Set-Alias         Set-Alias [-Name] <String> [...
```

You've already seen how to use the Get-Alias cmdlet to produce a list of aliases available in the current PowerShell session. The Export-Alias and Import-Alias cmdlets are used to export and import alias lists from one PowerShell session to another. Finally, the New-Alias and Set-Alias cmdlets allow you to define new aliases for the current PowerShell session.

> **NOTE**
>
> The alias implementation in PowerShell is limited. As mentioned earlier, an alias works only for cmdlets or executables, *not* for cmdlets and executables used with a parameter. However, there are methods to work around this limitation. One method is defining the command in a variable and then calling the variable from other commands. The problem with this approach is that the variable can be called only in the current PowerShell session, unless it's defined in the profile.ps1 file. The second but better method is placing your command in a function.

Creating Persistent Aliases

The aliases created when you use the New-Alias and Set-Alias cmdlets are valid only in the current PowerShell session. Exiting a PowerShell session discards any existing aliases. To have aliases persist across PowerShell sessions, you must define them in the profile.ps1 file, as shown in this example:

```
set-alias new new-object
set-alias time get-date
...
```

Although command shortening is appealing, the extensive use of aliases isn't recommended. One reason is that aliases aren't very portable. For example, if you use a lot of aliases in a script, you must include a Set-Aliases sequence at the start of the script to make sure those aliases are present, regardless of machine or session profile, when the script runs.

However, a bigger concern than portability is that aliases can often confuse or obscure the true meaning of commands or scripts. The aliases you define might make sense to you, but not everyone shares your logic in defining aliases. So if you want others to understand your scripts, you must be careful about using too many aliases. Instead, look into creating reusable functions.

> **NOTE**
>
> When creating aliases for scripts, use names that other people can understand. For example, there's no reason, other than to encode your scripts, to create aliases consisting of only two letters.

Escape Sequences

The grave-accent or backtick (`) acts as the PowerShell escape character. Depending on when this character is used, PowerShell interprets characters immediately following it in a certain way.

If the backtick character is used at the end of a line in a script, it acts as a continuation character. In other words, ` acts the same way & does in VBScript, allowing you to break long lines of code into smaller chunks, as shown here:

```
$Reg = get-wmiobject -Namespace Root\Default -computerName `
    $Computer -List ¦ where-object `
    {$_.Name -eq "StdRegProv"}
```

If the backtick character precedes a PowerShell variable, the characters immediately following it should be passed on without substitution or processing:

```
PS C:\> $String = "Does this work?"
PS C:\> write-host "The question is: $String"
The question is: Does this work?
PS C:\> write-host "The question is: `$String"
The question is: $String
PS C:\>
```

If the backtick character is used in a string or interpreted as part of a string, that means the next character should be interpreted as a special character. For example, if you want to place a TAB in your string, you use the `t escape character sequence, as shown:

```
PS C:\> $String = "Look at the tab:`t [TAB]"
PS C:\> write-host $string
Look at the tab:           [TAB]
PS C:\>
```

Table 2.5 lists the escape character sequences supported by PowerShell.

TABLE 2.5   PowerShell Escape Sequences

Character	Meaning
`'	Single quotation mark
`"	Double quotation mark
`0	Null character
`a	Alert (bell or beep signal to the computer speaker)
`b	Backspace
`f	Form feed (used for printer output)
`n	Newline
`r	Carriage return
`t	Horizontal tab (8 spaces)
`v	Vertical tab (used for printer output)

Understanding Scopes

A **scope** is a logical boundary in PowerShell that isolates the use of functions and variables. Scopes can be defined as global, local, script, and private. They function in a hierarchy in which scope information is inherited downward. For example, the local scope can read the global scope, but the global scope can't read information from the local scope. Scopes and their use are described in the following sections.

Global

As the name indicates, a **global scope** applies to an entire PowerShell instance. Global scope data is inherited by all child scopes, so any commands, functions, or scripts that run make use of variables defined in the global scope. However, global scopes are *not* shared between different instances of PowerShell.

The following example shows the $Processes variable being defined as a global variable in the ListProcesses function. Because the $Processes variable is being defined globally, checking $Processes.Count after ListProcesses completes returns a count of the number of active processes at the time ListProcesses was executed.

```
PS C:\> function ListProcesses {$Global:Processes = get-process}
PS C:\> ListProcesses
PS C:\> $Processes.Count
37
```

> **NOTE**
>
> In PowerShell, you can use an explicit scope indicator to determine the scope a variable resides in. For instance, if you want a variable to reside in the global scope, you define it as $Global:*variablename*. If a explicit scope indicator isn't used, a variable resides in the current scope for which it's defined.

Local

A **local scope** is created dynamically each time a function, filter, or script runs. After a local scope has finished running, information in it is discarded. A local scope can read information from the global scope but can't make changes to it.

The following example shows the locally scoped variable $Processes being defined in the ListProcesses function. After ListProcesses finishes running, the $Processes variable no longer contains any data because it was defined only in the ListProcesses function. As you can see, checking $Processes.Count after the ListProcesses function is finished produces no results.

```
PS C:\> function ListProcesses {$Processes = get-process}
PS C:\> ListProcesses
PS C:\> $Processes.Count
PS C:\>
```

Script

A **script scope** is created whenever a script file runs and is discarded when the script finishes running. To see an example of how a script scope works, create the following script and save it as ListProcesses.ps1:

```
$Processes = get-process
write-host "Here is the first process:" -Foregroundcolor Yellow
$Processes[0]
```

After you have created the script file, run it from a PowerShell session. Your output should look similar to this example:

```
PS C:\> .\ListProcesses.ps1
Here is the first process:

Handles  NPM(K)     PM(K)      WS(K) VM(M)   CPU(s)     Id ProcessName
-------  ------     -----      ----- -----   ------     -- -----------
    105       5      1992       4128    32              916 alg


PS C:\> $Processes[0]
Cannot index into a null array.
At line:1 char:12
+ $Processes[0 <<<< ]
PS C:\>
```

Notice that when the ListProcesses.ps1 script runs, information about the first process object in the $Processes variable is written to the console. However, when you try to access information in the $Processes variable from the console, an error is returned because the $Processes variable is valid only in the script scope. When the script finishes running, that scope and all its contents are discarded.

What if you want to use a script in a pipeline or access it as a library file for common functions? Normally, this isn't possible because PowerShell discards a script scope whenever a script finishes running. Luckily, PowerShell supports the **dot sourcing** technique, a term that originally came from UNIX. Dot sourcing a script file tells PowerShell to load a script scope into the calling parent's scope.

To dot source a script file, simply prefix the script name with a period (dot) when running the script, as shown here:

```
PS C:\> . .\myscript.ps1
```

Private

A **private scope** is similar to a local scope, with one key difference: Definitions in the private scope aren't inherited by any child scopes.

The following example shows the privately scoped variable $Processes defined in the ListProcesses function. Notice that during execution of the ListProcesses function, the $Processes variable isn't available to the child scope represented by the script block enclosed by { and } in lines 6-9.

```
PS C:\> function ListProcesses {$Private:Processes = get-process
>>      write-host "Here is the first process:" -Foregroundcolor Yellow
>>      $Processes[0]
>>      write-host
>>
>>      &{
>>          write-host "Here it is again:" -Foregroundcolor Yellow
>>          $Processes[0]
>>      }
>> }
>>
PS C:\> ListProcesses
Here is the first process:

Handles  NPM(K)    PM(K)      WS(K) VM(M)   CPU(s)     Id ProcessName
-------  ------    -----      ----- -----   ------     -- -----------
    105       5     1992       4128    32               916 alg

Here it is again:
Cannot index into a null array.
At line:7 char:20
+          $Processes[0 <<<< ]


PS C:\>
```

This example works because it uses the & call operator. With this call operator, you can execute fragments of script code in an isolated local scope. This technique is helpful for isolating a script block and its variables from a parent scope or, as in this example, isolating a privately scoped variable from a script block.

Your First Script

Most of the commands covered in this chapter are interactive, meaning you enter commands at the PowerShell prompt and then output is returned. Although using PowerShell interactively is helpful for tasks that need to be done only once, it's not an effective way to perform repetitive automation tasks. Fortunately, PowerShell has the capability to read in files containing stored commands, which enables you to compose, save, and recall a sequence of commands when needed. These sequences of stored commands are commonly referred to as **scripts**.

PowerShell scripts are simply text files stored with a .ps1 extension. You can use any text editor (such as Notepad) to create a text file containing commands that make up a PowerShell script. For example, open Notepad and type the following command:

```
get-service | where-object {$_.Status -eq "Stopped"}
```

Next, save this file with the name `ListStoppedServices.ps1` in a directory of your choice. For this example, the `C:\Scripts` directory is used.

Before you can run this script, you need to adjust PowerShell's execution policy because the default setting doesn't allow running scripts for protection against malicious scripts. To change this setting, you use the `Set-ExecutionPolicy` cmdlet as shown in the following example. You can also use the `Get-ExecutionPolicy` cmdlet to verify the current execution policy. (Chapter 3 discusses PowerShell security and best practices in more detail.)

```
PS C:\> set-executionpolicy RemoteSigned
PS C:\> get-executionpolicy
RemoteSigned
PS C:\>
```

The `RemoteSigned` policy allows scripts created locally to run without being digitally signed (a concept discussed in Chapter 4, "Code Signing"), but still requires scripts downloaded from the Internet to be digitally signed. These settings give you the flexibility to run unsigned scripts from your local machine yet provide some protection against unsigned external scripts.

After changing PowerShell's execution policy to `RemoteSigned`, you can run the script in any PowerShell session by simply typing the script's full directory path and filename. In the following example, entering the `C:\Scripts\ListStoppedServices.ps1` command produces this output:

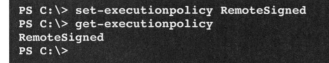

```
PS C:\> C:\Scripts\ListStoppedServices.ps1

Status    Name                DisplayName
------    ----                -----------
Stopped   Alerter             Alerter
Stopped   AppMgmt             Application Management
Stopped   aspnet_state        ASP.NET State Service
Stopped   BITS                Background Intelligent Transfer Ser...
Stopped   Browser             Computer Browser
Stopped   CiSvc               Indexing Service
Stopped   ClipSrv             ClipBook
Stopped   clr_optimizatio...  .NET Runtime Optimization Service v...
Stopped   COMSysApp           COM+ System Application
Stopped   dmadmin             Logical Disk Manager Administrative...
Stopped   FastUserSwitchi...  Fast User Switching Compatibility
Stopped   HidServ             Human Interface Device Access
Stopped   HTTPFilter          HTTP SSL
Stopped   IDriverT            InstallDriver Table Manager
Stopped   ImapiService        IMAPI CD-Burning COM Service
Stopped   mnmsrvc             NetMeeting Remote Desktop Sharing
Stopped   MSDTC               Distributed Transaction Coordinator
Stopped   MSIServer           Windows Installer
Stopped   MSSQLServerADHe...  MSSQLServerADHelper
```

```
Stopped    NetDDE               Network DDE
Stopped    NetDDEdsdm           Network DDE DSDM
Stopped    NGClient             Symantec Ghost Client Agent
Stopped    NtLmSsp              NT LM Security Support Provider
Stopped    NtmsSvc              Removable Storage
Stopped    OracleORA92Clie...   OracleORA92ClientCache
Stopped    ose                  Office Source Engine
Stopped    RasAuto              Remote Access Auto Connection Manager
Stopped    RDSessMgr            Remote Desktop Help Session Manager
Stopped    RemoteAccess         Routing and Remote Access
Stopped    rpcapd               Remote Packet Capture Protocol v.0 ...
Stopped    RpcLocator           Remote Procedure Call (RPC) Locator
Stopped    RSVP                 QoS RSVP
Stopped    SCardSvr             Smart Card
Stopped    SwPrv                MS Software Shadow Copy Provider
Stopped    SysmonLog            Performance Logs and Alerts
Stopped    TlntSvr              Telnet
Stopped    TrkWks               Distributed Link Tracking Client
Stopped    upnphost             Universal Plug and Play Device Host
Stopped    UPS                  Uninterruptible Power Supply
Stopped    vmount2              VMware Virtual Mount Manager Extended
Stopped    VSS                  Volume Shadow Copy
Stopped    WmdmPmSN             Portable Media Serial Number Service
Stopped    Wmi                  Windows Management Instrumentation ...
Stopped    WmiApSrv             WMI Performance Adapter
Stopped    wscsvc               Security Center
Stopped    xmlprov              Network Provisioning Service


PS C:\>
```

Although this basic one-line script is simple, it stills serves to illustrate how to write a script and use it in PowerShell. If needed, you can include more commands to have it perform an automation task. The following is an example:

```
param ([string] $StartsWith)

$StopServices = get-service ¦ where-object {$_.Status -eq "Stopped"}

write-host "The following $StartsWith services are stopped on" `
    "$Env:COMPUTERNAME:" -Foregroundcolor Yellow

$StopServices ¦ where-object {$_.Name -like $StartsWith} ¦ `
    format-table Name, DisplayName
```

The script then displays this output:

```
PS C:\> C:\Scripts\ListStoppedServices.ps1 N*
The following N* services are stopped on PLANX:

Name                                    DisplayName
----                                    -----------
NetDDE                                  Network DDE
NetDDEdsdm                              Network DDE DSDM
NtLmSsp                                 NT LM Security Support
Provider
NtmsSvc                                 Removable Storage


PS C:\>
```

This script is a little more complex because it can filter the stopped services based on the provided string to make the output cleaner. This script isn't a complicated piece of automation, but it does serve to illustrate just some of the power that PowerShell has. To use that power, you just need to gain a better understanding of PowerShell's features so that you can write more complex and meaningful scripts.

Summary

In this chapter, you have focused on learning the PowerShell basics. In learning these basics, you have gained insight into such concepts as PowerShell's different command types, what cmdlets are, how to use aliases variables and the CLI, and PowerShell scopes. After learning these concepts, you then moved on to learning the basics around PowerShell script writing and completed your first script. But, the most important concept that should be taken from this chapter is that you have downloaded PowerShell, installed it, and started using it.

By just using PowerShell, you have taken the first of many steps to becoming a master in PowerShell usage. This first step is after all the hardest, and once taken, the road should start to become easier and easier. As such, over the next couple chapters or maybe by the end of this book, you should notice your proficiency in PowerShell growing as more concepts are reviewed and a push is made to understand how PowerShell can be applied to meet automation needs.

# CHAPTER 3

PowerShell: A More In-Depth Look

Introduction

This chapter delves into some specifics of how PowerShell works that you need to understand for the later scripting chapters. Try not to get too bogged down in details; instead, focus on understanding the concepts. Because PowerShell is a change from Windows scripting of the past, you might also need to change your scripting methods. With practice, it will start to feel as familiar as Windows scripting via VBScript or JScript, which was the standard method for Windows automation tasks.

Object Based

Most shells operate in a text-based environment, which means you typically have to manipulate the output for automation purposes. For example, if you need to pipe data from one command to the next, the output from the first command usually must be reformatted to meet the second command's requirements. Although this method has worked for years, dealing with text-based data can be difficult and frustrating.

Often, a lot of work is necessary to transform text data into a usable format. Microsoft has set out to change the standard with PowerShell, however. Instead of transporting data as plain text, PowerShell retrieves data in the form of .NET Framework objects, which makes it possible for commands (cmdlets) to access object properties and methods directly. This change has simplified shell use. Instead of modifying text data, you can just refer to the required data by name. Similarly, instead of writing code to transform data into a usable format, you can simply refer to objects and manipulate them as needed.

Understanding the Pipeline

The use of objects gives you a more robust method for dealing with data. In the past, data was transferred from one command to the next by using the pipeline, which makes it possible to string a series of commands together to gather information from a system. However, as mentioned previously, most shells have a major disadvantage: The information gathered from commands is text based. Raw text needs to be parsed (transformed) into a format the next command can understand before being piped. To see how parsing works, take a look at the following Bash example:

```
$ ps -ef | grep "bash" | cut -f2
```

The goal is to get the process ID (PID) for the bash process. A list of currently running processes is gathered with the ps command and then piped to the grep command and filtered on the string "bash". Next, the remaining information is piped to the cut command, which returns the second field containing the PID based on a tab delimiter.

> **NOTE**
>
> A **delimiter** is a character used to separate data fields. The default delimiter for the cut command is a tab. If you want to use a different delimiter, use the -d parameter.

Based on the man information for the grep and cut commands, it seems as though the ps command should work. However, the PID isn't returned or displayed in the correct format.

The command doesn't work because the Bash shell requires you to manipulate text data to display the PID. The output of the ps command is text based, so transforming the text into a more usable format requires a series of other commands, such as grep and cut. Manipulating text data makes this task more complicated. For example, to retrieve the PID from the data piped from the grep command, you need to provide the field location and the delimiter for separating text information to the cut command. To find this information, run the first part of the ps command:

```
$ ps -ef | grep "bash"
   bob     3628        1 con  16:52:46 /usr/bin/bash
```
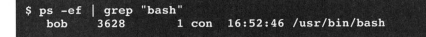

The field you need is the second one (3628). Notice that the ps command doesn't use a tab delimiter to separate columns in the output; instead, it uses a variable number of spaces or a whitespace delimiter, between fields.

> **NOTE**
>
> A **whitespace delimiter** consists of characters, such as spaces or tabs, that equate to blank space.

The cut command has no way to tell that spaces should be used as a field separator, which is why the command doesn't work. To get the PID, you need to use the awk scripting language. The command and output in that language would look like this:

```
$ ps -ef | grep "bash" | awk '{print $2}'
3628
```

The point is that although most UNIX and Linux shell commands are powerful, using them can be complicated and frustrating. Because these shells are text-based, often commands lack functionality or require using additional commands or tools to perform tasks. To address the differences in text output from shell commands, many utilities and scripting languages have been developed to parse text.

The result of all this parsing is a tree of commands and tools that make working with shells unwieldy and time consuming, which is one reason for the proliferation of management interfaces that rely on GUIs. This trend can be seen among tools Windows administrators use, too; as Microsoft has focused on enhancing the management GUI at the expense of the CLI.

Windows administrators now have access to the same automation capabilities as their UNIX and Linux counterparts. However, PowerShell and its use of objects fill the automation need Windows administrators have had since the days of batch scripting and WSH in a more usable and less parsing intense manner. To see how the PowerShell pipeline works, take a look at the following PowerShell example:

```
PS C:\> get-process bash | format-table id -autosize

  Id
  --
3628


PS C:\>
```

Like the Bash example, the goal of this PowerShell example is to display the PID for the bash process. First, information about the bash process is gathered by using the Get-Process cmdlet. Second, the information is piped to the Format-Table cmdlet, which returns a table containing only the PID for the bash process.

The Bash example requires complex shell scripting, but the PowerShell example simply requires formatting a table. As you can see, the structure of PowerShell cmdlets is much easier to understand and use.

Now that you have the PID for the bash process, take a look at the following example, which shows how to kill (stop) that process:

```
PS C:\> get-process bash | stop-process
PS C:\>
```

.NET Framework Tips

Before continuing, you need to know a few points about how PowerShell interacts with the .NET Framework. This information is critical to understanding the scripts you review in later chapters.

New-Object cmdlet

You use the New-Object cmdlet to create an instance of a .NET object. To do this, you simply provide the fully qualified name of the .NET class you want to use, as shown:

```
PS C:\> $Ping = new-object Net.NetworkInformation.Ping
PS C:\>
```

By using the New-Object cmdlet, you now have an instance of the Ping class that enables you to detect whether a remote computer can be reached via Internet Control Message Protocol (ICMP). Therefore, you have an object-based version of the Ping.exe command-line tool.

If you're wondering what the replacement is for the VBScript CreateObject method, it's the New-Object cmdlet. You can also use the comObject switch with this cmdlet to create a COM object, simply by specifying the object's programmatic identifier (ProgID), as shown here:

```
PS C:\> $IE = new-object –comObject InternetExplorer.Application
PS C:\> $IE.Visible=$True
PS C:\> $IE.Navigate("www.cnn.com")
PS C:\>
```

Square Brackets

Throughout this book, you'll notice the use of square brackets ([and]), which indicate that the enclosed term is a .NET Framework reference. These references can be one of the following:

- *A fully qualified class name*—[System.DirectoryServices.ActiveDirectory.Forest], for example

- *A class in the* System *namespace*—[string], [int], [boolean], and so forth

- *A type accelerator*—[ADSI], [WMI], [Regex], and so on

> **NOTE**
>
> Chapter 8, "PowerShell and WMI," explains type accelerators in more detail.

Defining a variable is a good example of when to use a .NET Framework reference. In this case, the variable is assigned an enumeration value by using an explicit cast of a .NET class, as shown in this example:

```
PS C:\> $SomeNumber = [int]1
PS C:\> $Identity = [System.Security.Principal.NTAccount]"Administrator"
PS C:\>
```

If an enumeration can consist of only a fixed set of constants, and you don't know these constants, you can use the System.Enum class's GetNames method to find this information:

```
PS C:\>
[enum]::GetNames([System.Security.AccessControl.FileSystemRights])
ListDirectory
ReadData
WriteData
CreateFiles
CreateDirectories
AppendData
ReadExtendedAttributes
WriteExtendedAttributes
Traverse
ExecuteFile
DeleteSubdirectoriesAndFiles
ReadAttributes
WriteAttributes
Write
Delete
ReadPermissions
Read
ReadAndExecute
Modify
ChangePermissions
TakeOwnership
Synchronize
FullControl
PS C:\>
```

3

Static Classes and Methods

Square brackets are used not only for defining variables, but also for using or calling static members of a .NET class. To do this, just use a double colon (::) between the class name and the static method or property, as shown in this example:

```
PS C:\> [System.DirectoryServices.ActiveDirectory.Forest]::
GetCurrentForest()


Name                     : taosage.internal
Sites                    : {HOME}
Domains                  : {taosage.internal}
GlobalCatalogs           : {sol.taosage.internal}
ApplicationPartitions    : {DC=DomainDnsZones,DC=taosage,DC=internal,
DC=ForestDns
                           Zones,DC=taosage,DC=internal}
ForestMode               : Windows2003Forest
RootDomain               : taosage.internal
Schema                   :
CN=Schema,CN=Configuration,DC=taosage,DC=internal
SchemaRoleOwner          : sol.taosage.internal
NamingRoleOwner          : sol.taosage.internal



PS C:\>
```

Reflection

Reflection is a feature in the .NET Framework that enables developers to examine objects and retrieve their supported methods, properties, fields, and so on. Because PowerShell is built on the .NET Framework, it provides this feature, too, with the Get-Member cmdlet. This cmdlet analyzes an object or collection of objects you pass to it via the pipeline. For example, the following command analyzes the objects returned from the Get-Process cmdlet and displays their associated properties and methods:

```
PS C:\> get-process | get-member
```

Developers often refer to this process as "interrogating" an object. It's a faster way to get information about objects than using the Get-Help cmdlet (which at the time of this writing provides limited information), reading the MSDN documentation, or searching the Internet.

```
PS C:\> get-process | get-member


    TypeName: System.Diagnostics.Process

Name                       MemberType      Definition
----                       ----------      ----------
Handles                    AliasProperty   Handles = Handlecount
Name                       AliasProperty   Name = ProcessName
NPM                        AliasProperty   NPM = NonpagedSystemMemorySize
PM                         AliasProperty   PM = PagedMemorySize
VM                         AliasProperty   VM = VirtualMemorySize
WS                         AliasProperty   WS = WorkingSet
add_Disposed               Method          System.Void add_Disposed(Event...
add_ErrorDataReceived      Method          System.Void add_ErrorDataRecei...
add_Exited                 Method          System.Void add_Exited(EventHa...
add_OutputDataReceived     Method          System.Void add_OutputDataRece...
BeginErrorReadLine         Method          System.Void BeginErrorReadLine()
BeginOutputReadLine        Method          System.Void BeginOutputReadLine()
CancelErrorRead            Method          System.Void CancelErrorRead()
CancelOutputRead           Method          System.Void CancelOutputRead()
Close                      Method          System.Void Close()
CloseMainWindow            Method          System.Boolean CloseMainWindow()
CreateObjRef               Method          System.Runtime.Remoting.ObjRef...
Dispose                    Method          System.Void Dispose()
Equals                     Method          System.Boolean Equals(Object obj)
get_BasePriority           Method          System.Int32 get_BasePriority()
get_Container              Method          System.ComponentModel.IContain...
get_EnableRaisingEvents    Method          System.Boolean get_EnableRaisi...
...
__NounName                 NoteProperty    System.String __NounName=Process
BasePriority               Property        System.Int32 BasePriority {get;}
Container                  Property        System.ComponentModel.IContain...
EnableRaisingEvents        Property        System.Boolean EnableRaisingEv...
ExitCode                   Property        System.Int32 ExitCode {get;}
ExitTime                   Property        System.DateTime ExitTime {get;}
Handle                     Property        System.IntPtr Handle {get;}
HandleCount                Property        System.Int32 HandleCount {get;}
HasExited                  Property        System.Boolean HasExited {get;}
Id                         Property        System.Int32 Id {get;}
MachineName                Property        System.String MachineName {get;}
MainModule                 Property        System.Diagnostics.ProcessModu...
MainWindowHandle           Property        System.IntPtr MainWindowHandle...
MainWindowTitle            Property        System.String MainWindowTitle ...
MaxWorkingSet              Property        System.IntPtr MaxWorkingSet {g...
MinWorkingSet              Property        System.IntPtr MinWorkingSet {g...
...
Company                    ScriptProperty  System.Object Company {get=$th...
CPU                        ScriptProperty  System.Object CPU {get=$this.T...
Description                ScriptProperty  System.Object Description {get...
FileVersion                ScriptProperty  System.Object FileVersion {get...
Path                       ScriptProperty  System.Object Path {get=$this....
Product                    ScriptProperty  System.Object Product {get=$th...
ProductVersion             ScriptProperty  System.Object ProductVersion {...


PS C:\>
```

3

This example shows that objects returned from the Get-Process cmdlet have additional property information that you didn't know. The following example uses this information to produce a report about Microsoft-owned processes and their folder locations. An example of such a report would be as follows:

```
PS C:\> get-process | where-object {$_.Company -match ".*Microsoft*"} |
format-table Name, ID, Path -Autosize

Name          Id Path
----          -- ----
ctfmon      4052 C:\WINDOWS\system32\ctfmon.exe
explorer    3024 C:\WINDOWS\Explorer.EXE
iexplore    2468 C:\Program Files\Internet Explorer\iexplore.exe
iexplore    3936 C:\Program Files\Internet Explorer\iexplore.exe
mobsync      280 C:\WINDOWS\system32\mobsync.exe
notepad     1600 C:\WINDOWS\system32\notepad.exe
notepad     2308 C:\WINDOWS\system32\notepad.exe
notepad     2476 C:\WINDOWS\system32\NOTEPAD.EXE
notepad     2584 C:\WINDOWS\system32\notepad.exe
OUTLOOK     3600 C:\Program Files\Microsoft Office\OFFICE11\OUTLOOK.EXE
powershell  3804 C:\Program Files\Windows PowerShell\v1.0\powershell.exe
WINWORD     2924 C:\Program Files\Microsoft Office\OFFICE11\WINWORD.EXE


PS C:\>
```

You wouldn't get nearly this much process information by using WSH with only a single line of code.

The Get-Member cmdlet isn't just for objects generated from PowerShell cmdlets. You can also use it on objects initialized from .NET classes, as shown in this example:

```
PS C:\> new-object System.DirectoryServices.DirectorySearcher
```

The goal of using the DirectorySearcher class is to retrieve user information from Active Directory, but you don't know what methods the returned objects support. To retrieve this information, run the Get-Member cmdlet against a variable containing the mystery objects, as shown in this example.

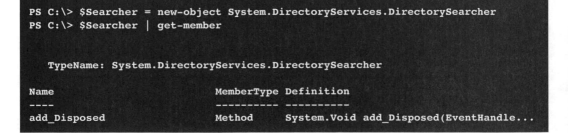

```
PS C:\> $Searcher = new-object System.DirectoryServices.DirectorySearcher
PS C:\> $Searcher | get-member


   TypeName: System.DirectoryServices.DirectorySearcher

Name                      MemberType Definition
----                      ---------- ----------
add_Disposed              Method     System.Void add_Disposed(EventHandle...
```

```
CreateObjRef                  Method      System.Runtime.Remoting.ObjRef Creat...
Dispose                       Method      System.Void Dispose()
Equals                        Method      System.Boolean Equals(Object obj)
FindAll                       Method      System.DirectoryServices.SearchResul...
FindOne                       Method      System.DirectoryServices.SearchResul...
...
Asynchronous                  Property    System.Boolean Asynchronous {get;set;}
AttributeScopeQuery           Property    System.String AttributeScopeQuery {g...
CacheResults                  Property    System.Boolean CacheResults {get;set;}
ClientTimeout                 Property    System.TimeSpan ClientTimeout {get;s...
Container                     Property    System.ComponentModel.IContainer Con...
DerefAlias                    Property    System.DirectoryServices.Dereference...
DirectorySynchronization      Property    System.DirectoryServices.DirectorySy...
ExtendedDN                    Property    System.DirectoryServices.ExtendedDN ...
Filter                        Property    System.String Filter {get;set;}
PageSize                      Property    System.Int32 PageSize {get;set;}
PropertiesToLoad              Property    System.Collections.Specialized.Strin...
PropertyNamesOnly             Property    System.Boolean PropertyNamesOnly {ge...
ReferralChasing               Property    System.DirectoryServices.ReferralCha...
SearchRoot                    Property    System.DirectoryServices.DirectoryEn...
SearchScope                   Property    System.DirectoryServices.SearchScope...
SecurityMasks                 Property    System.DirectoryServices.SecurityMas...
ServerPageTimeLimit           Property    System.TimeSpan ServerPageTimeLimit ...
ServerTimeLimit               Property    System.TimeSpan ServerTimeLimit {get...
Site                          Property    System.ComponentModel.ISite Site {ge...
SizeLimit                     Property    System.Int32 SizeLimit {get;set;}
Sort                          Property    System.DirectoryServices.SortOption ...
Tombstone                     Property    System.Boolean Tombstone {get;set;}
VirtualListView               Property    System.DirectoryServices.
                                          DirectoryVi...


PS C:\>
```

Notice the FindAll method and the Filter property. These are object attributes that can be used to search for information about users in an Active Directory domain. To use these attributes the first step is to filter the information returned from DirectorySearcher by using the Filter property, which takes a filter statement similar to what you'd find in a Lightweight Directory Access Protocol (LDAP) statement:

```
PS C:\> $Searcher.Filter = ("(objectCategory=user)")
```

Next, you retrieve all users from the Active Directory domain with the FindAll method:

```
PS C:\> $Users = $Searcher.FindAll()
```

At this point, the $Users variable contains a collection of objects holding the distinguished names for all users in the Active Directory domain:

```
PS C:\> $Users

Path                                         Properties
----                                         ----------
LDAP://CN=Administrator,CN=Users,DC=...      {homemdb, samaccounttype, countrycod...
LDAP://CN=Guest,CN=Users,DC=taosage,...      {samaccounttype, objectsid, whencrea...
LDAP://CN=krbtgt,CN=Users,DC=taosage...      {samaccounttype, objectsid, whencrea...
LDAP://CN=admintyson,OU=Admin Accoun...      {countrycode, cn, lastlogoff, usncre...
LDAP://CN=servmom,OU=Service Account...      {samaccounttype, lastlogontimestamp,...
LDAP://CN=SUPPORT_388945a0,CN=Users,...      {samaccounttype, objectsid, whencrea...
LDAP://CN=Tyson,OU=Acc...  {msmqsigncertificates, distinguished...
LDAP://CN=Maiko,OU=Acc...  {homemdb, msexchhomeservername, coun...
LDAP://CN=servftp,OU=Service Account...      {samaccounttype, lastlogontimestamp,...
LDAP://CN=Erica,OU=Accounts,OU...  {samaccounttype, lastlogontimestamp,...
LDAP://CN=Garett,OU=Accou...  {samaccounttype, lastlogontimestamp,...
LDAP://CN=Fujio,OU=Accounts,O...  {samaccounttype, givenname, sn, when...
LDAP://CN=Kiyomi,OU=Accounts,...  {samaccounttype, givenname, sn, when...
LDAP://CN=servsql,OU=Service Account...      {samaccounttype, lastlogon, lastlogo...
LDAP://CN=servdhcp,OU=Service Accoun...      {samaccounttype, lastlogon, lastlogo...
LDAP://CN=servrms,OU=Service Account...      {lastlogon, lastlogontimestamp, msmq...

PS C:\>
```

> **NOTE**
>
> The commands in these examples use the default connection parameters for the
> DirectorySearcher class. This means the connection to Active Directory uses the
> default naming context. If you want to connect to a domain other than the one specified
> in the default naming context, you must set the appropriate connection parameters.

Now that you have an object for each user, you can use the Get-Member cmdlet to learn what you can do with these objects:

```
PS C:\> $Users | get-member


   TypeName: System.DirectoryServices.SearchResult

Name              MemberType Definition
----              ---------- ----------
Equals            Method     System.Boolean Equals(Object obj)
get_Path          Method     System.String get_Path()
get_Properties    Method     System.DirectoryServices.ResultPropertyCollecti...
GetDirectoryEntry Method     System.DirectoryServices.DirectoryEntry GetDire...
GetHashCode       Method     System.Int32 GetHashCode()
```

```
GetType              Method       System.Type GetType()
ToString             Method       System.String ToString()
Path                 Property     System.String Path {get;}
Properties           Property     System.DirectoryServices.ResultPropertyCollecti...


PS C:\>
```

To collect information from these user objects, it seems as though you need to step
through each object with the GetDirectoryEntry method. To determine what data you
can retrieve from these objects, you use the Get-Member cmdlet again, as shown here:

```
PS C:\> $Users[0].GetDirectoryEntry() | get-member -MemberType Property


    TypeName: System.DirectoryServices.DirectoryEntry

Name                                MemberType  Definition
----                                ----------  ----------
accountExpires                      Property    System.DirectoryServices.Property...
adminCount                          Property    System.DirectoryServices.Property...
badPasswordTime                     Property    System.DirectoryServices.Property...
badPwdCount                         Property    System.DirectoryServices.Property...
cn                                  Property    System.DirectoryServices.Property...
codePage                            Property    System.DirectoryServices.Property...
countryCode                         Property    System.DirectoryServices.Property...
description                         Property    System.DirectoryServices.Property...
displayName                         Property    System.DirectoryServices.Property...
distinguishedName                   Property    System.DirectoryServices.Property...
homeMDB                             Property    System.DirectoryServices.Property...
homeMTA                             Property    System.DirectoryServices.Property...
instanceType                        Property    System.DirectoryServices.Property...
isCriticalSystemObject              Property    System.DirectoryServices.Property...
lastLogon                           Property    System.DirectoryServices.Property...
lastLogonTimestamp                  Property    System.DirectoryServices.Property...
legacyExchangeDN                    Property    System.DirectoryServices.Property...
logonCount                          Property    System.DirectoryServices.Property...
mail                                Property    System.DirectoryServices.Property...
mailNickname                        Property    System.DirectoryServices.Property...
mDBUseDefaults                      Property    System.DirectoryServices.Property...
memberOf                            Property    System.DirectoryServices.Property...
msExchALObjectVersion               Property    System.DirectoryServices.Property...
msExchHomeServerName                Property    System.DirectoryServices.Property...
msExchMailboxGuid                   Property    System.DirectoryServices.Property...
msExchMailboxSecurityDescriptor     Property    System.DirectoryServices.Property...
msExchPoliciesIncluded              Property    System.DirectoryServices.Property...
msExchUserAccountControl            Property    System.DirectoryServices.Property...
mSMQDigests                         Property    System.DirectoryServices.Property...
mSMQSignCertificates                Property    System.DirectoryServices.Property...
name                                Property    System.DirectoryServices.Property...
```

3

```
nTSecurityDescriptor              Property      System.DirectoryServices.Property...
objectCategory                    Property      System.DirectoryServices.Property...
objectClass                       Property      System.DirectoryServices.Property...
objectGUID                        Property      System.DirectoryServices.Property...
objectSid                         Property      System.DirectoryServices.Property...
primaryGroupID                    Property      System.DirectoryServices.Property...
proxyAddresses                    Property      System.DirectoryServices.Property...
pwdLastSet                        Property      System.DirectoryServices.Property...
sAMAccountName                    Property      System.DirectoryServices.Property...
sAMAccountType                    Property      System.DirectoryServices.Property...
showInAddressBook                 Property      System.DirectoryServices.Property...
textEncodedORAddress              Property      System.DirectoryServices.Property...
userAccountControl                Property      System.DirectoryServices.Property...
uSNChanged                        Property      System.DirectoryServices.Property...
uSNCreated                        Property      System.DirectoryServices.Property...
whenChanged                       Property      System.DirectoryServices.Property...
whenCreated                       Property      System.DirectoryServices.Property...


PS C:\>
```

> **NOTE**
>
> The MemberType parameter tells the Get-Member cmdlet to retrieve a specific type
> of member. For example, to display the methods associated with an object, use the
> get-member –MemberType Method command.

To use PowerShell effectively, you should make sure you're familiar with the Get-Member
cmdlet. If you don't understand how it works, figuring out what an object can and can't
do may be at times difficult.

Now that you understand how to pull information from Active Directory, it's time to put
together all the commands used so far:

```
PS C:\> $Searcher = new-object System.DirectoryServices.DirectorySearcher
PS C:\> $Searcher.Filter = ("(objectCategory=user)")
PS C:\> $Users = $Searcher.FindAll()
PS C:\> foreach ($User in $Users){$User.GetDirectoryEntry().sAMAccountName}
Administrator
Guest
krbtgt
admintyson
servmom
SUPPORT_388945a0
Tyson
Maiko
servftp
Erica
Garett
```

```
Fujio
Kiyomi
servsql
servdhcp
servrms
PS C:\>
```

Although the list of users in this domain isn't long, it shows that you can interrogate a set of objects to understand their capabilities.

The same is true for static classes, however, when attempting to use the Get-Member cmdlet in the same manner as before creates the following error:

```
PS C:\> new-object System.Net.Dns
New-Object : Constructor not found. Cannot find an appropriate constructor for
type System.Net.Dns.
At line:1 char:11
+ New-Object  <<<< System.Net.Dns
PS C:\>
```

As you can see, the System.Net.Dns class doesn't have a constructor, which poses a challenge when you're trying to find out what this class does. However, the Get-Member cmdlet can handle this challenge. With the Static parameter, you can gather information from static classes, as shown in this example:

```
PS C:\> [System.Net.Dns] | get-member -Static


    TypeName: System.Net.Dns

Name                   MemberType  Definition
----                   ----------  ----------
BeginGetHostAddresses  Method      static System.IAsyncResult BeginGetHostAddr...
BeginGetHostByName     Method      static System.IAsyncResult BeginGetHostByNa...
BeginGetHostEntry      Method      static System.IAsyncResult BeginGetHostEntr...
BeginResolve           Method      static System.IAsyncResult BeginResolve(Str...
EndGetHostAddresses    Method      static System.Net.IPAddress[] EndGetHostAdd...
EndGetHostByName       Method      static System.Net.IPHostEntry EndGetHostByN...
EndGetHostEntry        Method      static System.Net.IPHostEntry EndGetHostEnt...
EndResolve             Method      static System.Net.IPHostEntry EndResolve(IA...
Equals                 Method      static System.Boolean Equals(Object objA, O...
GetHostAddresses       Method      static System.Net.IPAddress[] GetHostAddres...
GetHostByAddress       Method      static System.Net.IPHostEntry GetHostByAddr...
GetHostByName          Method      static System.Net.IPHostEntry GetHostByName...
GetHostEntry           Method      static System.Net.IPHostEntry GetHostEntry(...
GetHostName            Method      static System.String GetHostName()
```

```
ReferenceEquals       Method      static System.Boolean ReferenceEquals(Objec...
Resolve               Method      static System.Net.IPHostEntry Resolve(Strin...


PS C:\>
```

Now that you have information about the System.Net.Dns class, you can put it to work. As an example, use the GetHostAddress method to resolve the IP address for the Web site www.digg.com:

```
PS C:\> [System.Net.Dns]::GetHostAddresses("www.digg.com")


IPAddressToString : 64.191.203.30
Address           : 516669248
AddressFamily     : InterNetwork
ScopeId           :
IsIPv6Multicast   : False
IsIPv6LinkLocal   : False
IsIPv6SiteLocal   : False


PS C:\>
```

NOTE

As you have seen, the Get-Member cmdlet can be a powerful tool. It can also be time consuming because it's easy to spend hours exploring what you can do with different cmdlets and classes. To help prevent Get-Member User Stress Syndrome (GUSS), try to limit your discovery sessions to no more than a couple of hours a day.

Extended Type System (ETS)

You might think that scripting in PowerShell is typeless because you rarely need to specify the type for a variable. PowerShell is actually type driven, however, because it interfaces with different types of objects from the less than perfect .NET to Windows Management Instrumentation (WMI), Component Object Model (COM), ActiveX Data Objects (ADO), Active Directory Service Interfaces (ADSI), Extensible Markup Language (XML), and even custom objects. However, you typically don't need to be concerned about object types because PowerShell adapts to different object types and displays its interpretation of an object for you.

In a sense, PowerShell tries to provide a common abstraction layer that makes all object interaction consistent, despite the type. This abstraction layer is called the PSObject, a common object used for all object access in PowerShell. It can encapsulate any base object (.NET, custom, and so on), any instance members, and implicit or explicit access to adapted and type-based extended members, depending on the type of base object.

Furthermore, it can state its type and add members dynamically. To do this, PowerShell uses the **Extended Type System (ETS),** which provides an interface that allows PowerShell cmdlet and script developers to manipulate and change objects as needed.

NOTE

When you use the `Get-Member` cmdlet, the information returned is from `PSObject`. Sometimes `PSObject` blocks members, methods, and properties from the original object. If you want to view the blocked information, use the `BaseObject` property with the `PSBase` standard name. For example, you could use the `$Procs.PSBase | get-member` command to view blocked information for the `$Procs` object collection.

Needless to say, this topic is fairly advanced, as `PSBase` is hidden from view. The only time you should need to use it is when the `PSObject` doesn't interpret an object correctly or you're digging around for hidden jewels in PowerShell.

Therefore, with ETS, you can change objects by adapting their structure to your requirements or create new ones. One way to manipulate objects is to adapt (extend) existing object types or create new object types. To do this, you define custom types in a custom types file, based on the structure of the default types file, `Types.ps1xml`.

In the `Types.ps1xml` file, all types are contained in a `<Type></Type>` node, and each type can contain standard members, data members, and object methods. Using this structure as a basis, you can create your own custom types file and load it into a PowerShell session by using the `Update-TypeData` cmdlet, as shown here:

```
PS C:\> Update-TypeData D:\PS\My.Types.Ps1xml
```

You can run this command manually during each PowerShell session or add it to your `profile.ps1` file.

CAUTION

The `Types.ps1xml` file defines default behaviors for all object types in PowerShell. Do *not* modify this file for any reason. Doing so might prevent PowerShell from working, resulting in a "Game over"!

The second way to manipulate an object's structure is to use the `Add-Member` cmdlet to add a user-defined member to an existing object instance, as shown in this example:

```
PS C:\> $Procs = get-process
PS C:\> $Procs | add-member –Type scriptProperty "TotalDays" {
>> $Date = get-date
>> $Date.Subtract($This.StartTime).TotalDays}
>>
PS C:\>
```

This code creates a `scriptProperty` member called `TotalDays` for the collection of objects in the $Procs variable. The `scriptProperty` member can then be called like any other member for those objects, as shown in the next example:

> **NOTE**
>
> The $This variable represents the current object when you're creating a script method.

```
PS C:\> $Procs | where {$_.name -Match "WINWORD"} | ft Name,
TotalDays -AutoSize

Name                TotalDays
----                ---------
WINWORD 5.1238899696898148


PS C:\>
```

Although the new `scriptProperty` member isn't particularly useful, it does demonstrate how to extend an object. Being able to extend objects from both a scripting and cmdlet development context is extremely useful.

Understanding Providers

Most computer systems are used to store data, often in a structure such as a file system. Because of the amount of data stored in these structures, processing and finding information can be unwieldy. Most shells have interfaces, or **providers**, for interacting with data stores in a predictable, set manner. PowerShell also has a set of providers for presenting the contents of data stores through a core set of cmdlets. You can then use these cmdlets to browse, navigate, and manipulate data from stores through a common interface. To get a list of the core cmdlets, use the following command:

```
PS C:\> help about_core_commands
…
    ChildItem CMDLETS
    Get-ChildItem

    CONTENT CMDLETS
    Add-Content
    Clear-Content
    Get-Content
    Set-Content

    DRIVE CMDLETS
    Get-PSDrive
    New-PSDrive
    Remove-PSDrive
```

```
    ITEM CMDLETS
    Clear-Item
    Copy-Item
    Get-Item
    Invoke-Item
    Move-Item
    New-Item
    Remove-Item
    Rename-Item
    Set-Item

    LOCATION CMDLETS
    Get-Location
    Pop-Location
    Push-Location
    Set-Location

    PATH CMDLETS
    Join-Path
    Convert-Path
    Split-Path
    Resolve-Path
    Test-Path

    PROPERTY CMDLETS
    Clear-ItemProperty
    Copy-ItemProperty
    Get-ItemProperty
    Move-ItemProperty
    New-ItemProperty
    Remove-ItemProperty
    Rename-ItemProperty
    Set-ItemProperty

    PROVIDER CMDLETS
    Get-PSProvider


PS C:\>
```

To view built-in PowerShell providers, use the following command:

```
PS C:\> get-psprovider

Name                    Capabilities                    Drives
----                    ------------                    ------
Alias                   ShouldProcess                   {Alias}
Environment             ShouldProcess                   {Env}
```

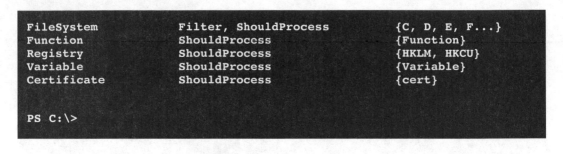

```
FileSystem              Filter, ShouldProcess        {C, D, E, F...}
Function                ShouldProcess                {Function}
Registry                ShouldProcess                {HKLM, HKCU}
Variable                ShouldProcess                {Variable}
Certificate             ShouldProcess                {cert}


PS C:\>
```

The preceding list displays not only built-in providers, but also the drives each provider currently supports. A **drive** is an entity that a provider uses to represent a data store through which data is made available to the PowerShell session. For example, the Registry provider creates a PowerShell drive for the HKEY_LOCAL_MACHINE and HKEY_CURRENT_USER Registry hives.

To see a list of all current PowerShell drives, use the following command:

```
PS C:\> get-psdrive

Name            Provider         Root
----            --------         ----
Alias           Alias
C               FileSystem       C:\
cert            Certificate      \
D               FileSystem       D:\
E               FileSystem       E:\
Env             Environment
F               FileSystem       F:\
Function        Function
G               FileSystem       G:\
HKCU            Registry         HKEY_CURRENT_USER
HKLM            Registry         HKEY_LOCAL_MACHINE
U               FileSystem       U
Variable        Variable


PS C:\>
```

Accessing Drives and Data

One way to access PowerShell drives and their data is with the Set-Location cmdlet. This cmdlet, shown in the following example, changes the working location to another specified location that can be a directory, subdirectory, location stack, or Registry location:

```
PS C:\> set-location hklm:
PS HKLM:\> set-location software\microsoft\windows
PS HKLM:\software\microsoft\windows>
```

Next, use the Get-ChildItem cmdlet to list the subkeys under the Windows key:

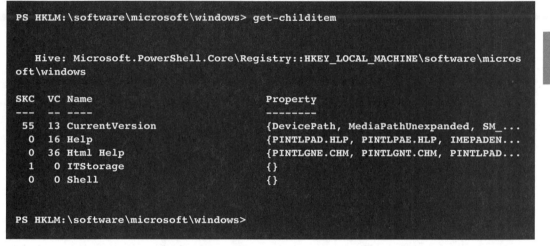

```
PS HKLM:\software\microsoft\windows> get-childitem


    Hive: Microsoft.PowerShell.Core\Registry::HKEY_LOCAL_MACHINE\software\micros
oft\windows

SKC  VC Name                         Property
---  -- ----                         --------
 55  13 CurrentVersion               {DevicePath, MediaPathUnexpanded, SM_...
  0  16 Help                         {PINTLPAD.HLP, PINTLPAE.HLP, IMEPADEN...
  0  36 Html Help                    {PINTLGNE.CHM, PINTLGNT.CHM, PINTLPAD...
  1   0 ITStorage                    {}
  0   0 Shell                        {}


PS HKLM:\software\microsoft\windows>
```

Note that with a Registry drive, the Get-ChildItem cmdlet lists only the subkeys under a key, not the actual Registry values. This is because Registry values are treated as properties for a key rather than a valid item. To retrieve these values from the Registry, you use the Get-ItemProperty cmdlet, as shown in this example:

```
PS HKLM:\software\microsoft\windows> get-itemproperty currentversion


PSPath                    : Microsoft.PowerShell.Core\Registry::HKEY_LOCAL_MACHI
                            NE\software\microsoft\windows\currentversion
PSParentPath              : Microsoft.PowerShell.Core\Registry::HKEY_LOCAL_MACHI
                            NE\software\microsoft\windows
PSChildName               : currentversion
PSDrive                   : HKLM
PSProvider                : Microsoft.PowerShell.Core\Registry
DevicePath                : C:\WINDOWS\inf
MediaPathUnexpanded       : C:\WINDOWS\Media
SM_GamesName              : Games
SM_ConfigureProgramsName  : Set Program Access and Defaults
ProgramFilesDir           : C:\Program Files
CommonFilesDir            : C:\Program Files\Common Files
ProductId                 : 76487-OEM-0011903-00101
WallPaperDir              : C:\WINDOWS\Web\Wallpaper
MediaPath                 : C:\WINDOWS\Media
```

```
ProgramFilesPath            : C:\Program Files
SM_AccessoriesName          : Accessories
PF_AccessoriesName          : Accessories
(default)                   :


PS HKLM:\software\microsoft\windows>
```

As with the Get-Process command, the data returned is a collection of objects. You can modify these objects further to produce the output you want, as this example shows:

```
PS HKLM:\software\microsoft\windows> get-itemproperty currentversion |
select ProductId

ProductId
----------
76487-OEM-XXXXXXX-XXXXX


PS HKLM:\software\microsoft\windows>
```

Accessing data from a FileSystem drive is just as simple. The same type of command logic is used to change the location and display the structure:

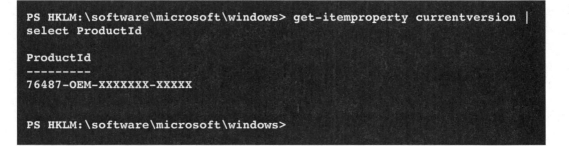

```
PS HKLM:\software\microsoft\windows> set-location c:
PS C:\> set-location "C:\WINDOWS\system32\windowspowershell\v1.0"
PS C:\WINDOWS\system32\windowspowershell\v1.0> get-childitem about_a*


    Directory: Microsoft.PowerShell.Core\FileSystem::C:\WINDOWS\system32\window
    spowershell\v1.0


Mode                LastWriteTime        Length Name
----                -------------        ------ ----
-----         9/8/2006     2:10 AM         5662 about_alias.help.txt
-----         9/8/2006     2:10 AM         3504 about_arithmetic_operators.help.txt
-----         9/8/2006     2:10 AM         8071 about_array.help.txt
-----         9/8/2006     2:10 AM        15137 about_assignment_operators.help.txt
-----         9/8/2006     2:10 AM         5622 about_associative_array.help.txt
-----         9/8/2006     2:10 AM         3907 about_automatic_variables.help.txt
...


PS C:\WINDOWS\system32\windowspowershell\v1.0>
```

What's different is that data is stored in an item instead of being a property of that item. To retrieve data from an item, use the Get-Content cmdlet, as shown in this example:

```
PS C:\WINDOWS\system32\windowspowershell\v1.0> get-content
about_Alias.help.txt
TOPIC
    Aliases

SHORT DESCRIPTION
    Using pseudonyms to refer to cmdlet names in the Windows PowerShell

LONG DESCRIPTION
    An alias is a pseudonym, or "nickname," that you can assign to a
    cmdlet so that you can use the alias in place of the cmdlet name.
    The Windows PowerShell interprets the alias as though you had
    entered the actual cmdlet name. For example, suppose that you want
    to retrieve today's date for the year 1905. Without an alias, you
    would use the following command:

        Get-Date -year 1905
...


PS C:\WINDOWS\system32\windowspowershell\v1.0>
```

> **NOTE**
>
> Not all drives are based on a hierarchical data store. For example, the Environment, Function, and Variable PowerShell providers aren't hierarchical. Data accessed through these providers is in the root location on the associated drive.

Mounting a Drive

PowerShell drives can be created and removed, which is handy when you're working with a location or set of locations frequently. Instead of having to change the location or use an absolute path, you can create new drives (also referred to as "mounting a drive" in PowerShell) as shortcuts to those locations. To do this, use the New-PSDrive cmdlet, shown in the following example:

```
PS C:\> new-psdrive -name PSScripts -root D:\Dev\Scripts -psp FileSystem

Name        Provider      Root                                CurrentLocation
----        --------      ----                                ---------------
PSScripts   FileSystem    D:\Dev\Scripts


PS C:\> get-psdrive
```

```
Name              Provider       Root                                   CurrentLocation
----              --------       ----                                   ---------------
Alias             Alias
C                 FileSystem     C:\
cert              Certificate    \
D                 FileSystem     D:\
E                 FileSystem     E:\
Env               Environment
F                 FileSystem     F:\
Function          Function
G                 FileSystem     G:\
HKCU              Registry       HKEY_CURRENT_USER                             software
HKLM              Registry       HKEY_LOCAL_MACHINE                    ...crosoft\windows
PSScripts         FileSystem     D:\Dev\Scripts
U                 FileSystem     U:\
Variable          Variable


PS C:\>
```

To remove a drive, use the `Remove-PSDrive` cmdlet, as shown here:

```
PS C:\> remove-psdrive -name PSScripts
PS C:\> get-psdrive

Name              Provider       Root                                   CurrentLocation
----              --------       ----                                   ---------------
Alias             Alias
C                 FileSystem     C:\
cert              Certificate    \
D                 FileSystem     D:\
E                 FileSystem     E:\
Env               Environment
F                 FileSystem     F:\
Function          Function
G                 FileSystem     G:\
HKCU              Registry       HKEY_CURRENT_USER                      software
HKLM              Registry       HKEY_LOCAL_MACHINE                     ...crosoft\windows
U                 FileSystem     U:\
Variable          Variable


PS C:\>
```

Understanding Errors

PowerShell errors are divided into two types: terminating and nonterminating.
Terminating errors, as the name implies, stop a command. **Nonterminating errors** are
generally just reported without stopping a command. Both types of errors are reported in

the $Error variable, which is a collection of errors that have occurred during the current PowerShell session. This collection contains the most recent error, as indicated by $Error[0] up to $MaximumErrorCount, which defaults to 256.

Errors in the $Error variable can be represented by the ErrorRecord object. It contains error exception information as well as a number of other properties that are useful for understanding why an error occurred

The next example shows the information that is contained in InvocationInfo property of an ErrorRecord object:

```
PS C:\> $Error[0].InvocationInfo


MyCommand          : Get-ChildItem
ScriptLineNumber   : 1
OffsetInLine       : -2147483648
ScriptName         :
Line               : dir z:
PositionMessage    :
                     At line:1 char:4
                     + dir  <<<< z:
InvocationName     : dir
PipelineLength     : 1
PipelinePosition   : 1


PS C:\>
```

Based on this information, you can determine a number of details about $Error[0], including the command that caused the error to be thrown. This information is crucial to understanding errors and handling them effectively.

Use the following command to see a full list of ErrorRecord properties:

```
PS C:\> $Error[0] | get-member -MemberType Property


    TypeName: System.Management.Automation.ErrorRecord

Name                     MemberType  Definition
----                     ----------  ----------
CategoryInfo             Property    System.Management.Automation.ErrorCategoryI...
ErrorDetails             Property    System.Management.Automation.ErrorDetails E...
Exception                Property    System.Exception Exception {get;}
FullyQualifiedErrorId    Property    System.String FullyQualifiedErrorId {get;}
```

```
InvocationInfo           Property    System.Management.Automation.InvocationInfo...
TargetObject             Property    System.Object TargetObject {get;}


PS C:\>
```

Table 3.1 shows the definitions for each of the ErrorRecord properties that are listed in the preceding example:

TABLE 3.1   ErrorRecord Property Definitions

Property	Definition
CategoryInfo	Indicates under which category an error is classified
ErrorDetails	Can be null, but when used provides additional information about the error
Exception	The error that occurred
FullyQualifiedErrorId	Identifies an error condition more specifically
InvocationInfo	Can be null, but when used explains the context in which the error occurred
TargetObject	Can be null, but when used indicates the object being operated on

Error Handling

Methods for handling errors in PowerShell can range from simple to complex. The simple method is to allow PowerShell to handle the error. Depending on the type of error, the command or script might terminate or continue. However, if the default error handler doesn't fit your needs, you can devise a more complex error-handling scheme by using the methods discussed in the following sections.

Method One: cmdlet Preferences

In PowerShell, **ubiquitous parameters** are available to all cmdlets. Among them are the ErrorAction and ErrorVariable parameters, used to determine how cmdlets handle *nonterminating* errors, as shown in this example:

```
PS C:\> get-childitem z: -ErrorVariable Err -ErrorAction SilentlyContinue
PS C:\> if ($Err){write-host $Err -Foregroundcolor Red}
Cannot find drive. A drive with name 'z' does not exist.
PS C:\>
```

The ErrorAction parameter defines how a cmdlet behaves when it encounters a *nonterminating* error. In the preceding example, ErrorAction is defined as SilentlyContinue, meaning the cmdlet continues running with no output if it encounters a *nonterminating* error. Other options for ErrorAction are as follows:

- `Continue`—Print error and continue (default action)

- `Inquire`—Ask users whether they want to continue, halt, or suspend

- `Stop`—Halt execution of the command or script

> **NOTE**
>
> The term *nonterminating* has been emphasized in this section because a terminating error bypasses the defined `ErrorAction` and is delivered to the default or custom error handler.

The `ErrorVariable` parameter defines the variable name for the error object generated by a *nonterminating* error. As shown in the previous example, `ErrorVariable` is defined as `Err`. Notice the variable name doesn't have the $ prefix. However, to access `ErrorVariable` outside a cmdlet, you use the variable's name with the $ prefix (`$Err`). Furthermore, after defining `ErrorVariable`, the resulting variable is valid for the current PowerShell session or associated script block. This means other cmdlets can append error objects to an existing `ErrorVariable` by using a + prefix, as shown in this example:

```
PS C:\> get-childitem z: -ErrorVariable Err -ErrorAction SilentlyContinue
PS C:\> get-childitem y: -ErrorVariable +Err -ErrorAction SilentlyContinue
PS C:\> write-host $Err[0] -Foregroundcolor Red
Cannot find drive. A drive with name 'z' does not exist.
PS C:\> write-host $Err[1] -Foregroundcolor Red
Cannot find drive. A drive with name 'y' does not exist.
PS C:\>
```

Method Two: Trapping Errors

When encountering a terminating error, PowerShell's default behavior is to display the error and halt the command or script execution. If you want to use custom error handling for a terminating error, you must define an exception trap handler to prevent the terminating error (`ErrorRecord`) from being sent to the default error-handling mechanism. The same holds true for *nonterminating* errors as PowerShell's default behavior is to just display the error and continue the command or script execution.

To define a trap, you use the following syntax:

```
trap ExceptionType {code; keyword}
```

The first part is *ExceptionType*, which specifies the type of error a trap accepts. If no *ExceptionType* is defined, a trap accepts all errors. The *code* part can consist of a command or set of commands that run after an error is delivered to the trap. Defining commands to run by a trap is optional. The last part, *keyword*, is what determines whether the trap allows the statement block where the error occurred to execute or terminate.

Supported keywords are as follows:

- Break—Causes the exception to be rethrown and stops the current scope from executing
- Continue—Allows the current scope execution to continue at the next line where the exception occurred
- Return [*argument*]—Stops the current scope from executing and returns the argument, if specified

If a keyword isn't specified, the trap uses the keyword Return [*argument*]; *argument* is the ErrorRecord that was originally delivered to the trap.

Trap Examples

The following two examples show how traps can be defined to handle errors. The first trap example shows a trap being used in conjunction with a *nonterminating* error that is produced from an invalid DNS name being given to the System.Net.Dns class. The second example shows a trap being again used in conjunction with a *nonterminating* error that is produced from the Get-Item cmdlet. However, in this case, because the ErrorAction parameter has been defined as Stop, the error is in fact a terminating error that is then handled by the trap.

Example one: errortraps1.ps1

```
$DNSName = "www.-baddnsname-.com"


trap [System.Management.Automation.MethodInvocationException]{
    write-host ("ERROR: " + $_) -Foregroundcolor Red; Continue}


write-host "Getting IP address for" $DNSName
write-host ([System.Net.Dns]::GetHostAddresses("www.$baddnsname$.com"))
write-host "Done Getting IP Address"
```

The $_ parameter in this example represents the ErrorRecord that was delivered to the trap.

Output:

```
PS C:\> .\errortraps1.ps1
Getting IP address for www.-baddnsname-.com
ERROR: Exception calling "GetHostAddresses" with "1" argument(s): "No such host
is known"
Done Getting IP Address
PS C:\>
```

Example two: `errortraps2.ps1`

```
write-host "Changing drive to z:"

trap {write-host("[ERROR] " + $_) -Foregroundcolor Red; Continue}

get-item z: -ErrorAction Stop
$TXTFiles = get-childitem *.txt -ErrorAction Stop

write-host "Done getting items"
```

3

> **NOTE**
>
> A cmdlet doesn't generate a terminating error unless there's a syntax error. This means a trap doesn't catch nonterminating errors from a cmdlet unless the error is transformed into a terminating error by setting the cmdlet's ErrorAction to Stop.

Output:

```
PS C:\> .\errortraps2.ps1
Changing drive to z:
[ERROR] Command execution stopped because the shell variable
"ErrorActionPreference" is set to Stop: Cannot find drive. A drive
with name 'z' does not exist.
Done getting items
PS C:\>
```

Trap Scopes

A PowerShell scope, as discussed in Chapter 2, "PowerShell Basics," determines how traps are executed. Generally, a trap is defined and executed within the same scope. For example, you define a trap in a certain scope; when a terminating error is encountered in that scope, the trap is executed. If the current scope doesn't contain a trap and an outer scope does, any terminating errors encountered break out of the current scope and are delivered to the trap in the outer scope.

Method Three: The Throw **Keyword**

In PowerShell, you can generate your own terminating errors. This doesn't mean causing errors by using incorrect syntax. Instead, you can generate a terminating error on purpose by using the throw keyword, as shown in the next example if a user doesn't define the argument for the MyParam parameter when trying to run the MyParam.ps1 script. This type of behavior is very useful when data from functions, cmdlets, data sources, applications, etc. is not what is expected and hence may prevent the script or set of commands from executing correctly further into the execution process.

Script:

```
param([string]$MyParam = $(throw write-host "You did not define MyParam"
-Foregroundcolor Red))

write-host $MyParam
```

Output:

```
PS C:\ .\MyParam.ps1
You did not define MyParam
ScriptHalted
At C:\MyParam.ps1:1 char:33
+ param([string]$MyParam = $(throw  <<<< write-host "You did not define MyParam
" -Foregroundcolor Red))
PS C:\>
```

PowerShell Profiles

A PowerShell **profile** is a saved collection of settings for customizing the PowerShell environment. There are four types of profiles, loaded in a specific order each time PowerShell starts. The following sections explain these profile types, where they should be located, and the order in which they are loaded.

The All Users Profile

This profile is located in %windir%\system32\windowspowershell\v1.0\profile.ps1. Settings in the All Users profile are applied to all PowerShell users on the current machine. If you plan to configure PowerShell settings across the board for users on a machine, then this would be the profile to use.

The All Users Host-Specific Profile

This profile is located in %windir%\system32\windowspowershell\v1.0*ShellID*_ profile.ps1. Settings in the All Users host-specific profile are applied to all users of the current shell (by default, the PowerShell console). PowerShell supports the concept of multiple shells or hosts. For example, the PowerShell console is a host and the one most users use exclusively. However, other applications can call an instance of the PowerShell runtime to access and run PowerShell commands and scripts. An application that does this is called a **hosting application** and uses a host-specific profile to control the PowerShell configuration. The host-specific profile name is reflected by the host's ShellID. In the PowerShell console, the ShellID is the following:

```
PS C:\ $ShellId
Microsoft.PowerShell
PS C:\
```

Putting this together, the PowerShell console's All Users host-specific profile is named `Microsoft.PowerShell_profile.ps1`. For other hosts, the `ShellID` and All Users host-specific profile names are different. For example, the PowerShell Analyzer (www.powershellanalyzer.com) is a PowerShell host that acts as a rich graphical interface for the PowerShell environment. Its `ShellID` is `PowerShellAnalyzer.PSA`, and its All Users host-specific profile name is `PowerShellAnalyzer.PSA_profile.ps1`.

The Current User's Profile

This profile is located in `%userprofile%\My Documents\WindowsPowerShell\profile.ps1`. Users who want to control their own profile settings can use the current user's profile. Settings in this profile are applied only to the user's current PowerShell session and doesn't affect any other users.

The Current User's Host-Specific Profile

This profile is located in `%userprofile%\My Documents\WindowsPowerShell\ShellID_ profile.ps1`. Like the All Users host-specific profile, this profile type loads settings for the current shell. However, the settings are user specific.

> **NOTE**
>
> When you start the shell for the first time, you might see a message indicating that scripts are disabled and no profiles are loaded. You can modify this behavior by changing the PowerShell execution policy, discussed in the following section.

Understanding Security

When WSH was released with Windows 98, it was a godsend for Windows administrators who wanted the same automation capabilities as their UNIX brethren. At the same time, virus writers quickly discovered that WSH also opened up a large attack vector against Windows systems.

Almost anything on a Windows system can be automated and controlled by using WSH, which is an advantage for administrators. However, WSH doesn't provide any security in script execution. If given a script, WSH runs it. Where the script comes from or its purpose doesn't matter. With this behavior, WSH became known more as a security vulnerability than an automation tool.

Execution Policies

Because of past criticisms of WSH's security, when the PowerShell team set out to build a Microsoft shell, the team decided to include an execution policy to mitigate the security threats posed by malicious code. An **execution policy** defines restrictions on how PowerShell allows scripts to run or what configuration files can be loaded. PowerShell has four execution policies, discussed in more detail in the following sections: Restricted, AllSigned, RemoteSigned, and Unrestricted.

Restricted

By default, PowerShell is configured to run under the Restricted execution policy. This execution policy is the most secure because it allows PowerShell to operate only in an interactive mode. This means no scripts can be run, and only configuration files digitally signed by a trusted publisher are allowed to run or load.

AllSigned

The AllSigned execution policy is a notch under Restricted. When this policy is enabled, only scripts or configuration files that are digitally signed by a publisher you trust can be run or loaded. Here's an example of what you might see if the AllSigned policy has been enabled:

```
PS C:\Scripts> .\evilscript.ps1
The file C:\Scripts\evilscript.ps1 cannot be loaded. The file
C:\Scripts\evilscript.ps1 is not digitally signed. The script will not
execute on the system. Please see "get-help about_signing" for more
details.
At line:1 char:16
+ .\evilscript.ps1 <<<<
PS C:\Scripts>
```

Signing a script or configuration file requires a code-signing certificate. This certificate can come from a trusted certificate authority (CA), or you can generate one with the Certificate Creation Tool (Makecert.exe). Usually, however, you want a valid code-signing certificate from a well-known trusted CA, such as Verisign, Thawte, or your corporation's internal public key infrastructure (PKI). Otherwise, sharing your scripts or configuration files with others might be difficult because your computer isn't a trusted CA by default.

> **NOTE**
>
> Chapter 4, "Code Signing," explains how to obtain a valid trusted code-signing certificate. Reading this chapter is strongly recommended because of the importance of digitally signing scripts and configuration files.

RemoteSigned

The `RemoteSigned` execution policy is designed to prevent remote PowerShell scripts and configuration files that aren't digitally signed by a trusted publisher from running or loading automatically. Scripts and configuration files that are locally created can be loaded and run without being digitally signed, however.

A remote script or configuration file can be obtained from a communication application, such as Microsoft Outlook, Internet Explorer, Outlook Express, or Windows Messenger. Running or loading a file downloaded from any of these applications results in the following error message:

```
PS C:\Scripts> .\interscript.ps1
The file C:\Scripts\interscript.ps1 cannot be loaded. The file
C:\Scripts\interscript.ps1 is not digitally signed. The script will
not execute on the system. Please see "get-help about_signing" for
more details..
At line:1 char:17
+ .\interscript.ps1 <<<<
PS C:\Scripts>
```

To run or load an unsigned remote script or configuration file, you must specify whether to trust the file. To do this, right-click the file in Windows Explorer and click Properties. In the General tab, click the Unblock button (see Figure 3.1).

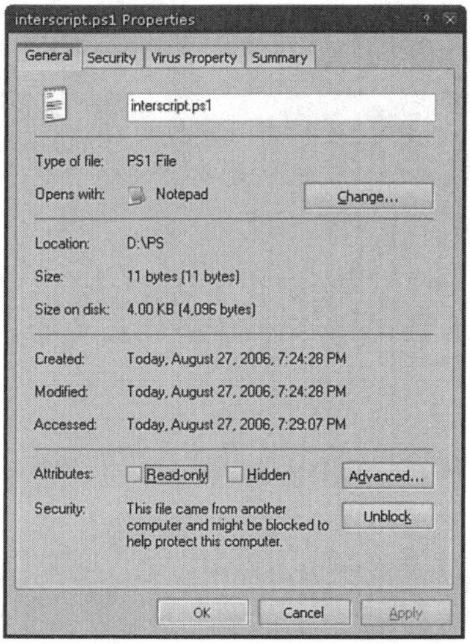

FIGURE 3.1   Trusting a remote script or configuration file

After you trust the file, the script or configuration file can be run or loaded. If it's digitally signed but the publisher isn't trusted, PowerShell displays the following prompt:

```
PS C:\Scripts> .\signed.ps1

Do you want to run software from this untrusted publisher?
File C:\Scripts\signed.ps1 is published by CN=companyabc.com, OU=IT,
O=companyabc.com, L=Oakland, S=California, C=US and is not trusted on
your system. Only run scripts from trusted publishers.
[V] Never run  [D] Do not run  [R] Run once  [A] Always run  [?] Help
(default is "D"):
```

In this case, you must choose whether to trust the file content.

> **NOTE**
>
> Chapter 4 explains the options in this prompt in more detail.

Unrestricted

As the name suggests, the Unrestricted execution policy removes almost all restrictions for running scripts or loading configuration files. All local or signed trusted files can run or load, but for remote files, PowerShell prompts you to choose an option for running or loading that file, as shown here:

```
PS C:\Scripts> .\remotescript.ps1

Security Warning
Run only scripts that you trust. While scripts from the Internet can
be useful, this script can potentially harm your computer. Do you want
to run
C:\Scripts\remotescript.ps1?
[D] Do not run  [R] Run once  [S] Suspend  [?] Help (default is "D"):
```

Setting the Execution Policy

To change the execution policy, you use the Set-ExecutionPolicy cmdlet, shown here:

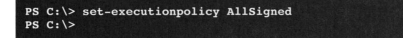

```
PS C:\> set-executionpolicy AllSigned
PS C:\>
```

If you want to know the current execution policy, use the Get-ExecutionPolicy cmdlet:

```
PS C:\> get-executionpolicy
AllSigned
PS C:\>
```

By default, when PowerShell is first installed, the execution policy is set to Restricted. As you know, default settings never stay default for long. In addition, if PowerShell is installed on many machines, the likelihood of its execution policy being set to Unrestricted increases.

Fortunately, you can control the PowerShell execution policy through a Registry setting. This setting is a REG_SZ value named ExecutionPolicy, which is located in the HKLM\SOFTWARE\Microsoft\PowerShell\1\ShellIds\Microsoft.PowerShell key. Controlling the execution policy through the Registry means you can enforce a policy setting across many machines managed by a Group Policy Object (GPO).

In the past, creating a GPO to control the execution policy was simple because the PowerShell installation includes a Group Policy Administrative Template (ADM). However, as of the PowerShell RC2 release, the ADM is no longer part of the installation and may or may not be available in a separate PowerShell download. If Microsoft doesn't provide an ADM to control the execution policy, you can always create your own, as shown in the following example:

```
CLASS MACHINE

CATEGORY !!PowerShell
    POLICY !!Security
        KEYNAME "SOFTWARE\Microsoft\PowerShell\1\ShellIds\Microsoft.PowerShell"

        EXPLAIN !!PowerShell_ExecutionPolicy

        PART !!ExecutionPolicy EDITTEXT REQUIRED
            VALUENAME "ExecutionPolicy"
        END PART
    END POLICY
END CATEGORY

[strings]
PowerShell=PowerShell
Security=Security Settings
PowerShell_ExecutionPolicy=If enabled, this policy will set the PowerShell
execution policy on a machine to the defined value.  Execution policy values can be
Restricted, AllSigned, RemoteSigned, and Unrestricted.
Executionpolicy=Execution Policy
```

You can find a working version of this ADM on the PowerShell Unleashed Reference Web site: www.samspublishing.com. Although the `PowerShellExecutionPolicy.adm` file has been tested and should work in your environment, note that the execution policy settings in this file are considered preference settings. Preference settings are GPOs that are Registry values found outside the approved Group Policy Registry trees. When a GPO containing preference settings goes out of scope, the preference settings aren't removed from the Registry.

> **NOTE**
>
> As with everything provided on the PowerShell Unleashed Reference Web site, test the ADM in a non-production environment before deploying a GPO that uses it.

To configure the `PowerShellExecutionPolicy.adm` file, follow these steps:

1. Log on to a GPO management machine as the GPO administrator.

2. Using the Group Policy MMC, create a GPO named **PowerShell**.

3. In the console tree, click to expand **Computer Configuration** and then **Administrative Templates**.

4. Right-click **Administrative Templates** and click **Add/Remove Templates** in the shortcut menu.

5. Navigate to the folder with the `PowerShellExecutionPolicy.adm` file. Select the file, click **Open**, and then click **Close**. The PowerShell node is then displayed under the Administrative Templates node.

6. Click the **Administrative Templates** node, and then click **View**, **Filtering** from the Group Policy MMC menu. Click to clear the **Only show policy settings that can be fully managed** checkbox. Clearing this option allows you to manage preference settings.

7. Next, click the **PowerShell** node under Administrative Templates.

8. In the details pane, right-click **Security Settings** and click **Properties** in the shortcut menu.

9. Click **Enabled**.

10. Set the **Execution Policy** to one of these values: Restricted, AllSigned, RemoteSigned, or Unrestricted.

11. Close the GPO, and then close the Group Policy MMC.

Controlling the execution policy through a GPO preference setting might seem like a less then perfect solution. After all, a preference setting doesn't offer the same level of security as an execution policy setting, so users with the necessary rights can modify it easily. This lack of security is probably why Microsoft removed the original ADM file from

PowerShell. A future release of PowerShell might allow controlling the execution policy with a valid GPO policy setting.

Additional Security Measures

Execution policies aren't the only security layer Microsoft implemented in PowerShell. PowerShell script files with the `.ps1` extension can't be run from Windows Explorer because they are associated with Notepad. In other words, you can't just double-click a `.ps1` file to run it. Instead, PowerShell scripts must run from a PowerShell session by using the relative or absolute path or through the cmd command prompt by using the PowerShell executable.

Another security measure, explained in Chapter 2, is that to run or open a file in the current directory from the PowerShell console, you must prefix the command with `.\` or `./`. This feature prevents PowerShell users from accidentally running a command or PowerShell script without specifying its execution explicitly.

Last, by default, there's no method for connecting to or calling PowerShell remotely. However, that doesn't mean you can't write an application that allows remote PowerShell connections. In fact, it has been done. If you're interested in learning how, download the PowerShell Remoting beta from www.gotdotnet.com/workspaces/workspace.aspx?id= ce09cdaf-7da2-4f1c-bed3-f8cb35de5aea.

The PowerShell Language

From this point on, this book varies from the usual format of many books on scripting languages, which try to explain scripting concepts instead of showing you actual working scripts. This book focuses on the practical applications of PowerShell.

It's assumed you have a basic understanding of scripting. In addition, because the PowerShell scripting language is similar to Perl, C#, and even VBScript, there's no need to spend time reviewing `for` loops, `if...then` statements, and other fundamentals of scripting.

Granted, there are some unique aspects to the PowerShell language, but you can consult the PowerShell documentation for that information. This is not a language reference book; it's about how PowerShell can be applied in the real world. For more detailed information about the PowerShell language, you can download the PowerShell User Guide from www.microsoft.com/downloads/details.aspx?FamilyId=B4720B00-9A66-430F-BD56-EC48BFCA154F&displaylang=en.

Summary

In this chapter, you have delved deeper into what PowerShell is and how it works. You reviewed such topics as Powershell's Providers, how it handles errors, its profiles, and its execution policies. However, of the items reviewed the most important concept to take from this chapter is that PowerShell is built from and around the .NET Framework. As such, PowerShell is not like other shells because it is an object-based shell that attempts to abstract all objects into a common form that can be used without modification (parsing) in your commands and scripts. Going forward this and the knowledge that you have learned from Chapters 2 and 3 will be the keystone from which you shall explore PowerShell scripting. Moving through each chapter, the scripts will increase in complexity as we review different aspects of how PowerShell can be used for Windows automation.

Code Signing

Introduction

In an effort to learn how to sign PowerShell scripts and configuration files, you have searched the Internet, read several blogs about code signing, reviewed the PowerShell documentation, and even browsed through some PowerShell books. Yet the more you read about code signing, the more confused you are. Finally, in frustration, you open your PowerShell console and enter the following command:

```
set-executionpolicy unrestricted
```

Before you enter this command, remember what you learned about execution policies in Chapter 3, "PowerShell: A More In-Depth Look." Using the Unrestricted setting negates an important security layer that was designed to prevent malicious code from running on your system. Code signing is another essential component of PowerShell security, but many people believe it's too complicated to learn and set their execution policies to Unrestricted to avoid having to use it. In response to an entry on script signing at Scott Hanselman's blog (www.hanselman.com/blog), one person commented that "Handling code signing certificates is way over the head of most users, including average developers and admins." This statement indicates a real need that should be addressed—hence this chapter devoted to code signing. Code signing seems complicated on the surface, but with some clear instructions, the process is easy to understand. Scripters, developers, and administrators should be familiar with it as an important part of their overall security efforts.

What Is Code Signing?

In short, **code signing** is the process of digitally signing scripts, executables, DLLs, and so forth to establish a level of trust for the code. The trust granted to digitally signed code is based on two assumptions. One, a signed piece of code ensures that the code hasn't been altered or corrupted since being signed. Two, the digital signature serves to prove the identity of the code's author, which helps you determine whether the code is safe for execution.

These two assumptions are a way to ensure the integrity and authenticity of code. However, these assumptions alone are no guarantee that signed code is safe to run. For these two assumptions to be considered valid, you need the digital signature and the infra-structure that establishes a mechanism for identifying the digital signature's originator.

A digital signature is based on public key cryptography, which has algorithms used for encryption and decryption. These algorithms generate a key pair consisting of a private key and a public key. The private key is kept secret so that only the owner has access to it, but the public key can be distributed to other entities through some form of secure inter-action. Depending on the type of interaction, one key is used to lock (encrypt) the communication, and the other key is used unlock (decrypt) the communication. In digital signatures, the private key is used to generate a signature, and the public key is used to validate the generated signature. The process is as follows:

1. A one-way hash of the content (documents, code, and so forth) being signed is generated by using a cryptographic digest.

2. The hash is then encrypted with the private key, resulting in the digital signature.

3. Next, the content is transmitted to the recipient.

4. The recipient then creates another one-way hash of the content and decrypts the hash by using the sender's public key.

5. Finally, the recipient compares the two hashes. If both hashes are the same, the digital signature is valid and the content hasn't been modified.

NOTE

A one-way hash (also known as a message digest, fingerprint, or compression function) is a cryptographic algorithm that turns data into a fixed-length binary sequence. The term one-way comes from the fact that it is difficult to derive the original data from the resulting sequence.

To associate an entity, such as an organization, a person, or a computer, with a digital signature, a digital certificate is used. A digital certificate consists of the public key and identifying information about the key pair owner. To ensure a digital certificate's integrity, it's also digitally signed. A digital certificate can be signed by its owner or a trustworthy third party called a **certificate authority (CA)**.

The act of associating code with the entity that created and published it removes the anonymity of running code. Furthermore, associating a digital signature with a code-signing certificate is much like using a brand name to establish trust and reliability. Armed with this information, users of PowerShell scripts and configuration files can make informed decisions about running a script or loading a configuration file. This, in a nutshell, is why code signing is an important aspect of the PowerShell security framework.

Obtaining a Code-Signing Certificate

There are two methods for obtaining a code-signing certificate: generating self-signed certificates and using a CA from a valid public key infrastructure (PKI).

Generating a self-signed certificate for signing your PowerShell scripts and configuration files is simpler and quicker and has the advantage of not costing anything. However, no independent third party verifies the certificate's authenticity, so it doesn't have the same level of trust that's expected from code signing. As a result, no other entity would trust your certificate by default. To distribute your PowerShell script or configuration file to other machines, your certificate would have to be added as a trusted root CA and a trusted publisher.

Although changing what an entity trusts is possible, there are two problems. One, entities outside your sphere of control might not choose to trust your certificate because there's no independent method for verifying who you are. Two, if the private key associated with your self-signed certificate becomes compromised or invalid, there's no way to manage your certificate's validity on other entities. Given these problems, limiting the use of self-signed certificates to a local machine or for testing purposes is recommended.

If you plan to digitally sign your scripts and configuration files so that they can be used in an enterprise or even the public realm, you should consider the second method of obtaining a code-signing certificate: a CA from a valid PKI. A valid PKI can mean a well-known and trusted commercial organization, such as www.globalsign.net, www.thawte.com, or www.verisign.com, or an internal PKI owned and operated by your organization. Obtaining a code-signing certificate from an external PKI can be quick and easy, as long as you keep a few caveats in mind.

First, a certificate must be purchased from the owner of the external PKI. Second, because you're purchasing the certificate from an outside entity, you're placing a lot of trust in the organization's integrity. For these reasons, code-signing certificates from commercial PKIs should be limited to certificates used to sign scripts and configuration files for public distribution.

Therefore, an internal PKI should be used for scripts and configuration files not meant for public consumption. Keep in mind that deploying and managing an internal PKI takes planning, effort, and money (Hardware Security Modules (HSMs), security consultants, and so forth can be expensive). Most organizations tend to shy away from the effort required to set up a PKI. Instead, they bring up CAs ad hoc, purchase certificates from commercial PKIs, or ignore PKI requirements. A commercial PKI might not provide the level of trust your organization needs, and the ad hoc approach isn't recommended because it reduces trust of certificates generated by rogue CAs, which are CAs that have a low level of assurance around their integrity. Having no valid PKI infrastructure could make internal distribution of digitally signed files difficult. Last, organizations that ignore PKI requirements illustrate another drawback of using an internal PKI: time.

If there's no PKI in your organization, obtaining a code-signing certificate might take an extended period of time. PKIs do not materialize overnight. If you have identified a PKI requirement for your scripts, there are probably additional PKI requirements in your organization. These requirements will need to be identified and considered before a PKI is deployed. Trying to drive a PKI deployment around your needs alone isn't the best approach for an infrastructure service that needs to meet the needs of an entire organization. After you have presented the PKI requirement to your organization, you might have to wait for the services to be provided. However, after the PKI is in place, you can obtain code-signing certificates knowing that the infrastructure fully supports the distribution of your signed PowerShell scripts and configuration files.

Method One: Self-Signed Certificate

This method of creating a self-signed certificate is based on using the makecert utility, which is part of the .NET Framework Software Development Kit (SDK). Follow these steps:

1. Download the latest Microsoft .NET Framework SDK from **http://msdn2.microsoft. com/en-us/netframework/aa731542.aspx**. At the time of this writing, the current .NET Framework SDK version is 2.0.

2. Install the SDK on the machine where you want to generate the self-signed certificate.

3. Locate the **makecert** utility on your system. The default location is C:\Program Files\Microsoft Visual Studio 8\SDK\v2.0\Bin.

4. Open up a cmd command prompt and change the working directory to the location of the makecert utility using the cd command.

5. Create a self-signed certificate by using the following command:

```
makecert -r -pe -n "CN=CertificateCommonName" -b 01/01/2000 -e 01/01/2099 –eku
1.3.6.1.5.5.7.3.3 -ss My
```

You should see output similar to the following:

```
C:\Program Files\Microsoft Visual Studio 8\SDK\v2.0\Bin>makecert -r -
pe -n "CN= Turtle Code Signing" -b 01/01/2000 -e 01/01/2099 -eku
1.3.6.1.5.5.7.3.3 -ss My
Succeeded
```

6. Finally, use the following PowerShell command to verify that the certificate was installed:

```
PS C:\> get-childitem cert:\CurrentUser\My -codesign


    Directory: Microsoft.PowerShell.Security\Certificate::CurrentUser\My


Thumbprint                                Subject
----------                                -------
944E910757A862B53DE3113249E12BCA9C7DD0DE  CN=Turtle Code Signing


PS C:\>
```

Method Two: CA Signed Certificate

This method is based on obtaining a code-signing certificate from a Microsoft Windows CA. These steps assume a PKI has been deployed at your organization. If not, installing Windows Certificate Services to meet your immediate need isn't recommended. Follow these steps to request a code-signing certificate:

1. Request that your PKI administrator create and enable a code-signing certificate template for your PowerShell scripts and configuration files.

2. Use Internet Explorer to access the Certificate Services Web Enrollment site at **https://CAServerName/certsrv** (replacing CAServerName with the name of your server).

3. Click the **Request a Certificate** link.

4. On the Request a Certificate page, click the **Advanced certificate request** link.

5. On the Advanced Certificate Request page, click the **Create and submit a request to this CA** link.

6. In the Certificate Template section, click to select the code-signing certificate your PKI administrator created.

7. Enter the rest of the identifying information and certificate request options according to your organization's certificate policy. You can use Figure 4.1 as a guideline.

8. Click the **Submit** button.

9. In the Potential Scripting Violation dialog box that opens (see Figure 4.2), click **Yes** to continue.

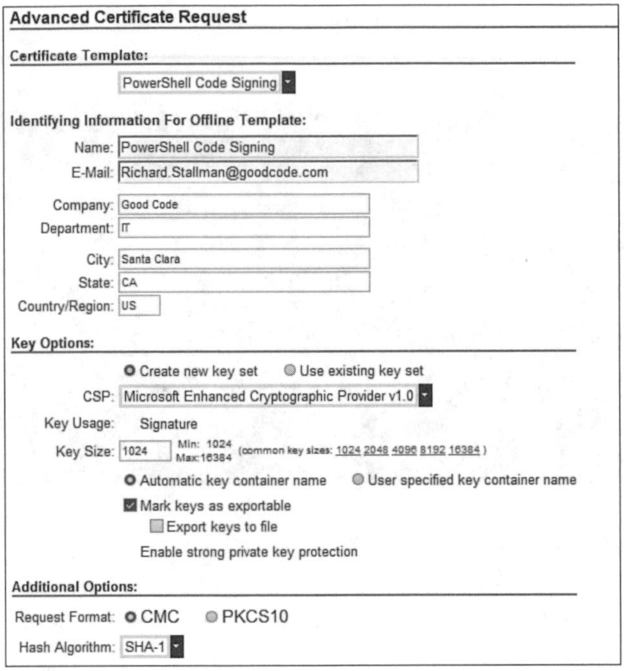
Advanced Certificate Request
Certificate Template:
PowerShell Code Signing
Identifying Information For Offline Template:
Name: PowerShell Code Signing
E-Mail: Richard.Stallman@goodcode.com
Company: Good Code
Department: IT
City: Santa Clara
State: CA
Country/Region: US
Key Options:
Create new key set
Use existing key set
CSP: Microsoft Enhanced Cryptographic Provider v1.0
Key Usage: Signature
Key Size: 1024
Min: 1024
Max:16384
(common key sizes: 1024 2048 4096 8192 16384)
Automatic key container name
User specified key container name
Mark keys as exportable
Export keys to file
Enable strong private key protection
Additional Options:
Request Format: CMC
PKCS10
Hash Algorithm: SHA-1

FIGURE 4.1 Example of requesting a code-signing certificate

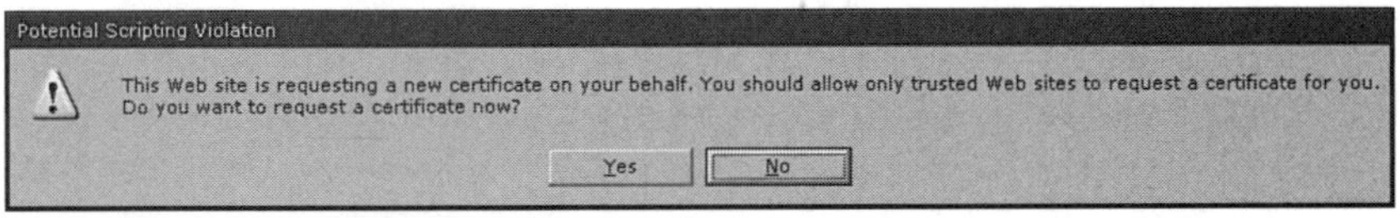
Potential Scripting Violation
This Web site is requesting a new certificate on your behalf. You should allow only trusted Web sites to request a certificate for you.
Do you want to request a certificate now?
Yes
No

FIGURE 4.2 Potential Scripting Violation message box

10. Next, if applicable, set the private key security level based on your organization's certificate policy (see Figure 4.3), and then click **OK**.

Creating a new RSA signature key
An application is creating a Protected item.
CryptoAPI Private Key
Security level set to Medium
Set Security Level...
OK
Cancel
Details...

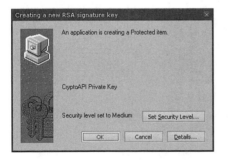

FIGURE 4.3 Creating a new RSA signature key dialog box

11. If your organization's certificate policy requires approval from a certificate manager, then ask your certificate manager to approve the certificate request you just submitted. If approval isn't required, go to step 16.

12. After the certificate request has been approved, use Internet Explorer to access the Certificate Services Web Enrollment site at **https://CAServerName/certsrv** (replacing CAServerName with the name of your server).

13. Click the **View the status of a pending certificate request** link.

14. On the next page, click the appropriate certificate request link.

15. On the Certificate Issued page, click the **Install this certificate** link.

16. In the Potential Scripting Violation dialog box that opens (see Figure 4.4), click **Yes** to continue.

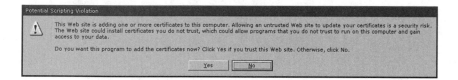

FIGURE 4.4   Potential Scripting Violation message box

17. Finally, the Certificate Services Web Enrollment site states that the certificate was installed successfully. Use the following PowerShell command to verify the certificate installation status:

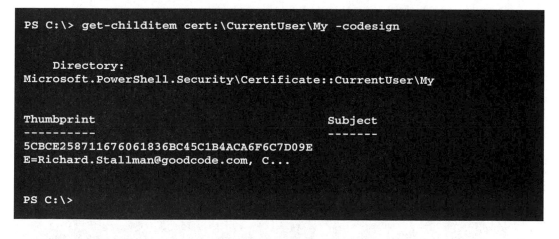

The PVK Digital Certificate Files Importer

When a digital certificate is generated, sometimes the private key is stored in a PVK (private key) file, and the corresponding digital certificate is stored in a Software Publishing Certificate (SPC) file. When a code-signing certificate has been obtained from

Verisign or Thawte, for example, the digital certificate is issued to you as a SPC and PVK file combination. If you want to use the code-signing certificate to digitally sign PowerShell scripts or configuration files, you must import the SPC and PVK file combination into your personal certificate store.

> **NOTE**
>
> A certificate store is a location that resides on a computer or device that is used to store certificate information. In Windows, you can use the Certificates MMC snap-in to display the certificate store for a user, a computer, or a service according. Your personal certificate store is referring to your own "user" certificate store.

To import the SPC+PVK, you use the Microsoft utility called PVK Digital Certificate Files Importer. You can download it from the Microsoft Download Web site at www.microsoft.com/downloads/details.aspx?FamilyID=F9992C94-B129-46BC-B240-414BDFF679A7&displaylang=EN.

Next, enter the following command to import the SPC+PVK, substituting your own filenames:

```
pvkimprt -IMPORT "mycertificate.spc" "myprivatekey.pvk"
```

Signing PowerShell Scripts

When signing a PowerShell script, you use the Set-AuthenticodeSignature cmdlet, which takes two required parameters. The first parameter, filePath, is the path and filename for the script or file to be digitally signed. The second parameter, certificate, is the X.509 certificate used to sign the script or file. To obtain the X.509 certificate in a format the Set-AuthenticodeSignature cmdlet understands, you retrieve the certificate as an object with the Get-ChildItem cmdlet, as shown in this example:

```
PS C:\> set-authenticodesignature –filePath signed.ps1 -certificate @(get-
childitem cert:\CurrentUser\My -codeSigningCert)[0] -includeChain "All"


    Directory: C:\


SignerCertificate                               Status        Path
-----------------                               ------        ----
5CBCE258711676061836BC45C1B4ACA6F6C7D09E  Valid         signed.ps1


PS C:\>
```

To retrieve the certificate you want from your own "user" certificate store, you use the Get-ChildItem cmdlet with the codeSigningCert SwitchParameter. This SwitchParameter can be used only with the PowerShell Certificate provider and acts as a filter to force the Get-ChildItem cmdlet to retrieve only code-signing certificates. Last, to ensure that the entire certificate chain is included in the digital signature, the includeChain parameter is used.

After the Set-AuthenticodeSignature cmdlet has been executed successfully, the signed file has a valid digital signature block containing the digital signature. A signature block in a PowerShell script or configuration file is always the last item in the file and can be found easily because it's enclosed between SIG # Begin signature block and SIG # End signature block, as shown here:

```
write-host ("This is a signed script!") -Foregroundcolor Green
# SIG # Begin signature block
# MIIIHQYJKoZIhvcNAQcCoIIIDjCCCAoCAQExCzAJBgUrDgMCGgUAMGkGCisGAQQB
# gjcCAQSgWzBZMDQGCisGAQQBgjcCAR4wJgIDAQAABBAfzDtgWUsITrck0sYpfvNR
# AgEAAgEAAgEAAgEAMCEwCQYFKw4DAhoFAAQUOBxWZ+ceVCY8SKcVLl/3iq2F
# w0OgggYVMIIGETCCBPmgAwIBAgIKcsuBWwADAAAAIzANBgkqhkiG9w0BAQUFADBE
...
# KwYBBAGCNwIBCzEOMAwGCisGAQQBgjcCARUwIwYJKoZIhvcNAQkEMRYEFG+QcdwH
# dHiuftHilhdyHCeSl0UgMA0GCSqGSIb3DQEBAQUABIGAZxItZJ+uo1E/cVhOCFex
# 9hinxULa3s0urQi362qa+NQ7yV3XczQOAPl0/kBIrEcwFN6YyS7PPm0wkCAPnfib
# 4J3uKxZK+4l9iHTiEVmp1ZO5G+P3KrqUS9ktFs7v9yTgqc8JLznxsRLvMwZpAMBO
# R2792YGWH5Jy4AwDYeljQ6Y=
# SIG # End signature block
```

NOTE

This process for digitally signing scripts also applies to PowerShell configuration files. As discussed in Chapter 3, configuration files, depending on the execution policy setting, might also need to be signed before they are loaded into a PowerShell session.

Verifying Digital Signatures

To verify the digital signature of PowerShell scripts and configuration files, you use the Get-AuthentiCodeSignature cmdlet. It returns a valid status or an invalid status, such as HashMismatch, indicating a problem with the file.

Valid status:

```
PS C:\> get-authenticodesignature signed.ps1


    Directory: C:\


SignerCertificate                               Status          Path
-----------------                               ------          ----
5CBCE258711676061836BC45C1B4ACA6F6C7D09E        Valid           signed.ps1


PS C:\> .\signed.ps1
This is a signed script!
PS C:\>
```

Invalid status:

```
PS C:\> Get-AuthenticodeSignature signed.ps1


    Directory: C:\


SignerCertificate                               Status          Path
-----------------                               ------          ----
5CBCE258711676061836BC45C1B4ACA6F6C7D09E        HashMismatch    signed.ps1


PS C:\ .\signed.ps1
File C:\signed.ps1 cannot be loaded. The contents of file D:\signed.ps1
may have been tampered because the hash of the file does not match the
hash stored in the digital signature. The script will not execute on the
system. Please see "get-help about_signing" for more details.
At line:1 char:12
+ .\signed.ps1 <<<<
PS C:\>
```

Based on the error in the preceding example, the script has been modified or tampered with or is corrupt. If the script has been modified by its owner, it must be signed again before it can be used. If the script has been tampered with or is corrupt, it should be discarded because its validity and authenticity can no longer be trusted.

Signed Code Distribution

Distributing signed PowerShell scripts and configuration files requires the user to determine whether to trust code from a particular publisher. The first step is to validate the publisher's identity based on a chain of trust. To establish a chain of trust, the user uses the publisher's code-signing certificate associated with the digital signature to verify that the certificate owner is indeed the publisher. For example, Figure 4.5 shows an unbroken path (or chain) of valid certificates from the publisher's certificate to a trusted root certificate (or trust anchor).

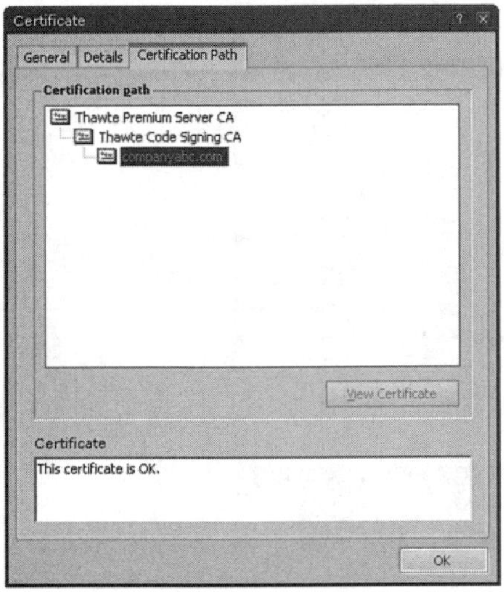

FIGURE 4.5   The certificate path

When a well-known trusted public root CA or internally trusted root CA is the trust anchor for the publisher's certificate, the user explicitly trusts that the publisher's identity claims are true.

For Windows users, if a root CA is considered trusted, that CA's certificate resides in the Trusted Root Certification Authorities certificate store (see Figure 4.6).

When a root CA is not a valid trust anchor or the certificate is self-signed, the user needs to decide whether to trust a publisher's identity claim. If the user determines the identity claim to be valid, the root CA's certificate or the self-signed certificate should be added to the Trusted Root Certification Authorities certificate store to establish a valid chain of trust.

After the publisher's identity has been verified or trusted, the next step is deciding whether the signed code is safe for execution. If a user has previously decided that code from a publisher is safe for execution, the code (PowerShell script or configuration file) runs without further user action.

For Windows users, if a publisher is considered trusted, their code-signing certificate resides in the Trusted Publishers certificate store (see Figure 4.7).

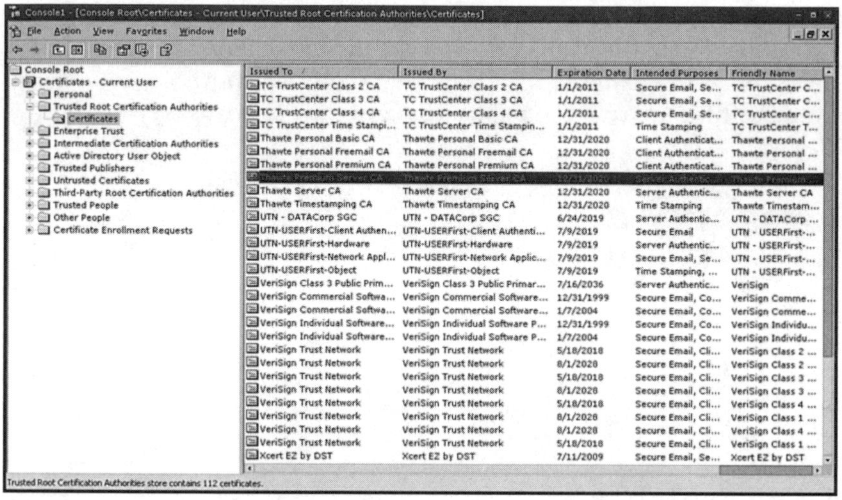

FIGURE 4.6   Trusted Root Certification Authorities certificate store

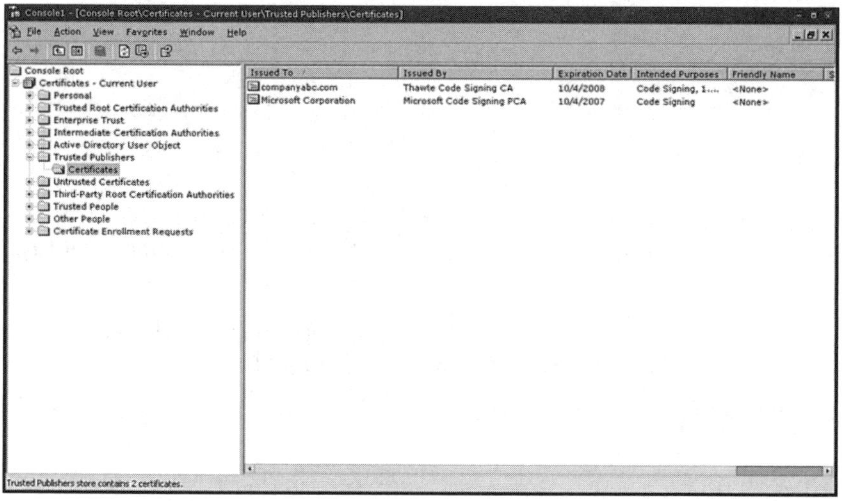

FIGURE 4.7   Trusted Publishers certificate store

If a publisher is not trusted, PowerShell prompts the user to decide whether to run signed code from that publisher, as shown in this example:

```
PS C:\> .\signed.ps1

Do you want to run software from this untrusted publisher?
File C:\signed.ps1 is published by CN=companyabc.com, OU=IT,
O=companyabc.com, L=Oakland, S=California, C=US and is not trusted on your
system. Only run scripts from trusted publishers.
[V] Never run   [D] Do not run   [R] Run once   [A] Always run   [?] Help
(default is "D"):
```

The following list explains the available options:

▶ *[V] Never run*—This option places the publisher's certificate in the user's Untrusted Certificates certificate store. After a publisher's certificate has been determined to be untrusted, PowerShell never allows code from that publisher to run unless the certificate is removed from the Untrusted Certificates certificate store or the execution policy is set to `Unrestricted` or `RemoteSigned`.

▶ *[D] Do not run*—This option, which is the default, halts execution of the untrusted code.

▶ *[R] Run once*—This option allows one-time execution of the untrusted code.

▶ *[A] Always run*—This option places the publisher's certificate in the user's Trusted Publishers certificate store. Also, the root CA's certificate is placed in the Trusted Root Certification Authorities certificate store, if it isn't already there.

Enterprise Code Distribution

You might be wondering how to control what code is considered trusted in your organization. Obviously, having users or machines decide what to trust defeats the purpose of distributing signed code in a managed environment. If your environment is managed, your PKI deployment should have methods for controlling what's trusted in an organization. If your organization is a Windows environment, the most common method is through GPO. For example, you can define trusted publishers by using a Certificate Trust List (CTL) or manage them through the Internet Explorer Maintenance extension.

Public Code Distribution

Determining trust in the public realm is entirely different. When establishing trust between two private entities, they are able to define what is and isn't trusted. When dealing with public entities, you don't have this level of control. It is up to those public entities to determine what they do or do not trust.

Summary

In summary, this chapter, as its name suggested, was an in-depth exploration into code signing. Based on the information that you have gleaned from this chapter, you should now have an understanding for just how important code signing is to PowerShell security and how to use it. If you haven't come to this realization, then it is again stressed that code signing be understood and used in conjunction with your script development activities.

In addition to stressing the use of code signing, you should also now have a better understanding for the infrastructure that is required to make code signing a viable method for trusting code within an organization. Granted, while PKI can be difficult to understand, one of the main goals of this chapter was to explain PKI from the perspective that was related to your scripting activities—an approach that was taken in an effort to reduce the amount of bewilderment, on your part, by relating PKI to something that is applicable to how it would be used with PowerShell. With this knowledge, you should now be able to determine, or at least convey, a PKI need and hopefully move a project forward such that the scripts you developed can be trusted at your organization.

CHAPTER 5

PowerShell Scripting Best Practices

Introduction

Many helpful guides are available for learning what scripting practices to follow. Often these guides cover best practices for a particular language, general scripting concepts, or even one scripter's views on what's considered good scripting. No matter what type of guide you consult, your goal should always be to seek improvements in how you script.

This chapter is intended to provide guidelines based on experience for scripting best practices that tie into software development best practices. Scripting is similar to software development, in that it involves writing and developing code in a way that makes sense. Furthermore, many aspects of a software development project apply to scripting projects. Extending software development guidelines to scripting best practices can give you a good foundation for improving your script writing.

Script Development

The following sections offer best practices for script development that applies to scripting in general. It is highly recommended that when you are developing your own scripts that the practices discussed in these sections be followed to some extent or another. By doing this, you should find that your scripts will start to meet stated project requirements, take less time to develop, and have fewer issues when deployed into production.

Treat Scripting Projects as Actual Projects

Developing a script can take as much effort as any software development project. For example, you should make sure to incorporate some prototyping and testing to prevent the script from having any negative impact on an environment. So whenever you write a script, check the scope of the effect it might have. If the script is complex, takes more than a few minutes to complete its tasks, requires more resources than yourself (such as other people), or carries a high level of risk when its runs, turning the script job into a project might be appropriate.

Use a Development Life Cycle Model

As with all software development projects, you should choose a development life cycle model that fits the needs of your scripting project. These models range from the traditional waterfall model to newer models such as Agile, Extreme Programming (XP), Spiral, Iterative, and so forth. The choice of a model isn't as important as having a formal process for managing your scripting projects, however.

If the models mentioned here seem overly complex for a scripting project, Figure 5.1 shows a simple series of steps developed for scripting projects.

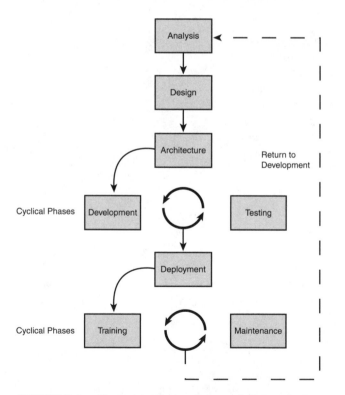

FIGURE 5.1   The process map for a scripting project

Although similar to a full development life cycle model, the steps are simply pointers to tasks that need to be completed for a typical scripting project. You can follow this scripting model or develop your own, but the point of this practice is to choose a method for managing your scripting projects.

Design and Prototype Your Scripts by Using Pseudocode

The idea behind designing and prototyping a script by using pseudocode is that it enables you to develop a script's structure and logic before writing any code. Working out the structure and logic beforehand helps you ensure that your script meets its requirements and helps you detect possible logic flaws early in the process. Furthermore, pseudocode is language independent and can be written so that other people, especially those who need to give input on the script design, can read and understand it easily. The following is an example of pseudocode:

```
Param domain
Param resource account CSV file

Bind to domain
Open and read CSV file

For each resource account in CSV file:
    -Create a new account in the specified OU.
    -Set the password (randomly generated complex 14-character password).
    -Log password to admin password archive.
    -Set the user account attributes based on CSV file information.
    -Mail-enable the account.
    -Add the user to the appropriate groups based on CSV file information.
Next
```

Gather Script Requirements Effectively

As with any project, you need to define the problem your script will be solving to determine what's required of it. Sometimes a script just solves a simple automation need, as such its requirements are easy to determine. When a script needs to solve more complex business automation needs, however, you might need to learn more about the business processes being automated to determine its requirements. In either case, identifying the requirements for a script and having all parties sign off on those requirements is pivotal to ensuring its success. Overlooking these steps in the development process may mean that your final script fails to meet its requirements and is then rejected as a solution for the original business need.

Don't Develop Scripts in a Production Environment

Most scripts are designed to make changes to a system, so there's always the chance that running a script in a production environment could have unwanted or possibly damaging results. Even if a script makes no changes, it could have an undesirable effect, or you might not fully understand the impact. Even worse, when you run the script to test its functionality, you might accidentally run the script outside your designated testing scope and perhaps affect production systems. Therefore, developing your scripts in a production environment isn't a good idea.

Test, Test, Test

Scripts are usually written to perform some type of automation task, such as modifying an attribute on every user in an Active Directory domain. The automation task might carry a high or low level of impact, but some form of quality assurance testing should be conducted on the code before running it in a production environment. Scripts in particular should be tested thoroughly because of their potential effect on an environment.

Keep Your Scripts Professional

Many scripters tend to view scripting as a quick and easy way to complete tasks and don't see the need for professional considerations, such as planning, documentation, and standards. This mindset is likely a holdover from the days when scripting was considered a clandestine task reserved for UNIX and Linux coders. Clearly, this view is changing with Microsoft's release of PowerShell. CLI use, scripting, and automation are becoming the foundation for how Windows systems administrators manage their environments. With this change, scripting, with its flexibility and raw power, will be increasingly viewed as a solution to business automation needs and, therefore, a task that should be done with professionalism.

To be professional when creating scripts, you should make sure your work meets a certain level of quality by developing standards for all your scripts to meet, writing clear and concise documentation, following best practices in planning and layout, testing thoroughly, and so forth. Adhering to professional standards can also ensure that others accept your work more readily and consider it more valuable.

Script Design

The following sections offer best practices for PowerShell script design. The term "design" is used lightly here as the goal is to provide insight into design aspects that should and should not be done when writing a PowerShell script. For example, when writing a script, you should validate information that is provided to the script. Again, it is highly recommended that the practices reviewed in these sections be applied, in some form, to scripts that you develop. Following these practices will help make your scripts more readable, usable, robust, and less buggy.

Put Configuration Information at the Beginning of Script

When setting variables, parameters, and so on that control script configuration, you should always place them near the beginning of a script to make locating these items easy for anyone using, reading, or editing the script, as shown in this example:

```
#-------------------
# Set Vars
#-------------------
$Owner = "Administrators"
$Targets = import-csv $ImportFile


#-------------------
# Script Body
#-------------------
...
```

Another reason for this practice is to reduce the number of errors introduced when editing the script configuration. If configuration information is spread throughout a script, it's more likely to be misconfigured, declared multiple times, or forgotten.

Use Comments

You can't assume users will understand the logic you've used in a script or be familiar with the methods you used to perform tasks. Therefore, using comments to assist users in understanding your script is a good practice. Comments don't have to be as lengthy as a novel, but should provide enough information to help users see how the script logic flows. In addition, if your script includes a complex method, class, or function, adding a comment to explain what it does is helpful. Another benefit of comments is that the information makes it easier for you to review or update a script. The following example shows the use of comments to provide helpful information:

```
#---------------------------------------------------
# Add-DACL
#---------------------------------------------------
# Usage:        Grants rights to a folder or file.
# $Object:      The directory or file path.  ("c:\myfolder" or
#               "c:\myfile.txt")
# $Identity:    User or Group name. ("Administrators" or
#               "mydomain\user1"
# $AccessMask:  The access rights to use when creating the access rule.
#               ("FullControl", "ReadAndExecute, Write", etc.)
# $Type:        Allow or deny access. ("Allow" or "Deny")
```

Avoid Hard-Coding Configuration Information

Hard-coding configuration information is a common mistake. Instead of asking users to supply the required information, the configuration information is hard-coded in variables or randomly scattered throughout the script. Hard-coding requires users to manually edit scripts to set the configuration information, which increases the risk of mistakes that result in errors when running the script. Remember that part of your goal as a scripter is to provide usable scripts; hard-coding information makes using a script in different environments difficult. Instead, use parameters or configuration files, as shown in the following example, so that users can set configuration information more easily.

```
param([string] $ADSISearchPath=$(throw "Please specify the ADSI Path!"))
```

When Necessary, Use Variables

If configuration information does need to be hard-coded in a script, use variables to represent the information. Defining configuration information in a variable in one place instead of several places throughout a script decreases the chance of introducing errors when the information needs to be changed. Furthermore, having configuration information in a single place, particularly at the beginning of a script, helps reduce the time to reconfigure a script for different environments.

Provide Instructions

Most scripts are written for use by others. In many cases, the user is an administrator who isn't comfortable with code and command-line interfaces. This means that your scripts have to be usable as well as useful. If you don't include instructions to make sure even a novice can run the script and understand what it does, you haven't succeeded as a scripter.

It's common to see scripts without any instructions, with incorrect instructions, or with little explanation of what the script does. For users, these scripts are usually frustrating. Even worse, they might have no clue what impact a script could have on their environment, and running it could result in a disaster.

The following example includes instructions that might be included in a readme file on the script's purpose and how it works:

```
=====================================================================
Script Info
=====================================================================
Name: AddProxyAddress.ps1
Author: Tyson Kopczynski
Date: 6/02/2006

Description:
Use this script to add secondary proxy addresses to users based on a CSV import
file. When trying to add the additional proxy addresses, this script checks the
following conditions:
```

```
    Does the user exist?
    Is the user mail-enabled?
    Does the proxy address currently exist?

This script will create a log file each time it is run.

CSV file format:
[sAMAccountName],[ProxyAddresses]
tyson,tyson@cco.com;tyson@taosage.net
maiko,maiko@cco.com
bob,bob@cco.com
erica,erica@cco.com

The ProxyAddresses column is ; delimited for more than one proxy address.
```

Perform Validity Checking on Required Parameters

Failing to perform basic validity checks on required parameters is a common mistake. If your script requires input from users, neglecting these validity checks could mean that users enter the wrong input, and the script halts with an error. This oversight might not be a major issue with small scripts, but, with large, complex scripts, it could seriously affect their usability.

Say you have written a script that performs a software inventory. In your development environment consisting of a few machines, you run the script but fail to provide the correct information for a required parameter. The script runs, and a couple of seconds later, it fails. You realize that you mistyped a parameter, so you correct your mistake and rerun the script.

Then the systems administrator runs your script against thousands of machines; it runs for six hours and then fails. Reviewing the error information, the administrator discovers the script failed because of a mistyped parameter. At that point, the administrator has already invested six hours only to encounter an error and might conclude your script isn't usable. In other words, you wrote a script that works for your environment but not the administrator's environment. To prevent this problem, make sure you perform validity checking on required parameters, as shown in the following example:

```
param([string] $TemplatePath = $(throw write-host `
    "Please specify the source template path of the folder structure to" `
    "be copied." -Foregroundcolor Red), [string] $ImportFile = $(throw `
    write-host "Please specify the import CSV filename." `
    -Foregroundcolor Red))

write-host "Checking Template Path" -NoNewLine
```

```
if (!(test-path $TemplatePath)){
    throw write-host `t "$TemplatePath is not a valid directory!" `
        -Foregroundcolor Red
    }
else {
    write-host `t "[OK]" -Foregroundcolor Green
    }

write-host "Checking Import File" -NoNewLine

if (!(test-path $ImportFile)){
    throw write-host `t "$ImportFile is not a valid file!" -Foregroundcolor Red
    }
else {
    write-host `t "[OK]" -Foregroundcolor Green
    }
```

Make Scripts and Functions Reusable

If you have spent time developing sophisticated script functionality, you should take the time to make that functionality reusable. With a common set of scripts or functions, you can also save time when you need to create new scripts. For example, in one script you have created logic for parsing data from a comma separated value (CSV) file to create an HTML table. Instead of copying and modifying that logic for new scripts, you can create a script or library file that includes this logic so that it can be reused in any script.

Reusability is an important best practice. In PowerShell, the concept of reusability makes even more sense because scripts and library files can be ported easily by calling reusable code from a PowerShell console session or loading the script or library file with a dot sourced statement. The following example shows a series of script files being called from the PowerShell console as part of the pipeline.

```
PS C:\> .\get-invalidusers.ps1 mydomain.com | .\out-html.ps1 | .\out-ie.ps1
```

Use Descriptive Names Rather Than Aliases

Using aliases in PowerShell can save time but make your scripts difficult for users to read. The PowerShell language is designed to be easy to write and read, but your naming standards and use of aliases have an effect on readability. To ensure readability, follow consistent naming standards and use descriptive names rather than aliases, when possible.

Making your code more readable benefits users trying to understand it and means future updates and changes will be easier for you, too. If you take the time to follow consistent naming standards and avoid the overuse of aliases, making modifications to the script should be a breeze.

Provide Status Information for Script Users

Providing status information in an automation script is essential so that users understand how the script is progressing during execution and know whether script tasks have been completed successfully. Status information also lets users know whether any errors have occurred and can even indicate how much longer until the script has finished running.

You can provide status information to users in the form of console displays, as shown in Figure 5.2, by using the Write-Host and Write-Progress cmdlets, written to a log file, or Windows Forms.

FIGURE 5.2   Example of how a script can provide status information

NOTE

Regardless of the method, the idea is to provide enough status information without overloading users with useless details. If you need different levels of detail when displaying information to users, you can use the Write-Verbose and Write-Debug cmdlets, the Verbose and Debug parameters, or custom output.

Use the WhatIf and Confirm Parameters

As discussed in Chapter 2, "PowerShell Basics," two cmdlet parameters are designed to help prevent scripters and systems administrators from making unwanted changes. The WhatIf parameter is designed to return information about changes that would occur if the cmdlet runs yet doesn't actually make those changes, as shown in this example:

```
What if: Performing operation "Stop-Process" on Target "explorer (2172)".
```

In this example, the process object returned from the Get-Process cmdlet is explorer.exe. Normally, if a process object is then piped to the Stop-Process cmdlet, the received process stops. However, when using the WhatIf parameter with the Stop-Process cmdlet, the command returns information about the changes that would have happened instead of carrying out the command. For example, say you entered this command:

WARNING

Do not run the following command as it is only meant as an example of what not to do.

```
PS C:\> get-process | stop-process
```

Without the WhatIf parameter, this command would stop your PowerShell console session as well as your system. Adding the WhatIf parameter gives you information warning that the command would likely result in a system crash, as shown here:

```
PS C:\> get-process | stop-process -WhatIf
What if: Performing operation "Stop-Process" on Target "alg (1048)".
What if: Performing operation "Stop-Process" on Target "ati2evxx (1400)".
What if: Performing operation "Stop-Process" on Target "ati2evxx (1696)".
What if: Performing operation "Stop-Process" on Target "atiptaxx (3644)".
What if: Performing operation "Stop-Process" on Target "BTSTAC~1 (2812)".
What if: Performing operation "Stop-Process" on Target "BTTray (3556)".
What if: Performing operation "Stop-Process" on Target "btwdins (1652)".
What if: Performing operation "Stop-Process" on Target "csrss (1116)".
What if: Performing operation "Stop-Process" on Target "ctfmon (1992)".
What if: Performing operation "Stop-Process" on Target "eabservr (3740)".
What if: Performing operation "Stop-Process" on Target "explorer (2172)".
What if: Performing operation "Stop-Process" on Target "googletalk
(1888)".
What if: Performing operation "Stop-Process" on Target
"GoogleToolbarNotifier (2236)".
...
```

The Confirm parameter prevents unwanted modifications by forcing PowerShell to prompt users before making any changes, as shown in this example:

```
PS C:\> get-process expl* | stop-process -confirm

Confirm
Are you sure you want to perform this action?
Performing operation "Stop-Process" on Target "explorer (2172)".
[Y] Yes  [A] Yes to All  [N] No  [L] No to All  [S] Suspend  [?] Help
(default is "Y"):
```

As a best practice, you should use the WhatIf and Confirm parameters whenever possible to identify potentially harmful changes and give users a choice before making these changes.

> **NOTE**
>
> The WhatIf and Confirm parameters are valid only with cmdlets that make modifications.

Script Security

Security is often an item that is not considered during the development of software. The same is true with scripting. Unfortunately, considering for and incorporating security into your scripts is very good best practice. That is why the next three sections may be the most important sections within this chapter because they deal with PowerShell script security best practices.

Digitally Sign PowerShell Scripts and Configuration Files

As emphasized in Chapter 4, "Code Signing," you should always digitally sign your PowerShell scripts and configuration files so that users and machines running your scripts can trust that the code is actually from you and hasn't been tampered with or corrupted. Adhering to this practice also means you can keep the PowerShell execution policy on your machine and others in your organization set to AllSigned.

> **NOTE**
>
> Code signing doesn't apply just to PowerShell scripts and configuration files. You can apply the principles of code signing to other items, such as executables, macros, DLLs, other scripts, device drivers, firmware images, and so forth. Other code can benefit from the security of digital signatures, and you can further limit the possibility of untrusted code running in your environment.

Never Set Execution Policies to Unrestricted

Setting your execution policy to Unrestricted is like leaving an open door for malicious code to run on your systems. Because of this risk, you should set your execution policy to RemoteSigned at a minimum. This setting still allows you to run scripts and load configuration files created locally on your machine but prevents remote code that hasn't been signed and trusted from running. However, the RemoteSigned setting isn't foolproof and could allow some remote code to run through PowerShell.

Following these guidelines and becoming proficient in code signing are crucial to guaranteeing that your PowerShell environment doesn't become a target for malicious code. Setting your execution policy to AllSigned increases security even more because it requires that all scripts and configuration files be signed by a trusted source before running or loading them.

Try to Run Scripts with the Minimum Required Rights

IT security practices include following the principle of least privileges, which ensures that entities such as users, processes, and software are granted only the minimum rights needed to perform a legitimate action. For example, if a user doesn't need administrative rights to run a word processing program, there's no reason to grant that user administrative rights.

The principle of least privileges also applies to scripting. When you're developing a script, make an effort to code in a manner that requires the minimum rights to run the script. In addition, document the required rights to run your script in case they aren't apparent to users. If users don't know the required rights to run a script, they might try running it with administrative rights, which increases the possibility of causing unwanted and possibly damaging changes to your environment.

Standards for Scripting

As in software development, your scripting practices should incorporate some form of standardization. The term "standardization" as used here doesn't mean a formal standard, such as one from the International Organization for Standardization (ISO) or Institute of Electrical and Electronics Engineers (IEEE). Instead, it refers to using consistent methods for how your scripts are named, organized, and structured; how they function; and how they handle errors. Standardizing these aspects of your scripts ensures consistency in how others interact with, troubleshoot, and use your scripts.

Using a consistent naming standard across scripts or even within a single script can improve a script's readability. Another standardization practice, using a standard script layout, benefits those trying to read, troubleshoot, or modify your script. Standardization can also reduce the time you need to develop new scripts. For example, you can create standard forms for common tasks such as error handling, log file creation, and output formatting and reuse that functionality.

This Book's Scripting Standards

Subsequent chapters in this book focus on real-world examples for PowerShell scripts. So, working scripts have been pulled from actual projects developed to meet business requirements and are used throughout the remainder of this book. While the full source code for these scripts is presented in the remaining chapters, the source code has also been provided on the PowerShell Unleashed Reference Web site which allows you to examine the scripts in usable format. The URL for this Web site is: www.samspublishing.com/.

In addition, this book's reference Web site also contains several utilities used with scripts as well as the original source code. You can download a .zip file, which contains the `Scripts` file for each chapter. Each chapter subfolder contains another subfolder for a script and any related files.

To access the downloadable scripts, go to www.samspublishing.com/title/0672329530.

To address a few potential problems of standardization, some choices were made for how to present scripts in this books. First, scripts are limited to the PowerShell and VBScript languages to reduce the complexity of dealing with many different scripting languages. Second, VBScript scripts reside in a Windows Scripting File (WSF). Third, each PowerShell and VBScript is structured with a common layout that's easy to comprehend. Figures 5.3 and 5.4 are examples of the layouts used in this book.

Fourth, a digital code-signing certificate from Thawte was purchased, and all PowerShell scripts have been signed by the entity companyabc.com. If you have followed best practices for your execution policy setting, you need to configure companyabc.com as a trusted publisher to run the PowerShell scripts.

> **CAUTION**
>
> The scripts provided with this book are functioning scripts. They have been tested and should perform according to their intended purposes. However, this doesn't mean the scripts can be used in a production environment. If you plan to run one of these scripts in a production environment, conducting testing on that script first is strongly recommended.

Last, PowerShell and VBScript scripts tend to provide the same type of interaction for input and output, although there are differences occasionally when new concepts are introduced. Overall, however, methods for providing input and output are clear and concise through use of the PowerShell console, log files, and Windows Forms.

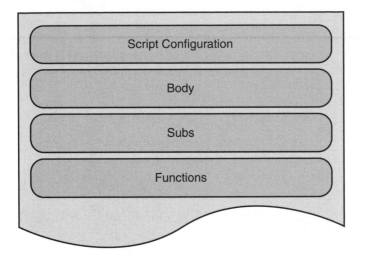

FIGURE 5.3   WSF script layout

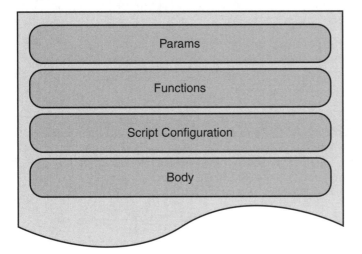

FIGURE 5.4   PowerShell script layout

Summary

In this chapter, you were presented with a number of PowerShell scripting best practices. These practices focused on how you develop, design, and secure your scripts so that your overall ability as a scripter will improve. The sources for these practices are based both from software development best practices and real-world scripting experience. They are by no means all inclusive or set in stone to how they apply to your own scripting practices.

If anything, the real goal of this chapter was to act as a prompt for your own thought processes around what is considered a good scripting practice. In the end, you may choose to expand on or add to these practices as long as you consider them when sitting down to write your next PowerShell script. After all, the PowerShell team went through all the trouble to produce the perfect shell. That favor should be repaid by trying to produce a well thought-out, well-designed, and secure script.

5

PART II

Translating Your Existing Knowledge into PowerShell

IN THIS CHAPTER

PowerShell and the File System

Introduction

This chapter explains how PowerShell can be used to manage the Windows file system. To do this, the chapter explores in-depth examples of managing the file system using both Windows Script Host (WSH) and PowerShell. These examples are presented from both perspectives in an effort to give the reader a path to learn PowerShell based on existing Windows scripting knowledge. In addition to the example-based comparisons, this chapter also presents a working file-management script based on a real-world situation. The goal, like the rest of the chapters in this book, is to give the reader a chance to learn how PowerShell scripting techniques can be applied to meet real-world automation needs.

File System Management in WSH and PowerShell

WSH offers several methods for manipulating the Windows file system. The FileSystemObject (FSO) object model, Windows Management Instrumentation (WMI), and utilities such as copy, calcs, and xcalcs are just a few examples. Using this plethora of tools, you can perform tasks such as copying, creating, and deleting files and folders. Most scripters use the FSO model to work with file systems.

FSO is part of the WSH object model. The FileSystemObject object acts as the root object for a hierarchy of COM objects, methods, and collections for working with the file system. FSO usually allows scripters to manipulate the file system as they see fit, but in some instances, it doesn't provide enough features, so additional tools and methods are needed for certain tasks.

PowerShell, on the other hand, has a built-in provider, the PowerShell FileSystem provider, for interfacing with the Windows file system. The abstraction layer this provider furnishes between PowerShell and the Windows file system gives the file system the appearance of a hierarchical data store. Therefore, interfacing with the file system is the same as with any other data store that's accessible through a PowerShell provider. As discussed in Chapter 3, "PowerShell: A More In-Depth Look," the core set of cmdlets for accessing and manipulating other data stores are also used with the file system. The following command that you've seen previously retrieves a list of the core cmdlets for manipulating data stores available via PowerShell providers:

```
PS C:\> help about_core_commands
```

Working with Drives

In WSH, you can use the FSO Drive object to retrieve information about available drives on a system, as shown in this example:

```
Dim FSO, objFolder
Set FSO = CreateObject("Scripting.FileSystemObject")
Set objDrive = fso.GetDrive(fso.GetDriveName("C:\"))

WScript.Echo "Total Space: " & FormatNumber(objDrive.TotalSize / 1024, 0)
```

In PowerShell, you can access some drive information with the Get-PSDrive and Get-Item cmdlets. However, as discussed in Chapter 3, PowerShell treats drives differently than WSH does. So if you want to access the same information available with the FSO Drive object, you need to use the appropriate .NET class, as shown in this next example, or WMI:

```
PS C:\> $CDrive = new-object System.IO.DriveInfo C
PS C:\> $DriveSize = ($CDrive.TotalSize / 1024) / 1000 /1000
PS C:\> $DriveSize = "{0:N0}" -f $DriveSize
PS C:\> write-host "The C Drive is $DriveSize GB."
The C Drive is 69 GB.
PS C:\>
```

Working with Folders

In WSH, you can access folder information and create, delete, copy, and move folders by using the FSO Folder object, as in this example:

```
Dim FSO, objFolder
Set FSO = CreateObject("Scripting.FileSystemObject")
Set objFolder = FSO.GetFolder("C:\tools")

WScript.Echo objFolder.DateLastAccessed
```

In PowerShell, you use the core cmdlets to perform the same tasks, as shown in this example:

```
PS C:\> get-item C:\tools | select LastAccessTime

LastAccessTime
--------------
9/10/2006 10:58:51 PM


PS C:\>
```

Working with Files

In WSH, you can access file information and create, modify, read, copy, move, and delete files by using the FSO `File` object, as shown here:

```
Dim FSO
Set FSO = CreateObject("Scripting.FileSystemObject")
strExtensionName = FSO.GetExtensionName("C:\tools\World_Domination_Plans_R1.doc")

WScript.Echo strExtensionName
```

In PowerShell, you use the core cmdlets to access file information and manipulate files, as in this example:

```
PS C:\tools> $File = get-item World_Domination_Plans_R1.doc
PS C:\tools> $File.extension
.doc
PS C:\tools>
```

As you can see from these examples, the methods for working with the Windows file system are similar in FSO and PowerShell, and the core cmdlets in PowerShell can perform many of the same tasks as FSO objects.

Working with Permissions

Working with file system permissions in WSH has limitations. For example, there's no straightforward method for changing permissions on a file or folder. Scripters must choose between using an external utility, such as cacls, Xcacls, Xcalcs.vbs, or SubInACL, or using ADsSecurity.dll or the WMI Win32_LogicalFileSecuritySetting class. Neither method offers a complete or standard solution for working with file system permissions in WSH. Usually, a scripting workaround is needed to compensate for a lack of features.

Setting Permissions with SubInACL

Given the limitations of WSH, the SubInACL utility is often used for file system permission changes. This tool isn't perfect, but if you script around its shortcomings, it's usually satisfactory for making permission changes. In addition, SubInACL supports files, directories, file shares, and printer shares and can be used on the Registry, system services, and even the Internet Information Services (IIS) metabase. You can download SubInACL from www.microsoft.com/downloads/details.aspx?FamilyId=E8BA3E56-D8FE-4A91-93CF-ED6985E3927B&displaylang=en.

The syntax for SubInACL consists of [/Option] /object_type object_name [[/Action[=Parameter]..]. Although the syntax seems simple, SubInACL is actually a complex permissions tool that can handle a variety of situations.

No matter what tool you use, the following permission changes are the ones most commonly needed:

▶ Take ownership

▶ Dump permissions

▶ Add permissions

▶ Remove permissions

This list isn't exhaustive, but it does give you a foundation for developing functions that are used frequently. Developing reusable functions is a highly recommended best practice. They can be used in many scripts and reduce the time needed to develop a script. For file system permission changes, developing reusable functions makes even more sense because working with the supported interfaces in WSH or existing tools can be time consuming. Therefore, the functions for SubInACL explained in the next section have been created for reuse in scripts.

SubInACL Functions

There are four SubInACL functions: SetOwner, DumpPerm, AddPerm, and RemovePerm. Each function takes arguments and builds a command string for the SubInACL utility. Then using a WshShell object the SubInACL utility is executed using the constructed command string. Next, output in the log.temp file from SubInACL is read for errors by using the ParseTempFile function. Based on the error information derived from log.temp, a success or failure status is then written to the console, as shown in this example:

```
Function SetOwner(path, account)
    'Used to set the owner on a folder or subfolders.
    On Error Resume Next
    strCommand = "subinacl /verbose /output=log.temp " _
        & "/subdirectories """ & path & """ /setowner=""" & account & """"

    ErrorCode = objWS.Run(strCommand, 0, TRUE)

    If ErrorCode <> 0 Then
        StdOut.Write("  " & account & ":" _
            & " [SetOwner Failed] on " & path)
    Else
        return = inStr(1, ParseTempFile("log.temp"), "will not be processed")

        If Not return = 0 Then
        StdOut.Write("  " & account & ":" _
            & " [SetOwner Failed] on " & path)
        Else
        StdOut.Write("  " & account & ":" _
            & " [SetOwner OK] on " & path)
        End If
    End If

    ErrorCode = vbNullString
End Function


Function DumpPerm(path)
    ' Used to clear permissions from a folder or subfolders.
    On Error Resume Next
    strCommand = "subinacl /verbose /output=log.temp " _
        & "/subdirectories """ & path & """ /perm"

    ErrorCode = objWS.Run(strCommand, 0, TRUE)

    If ErrorCode <> 0 Then
        StdOut.Write("  Dropped perm on " & path)
    Else
        StdOut.Write("  Dropped perm on " & path)
    End If

    ErrorCode = vbNullString
End Function
```

6

```
Function AddPerm(path, account, access)
    ' Used to grant a user's rights to a folder or subfolders.
    On Error Resume Next
    strCommand = "subinacl /verbose /output=log.temp" _
        & " /subdirectories """ & path & """ /grant=""" _
        & account & """ =" & access


    ErrorCode = objWS.Run(strCommand, 0, TRUE)


    If ErrorCode <> 0 Then
        StdOut.Write("  " & account & ": " & access _
            & " [AddPerm Failed] on " & path)
    Else
        return = inStr(1, ParseTempFile("log.temp"), "will not be processed")

        If Not return = 0 Then
            StdOut.Write("  " & account & ": " & access _
                & " [AddPerm Failed] on " & path)
        Else
            StdOut.Write("  " & account & ": " & access _
                & " [AddPerm OK] on " & path)
        End If
    End If


    ErrorCode = vbNullString
End Function


Function RemovePerm(path, account, access)
    ' Used to remove a user's rights to a folder or subfolders.
    On Error Resume Next
    strCommand = "subinacl /verbose /output=log.temp" _
        & " /subdirectories """ & path & """ /revoke=""" _
        & account & """ =" & access


    ErrorCode = objWS.Run(strCommand, 0, TRUE)


    If ErrorCode <> 0 Then
        StdOut.Write("  " & account & ": " & access _
            & " [AddPerm Failed] on " & path)
    Else
        return = inStr(1, ParseTempFile("log.temp"), "will not be processed")

        If Not return = 0 Then
            StdOut.Write("  " & account & ": " & access _
```

```
                & " [AddPerm Failed] on " & path)
        Else
            StdOut.Write("   " & account & ": " & access _
                & " [AddPerm OK] on " & path)
        End IF
    End If


    ErrorCode = vbNullString
End Function
```

Setting Permissions in PowerShell

With two built-in cmdlets named Get-ACL and Set-ACL, you might think managing file system permissions is easier in PowerShell. However, the Set-ACL cmdlet requires a security descriptor object defined by the System.Security.AccessControl.ObjectSecurity class. Constructing a security descriptor isn't difficult, but managing permissions isn't as straightfoward to script as you might have hoped. When faced with terms such as security descriptors and access control rules (ACLs), you might be tempted to stick with more familiar tools, such as SubInACL. If you sit down and go through the process step by step, however, it's not as complex as it seems at first glance. It consists of these basic steps:

1. Get the security descriptor (ACL) for an object by using Get-ACL.

2. Build the ACL with access control entries (ACEs).

3. Add the ACL to the security descriptor.

4. Bind the new security descriptor to the object by using Set-ACL.

The following code is an example of using these steps:

```
PS C:\> $SD = get-acl "Helena's Programs.csv"
PS C:\> $Rule = new-object
System.Security.AccessControl.FileSystemAccessRule("maiko",
"FullControl","Allow")
PS C:\> $SD.AddAccessRule($Rule)
PS C:\> set-acl "Helena's Programs.csv" $SD
PS C:\>
```

The hardest step to understand in this example is building the access rule. An access rule consists of three parameters to define user or group, access right, and access control type. The first parameter, Identity, is easy to define because you know the user or group to be added to an access rule. The second parameter, FileSystemRights, is more difficult because it requires understanding file system rights to define the access. However, you can use the following command to produce a list of supported rights:

```
[enum]::GetNames([System.Security.AccessControl.FileSystemRights])
ListDirectory
ReadData
WriteData
CreateFiles
CreateDirectories
AppendData
ReadExtendedAttributes
WriteExtendedAttributes
Traverse
ExecuteFile
DeleteSubdirectoriesAndFiles
ReadAttributes
WriteAttributes
Write
Delete
ReadPermissions
Read
ReadAndExecute
Modify
ChangePermissions
TakeOwnership
Synchronize
FullControl
PS C:\>
```

From this list, you can define a single right, such as Modify, or string rights together into a list, such as Read, Write, and Delete. The third parameter, AccessControlType, is easy to define because it can be only Allow or Deny.

PowerShell Functions

As with the SubInACL utility, a set of reusable permission management functions can be developed for use in your scripts. Examples of such functions are as follows:

```
#----------------------------------------------------
# Clear-Inherit
#----------------------------------------------------
# Usage:        Used to protect against inherited access rules
#               and remove all inherited explicitly defined rules.
# $Object:      The directory or file path. ("c:\myfolder" or
#               "c:\myfile.txt")

function Clear-Inherit{
    param ($Object)

    $SD = get-acl $Object
    $SD.SetAccessRuleProtection($True, $False)
    set-acl $Object $SD
    }
```

Clear-Inherit is probably the wrong name for this function because in addition to preventing inherited permissions from being applied from the parent object and clearing inherited permissions from the root object and subobjects, it clears explicitly defined permissions on subobjects. Therefore, before using the Clear-Inherit function, it's a good practice to take ownership of the object or make sure you have explicitly defined rights for yourself on the root file system object. If you don't ensure that you have access to file system objects, you might see "access denied" messages after clearing inherited rights.

The next function, Set-Owner, as its name might imply, is used to set the owner on a file system object:

```
#-----------------------------------------------------
# Set-Owner
#-----------------------------------------------------
# Usage:        Used to set the owner on a folder or file.
# $Object:      The directory or file path.  ("c:\myfolder" or
#               "c:\myfile.txt")
# $Identity:    User or Group name. ("Administrators" or
#               "mydomain\user1"

function Set-Owner{
    param ($Object,
        [System.Security.Principal.NTAccount]$Identity)

    # Get the item that will be changed
    $Item = get-item $Object

    # Set the owner
    $SD = $Item.GetAccessControl()
    $SD.SetOwner($Identity)
    $Item.SetAccessControl($SD)
    }
```

Next, the Clear-SD function is used to clear the security descriptor for a file system object:

```
#-----------------------------------------------------
# Clear-SD
#-----------------------------------------------------
# Usage:        Used to drop all permissions on a folder or file.
# $Object:      The directory or file path.  ("c:\myfolder" or
#               "c:\myfile.txt")
```

```
function Clear-SD{
    param ($Object)

    # Get the security descriptor for the object
    $SD = get-acl $Object

    # Set the SD to Everyone - Full Control
    #
    # Yes, this isn't a best practice; if you don't like it, then
    # set the SD to the current user.
    $SD.SetSecurityDescriptorSddlForm("D:PAI(A;OICI;FA;;;WD)")
    set-acl $Object $SD
    }
```

Although the Clear-SD function isn't used in the file system management script later in this chapter, it's a good illustration of how you can set a security descriptor with **Security Descriptor Definition Language (SDDL)**. SDDL is used to describe a security descriptor as a text string. If the Clear-SD function is used, an object's security descriptor is cleared and then set to FullControl for the Everyone group by using the string "D:PAI(A;OICI;FA;;;WD)".

> **NOTE**
>
> For more information on constructing a security descriptor with the **Security Descriptor String Format**, refer to http://msdn.microsoft.com/library/default.asp?url=/library/en-us/secauthz/security/security_descriptor_string_format.asp.

The next function, Add-ACE, is used to grant rights to a file system object for a user or group. This function, while very similar to the example at the beginning of this section, also shows how to control inheritance settings for a new Access Control Entry (ACE) with System.Security.AccessControl.PropagationFlags and System.Security.AccessControl.InheritanceFlags enumerations:

```
#-------------------------------------------------
# Add-ACE
#-------------------------------------------------
# Usage:        Grants rights to a folder or file.
# $Object:      The directory or file path. ("c:\myfolder" or
#               "c:\myfile.txt")
# $Identity:    User or Group name. ("Administrators" or
#               "mydomain\user1"
# $AccessMask:  The access rights to use when creating the access rule.
#               ("FullControl", "ReadAndExecute, Write", etc.)
```

```
# $Type:         Allow or deny access. ("Allow" or "Deny")

function Add-ACE{
    param ($Object,
    [System.Security.Principal.NTAccount]$Identity,
    [System.Security.AccessControl.FileSystemRights]$AccessMask,
    [System.Security.AccessControl.AccessControlType]$Type)

    $InheritanceFlags = `
        [System.Security.AccessControl.InheritanceFlags]`
        "ContainerInherit, ObjectInherit"
    $PropagationFlags = `
        [System.Security.AccessControl.PropagationFlags]"None"

    # Get the security descriptor for the object
    $SD = get-acl $Object

    # Add the AccessRule
    $Rule = new-object `
        System.Security.AccessControl.FileSystemAccessRule($Identity, `
        $AccessMask, $InheritanceFlags, $PropagationFlags, $Type)

    $SD.AddAccessRule($Rule)
    set-acl $Object $SD
    }
```

Don't let the name of these flags confuse you as they control how an ACE is applied to an object and all objects under that object. In the Add-ACE function, the flags are set so that an ACE is applied to file system objects as "This folder, subfolders, and files." This means that the ACE will be applied not only to the object being modified, but it will also be propagated to all objects under that object. Propagating the ACE as defined in the Add-ACE function should be sufficient for most file system management tasks. If not, you can modify the function so that it accepts inheritance settings as an argument.

The last function is the Remove-ACE function. This function is used to remove an ACE from an ACL:

```
#-------------------------------------------------
# Remove-ACE
#-------------------------------------------------
# Usage:       Removes rights to a folder or file.
# $Object:     The directory or file path.  ("c:\myfolder" or
#              "c:\myfile.txt")
```

```
# $Identity:    User or Group name. ("Administrators" or
#               "mydomain\user1"
# $AccessMask:  The access rights to use when creating the access rule.
#               ("FullControl", "ReadAndExecute, Write", etc.)
# $Type:        Allow or deny access. ("Allow" or "Deny")

function Remove-ACE{
    param ($Object,
        [System.Security.Principal.NTAccount]$Identity,
        [System.Security.AccessControl.FileSystemRights]$AccessMask,
        [System.Security.AccessControl.AccessControlType]$Type)

    # Get the security descriptor for the object
    $SD = get-acl $Object

    # Remove the AccessRule
    $Rule = new-object `
        System.Security.AccessControl.FileSystemAccessRule($Identity, `
        $AccessMask, $Type)
    $SD.RemoveAccessRule($Rule)
    set-acl $Object $SD
    }
```

From VBScript to PowerShell

In addition to showing practical applications for PowerShell, this book demonstrates how to convert VBScript scripts to PowerShell scripts. The first example is an account provisioning script for companyabc.com, a fast-growing ISP. When provisioning new user accounts, companyabc.com creates a Web site folder for each account. The folder structure is based on a template that's copied to new users' Web site folders. In the past, companyabc.com hired interns or contractors to manually create new Web site folders and set permissions on the folder structure.

After several errors in permission configuration and accidental folder deletions, IT management decided that using interns or contractors to create Web folders wasn't the best method for new account provisioning. To replace the manual process, the IT management staff wanted an automated method for creating a user's Web folder, copying the template folder structure to the new Web folder, and setting folder permissions.

The `ProvisionWebFolders.wsf` Script

`ProvisionWebFolder.wsf` is a VBScript based Windows Script File (WSF) script developed to meet companyabc.com's user-provisioning automation needs. A working copy is in the `Scripts\Chapter 6\ProvisionWebFolders` folder and is downloadable at www.samspublishing.com. This script requires that two parameters be defined.

First, `templatepath` should have its argument set to is the source path of the template folder structure copied to new users' Web folders. Second, `importfile` should have its argument set to the name of the CSV import file used to define new users and their Web folder locations. Here's the command to run the `ProvisionWebFolders.wsf` script, with sample output shown in Figure 6.1:

```
cscript ProvisionWebFolders.wsf /templatepath:".\Template" /importfile:"
.\users.csv"
```

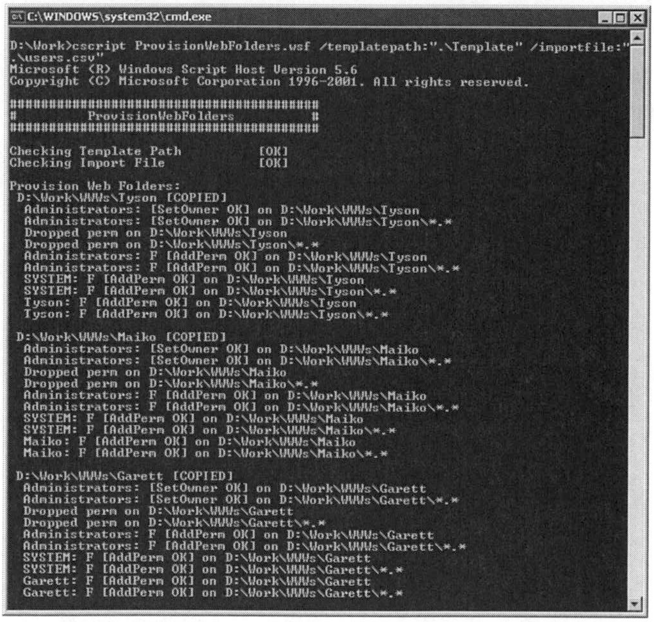

FIGURE 6.1   The `ProvisionWebFolder.wsf` script being executed

The `ProvisionWebFolder.wsf` script performs the following sequence of actions:

1. The script verifies the template folder path.

2. Next, the script opens and reads the CSV file's contents (new users and folder locations) into an array.

3. For each user in the array, the script uses `xcopy` to copy the template folder structure to the new user's Web folder.

4. The script then uses `SubInACL` to set permissions on each folder, such as the following:

   ▶ Administrators: Owner

   ▶ Administrators: FullControl

- ▶ System: FullControl
- ▶ NewUser: FullControl

NOTE

Used throughout this script are a set of common console or log file output functions named Mess, StatStart, and StatDone. When writing scripts for administrators who aren't scripters, try to make user interaction consistent throughout to improve scripts' usability and maintain a professional appearance. The source for these functions are found at the end of this script.

The first code sample consists of the initial XML elements for a WSF. These elements are used to define the allowed parameters, the script's description, examples on the script's operation, and the scripting language being used:

```
<?xml version="1.0" ?>
<package>
<job id="ProvisionWebFolders">
    <runtime>
        <description>
*************************************************************
This script provisions user Web folders based on a user list.
*************************************************************
        </description>
        <named name="templatepath" helpstring="The source template path of the
folder structure to be copied." type="string" required="1" />
        <named name="importfile" helpstring="The path\name of the CSV import file."
type="string" required="1" />
        <example>
Example:
cscript ProvisionWebFolders.wsf /templatepath:"C:\Template Folders\Folder1"
/importfile:"c:\temp\importfile.csv"
        </example>
    </runtime>
<script language="VBScript">
<![CDATA[
```

Next, the script checks to see if arguments have been defined for the required parameters `templatepath` and `importfile`. If the arguments are not present the script returns the script usage information (defined in the previous code sample) to the console and quits. If arguments are defined, the script then sets up the script environment by defining the variables that will be used throughout the rest of the script:

```
On Error Resume Next

'========================================================================
' Check required args
'========================================================================
If WScript.Arguments.Named.Exists("templatepath") = FALSE Then
    WScript.Arguments.ShowUsage()
    WScript.Quit
End If

If WScript.Arguments.Named.Exists("importfile") = FALSE Then
    WScript.Arguments.ShowUsage()
    WScript.Quit
End If


'========================================================================
' Set up job env
'========================================================================
Const ForReading = 1
ReDim arrTargs(0)
Dim StdOut
Dim FSO, objWS
Dim strTemplatePath, strImportFile

Set StdOut = WScript.StdOut
Set FSO = CreateObject("Scripting.FileSystemObject")
Set objWS = CreateObject("WScript.Shell")

strTemplatePath = WScript.Arguments.Named("templatepath")
strImportFile = WScript.Arguments.Named("importfile")
```

The next code sample is the beginning of the actual automation portion of the script.
First, the script writes the script header to the console, then checks to see if the
templatepath is a valid file system path. If the path is valid the script continues. If the
path is not valid the script quits. Notice how information about the validity of the
templatepath and the status of the script execution is written to the console functions for
the script operator to review using the StatStart and StatDone functions:

```
'========================================================================
' Start job
'========================================================================
Mess "####################################"
Mess "#         ProvisionWebFolders          #"
```

```
Mess "#######################################"
Mess vbNullString
'==================================================================
Mess vbNullString

'.....................
' Confirm that TemplatePath exists
'.....................
StatStart "Checking Template Path"

If (FSO.FolderExists(strTemplatePath)) Then
    StatDone
Else
    StdOut.WriteLine(" Critical Error: Template Path doesn't exist...")
    WScript.Quit()
End If
```

The ParseFile function in the following code sample reads each line (but skips the first line) in the CSV file and adds that line as an item to an existing array. This function is written such that if there is an error encountered the function Xerror will be called. The Xerror function will stop execution, write the error to the console, and quit the script:

```
'.....................
' Check csv Import File
'.....................
StatStart "Checking Import File"
    ParseFile strImportFile, arrTargs
StatDone
```

In the following code sample, the script uses the xcopy utility to create a user's Web folder and copy the template folder structure to it:

```
'.....................
' Provision Web Folders
'.....................
Mess vbNullString
Mess "Provision Web Folders:"

For Each Targ In arrTargs
    arrTargRecord = split(Targ, ",")
```

```
strUserName = arrTargRecord(0)
strPath = arrTargRecord(1)

StdOut.Write(" " & strPath)
StdOut.Write("\" & strUserName)

strCommand = "xcopy """ & strTemplatePath & """ """ & strPath & "\" _
    & strUserName & """ /O /E /I /Y"

ErrorCode = objWS.Run(strCommand, 0, TRUE)

If ErrorCode <> 0 Then
    StdOut.WriteLine(" [FAILED][Command used: " & strCommand & "]")
Else
    StdOut.WriteLine(" [COPIED]")
```

When calling the xcopy utility, the script uses a defined command string (strCommand) and a WScript.Shell object called objWS. The same results could have been achieved with an FSO object, but the xcopy utility reduces the lines of code needed to perform the task.

Now that the Web folder has been created for the user, the next task is to set the permissions for that folder. To do this, the script makes use of the SubInACL utility by calling the DumpPerm, SetOwner, AddPerm functions. Pay particular attention in the next code sample how the functions are called twice for each instance where an object's permissions are modified:

```
    ' Set Administrators as owner of folder
    SetOwner strPath & "\" & strUserName, "Administrators"
    Mess vbNullString

    ' Set Administrators as owner on everything below
    SetOwner strPath & "\" & strUserName & "\*.*", "Administrators"
    Mess vbNullString

    ' Dump permissions on the folder
    DumpPerm strPath & "\" & strUserName
    Mess vbNullString

    ' Dump permissions on everything below
    DumpPerm strPath & "\" & strUserName & "\*.*"
    Mess vbNullString
```

```
        ' Add Administrators
        AddPerm strPath & "\" & strUserName, "Administrators", "F"
        Mess vbNullString

        ' Add Administrators on everything below
        AddPerm strPath & "\" & strUserName & "\*.*", "Administrators", "F"
        Mess vbNullString

        ' Add SYSTEM
        AddPerm strPath & "\" & strUserName, "SYSTEM", "F"
        Mess vbNullString

        ' Add SYSTEM on everything below
        AddPerm strPath & "\" & strUserName & "\*.*", "SYSTEM", "F"
        Mess vbNullString

        ' Add the User
        AddPerm strPath & "\" & strUserName, strUserName, "F"
        Mess vbNullString

        ' Add the User on everything below
        AddPerm strPath & "\" & strUserName & "\*.*", strUserName, "F"
        Mess vbNullString

    End If

    Mess vbNullString

    ErrorCode = vbNullString
Next

Mess "Done Provisioning Web Folders:"
```

The first SubInACL call is to change permissions on the root folder, and the second SubInACL call is to modify permissions for all subfolders and files under the root folder. Granted, the second call probably isn't needed after permissions have been dumped from the root folder. However, dumping permissions from a folder structure doesn't always set inheritance settings correctly, and some subfolders and files may not inherit the root folder's permissions. Calling SubInACL for the second time to modify permissions for subfolders and files under the root folder seems to solve the inheritance problem.

The last code sample consists of the Subs and Functions that are used throughout the script and the closing XML elements for the script. Further review of the final section of the script is not needed because these Subs and Functions are either fairly self explanatory or have been previously discussed:

```vbscript
'=====================================================================
' Subs
'=====================================================================
'....................
' General Message Sub
'....................
Sub Mess(Message)
    ' Write to console
    StdOut.WriteLine(Message)
End Sub


'....................
' General Start Message Sub
'....................
Sub StatStart(Message)
    ' Write to console
    StdOut.Write(Message)
End Sub


'....................
' General Finish Message Sub
'....................
Sub StatDone
    ' Write to console
    StdOut.Write(vbTab & vbTab)
    StdOut.WriteLine("[OK]")
End Sub


'....................
' General Xerror Sub
'....................
Sub Xerror
    If Err.Number <> 0 Then
        ' Write to console
        StdOut.WriteLine(" Critical Error: " & CStr(Err.Number) _
            & " " & Err.Description)

        WScript.Quit()
    End If
End Sub
```

```
'=======================================================================
' Functions
'=======================================================================
Function ParseFile(file, arrname)
    ' This function parses a file and gives you back an array
    ' (Skips the first line!!!)
    On Error Resume Next
    count = -1

    ' Open file for reading
    Set objFile = FSO.OpenTextFile(file, ForReading)
    objFile.SkipLine 'note: This will always be the col headers
    Xerror

    ' Reads each line in the file and places it into an array
    Do While objFile.AtEndOfStream <> True
        count = count + 1
        If count > UBound(arrname) Then ReDim Preserve arrname(count)
            arrname(count) = objFile.Readline
    Loop
    Xerror

    ' Close the file because you are done with it.
    objFile.Close()
    Set objFile = Nothing
    count = 0
End Function

Function ParseTempFile(path)
    ' Open file for reading
    Set objFile = FSO.OpenTextFile(path, ForReading)

    tempfileinfo = vbNullString

    Do While objFile.AtEndOfStream <> True
        tempfileinfo = tempfileinfo & objFile.Readline
    Loop

    ParseTempFile = tempfileinfo

    objFile.Close()
    Set objFile = Nothing
End Function
```

```
Function SetOwner(path, account)
    ' Used to set the owner on a folder or subfolders.
    On Error Resume Next
    strCommand = "subinacl /verbose /output=log.temp " _
        & "/subdirectories """ & path & """ /setowner=""" & account & """"

    ErrorCode = objWS.Run(strCommand, 0, TRUE)


    If ErrorCode <> 0 Then
        StdOut.Write("  " & account & ":" _
            & " [SetOwner Failed] on " & path)
    Else
        return = inStr(1, ParseTempFile("log.temp"), "will not be processed")

        If Not return = 0 Then
        StdOut.Write("  " & account & ":" _
            & " [SetOwner Failed] on " & path)
        Else
        StdOut.Write("  " & account & ":" _
            & " [SetOwner OK] on " & path)
        End If
    End If


    ErrorCode = vbNullString
End Function


Function DumpPerm(path)
    ' Used to clear permissions from a folder or subfolders.
    On Error Resume Next
    strCommand = "subinacl /verbose /output=log.temp " _
        & "/subdirectories """ & path & """ /perm"

    ErrorCode = objWS.Run(strCommand, 0, TRUE)


    If ErrorCode <> 0 Then
        StdOut.Write("  Dropped perm on " & path)
    Else
        StdOut.Write("  Dropped perm on " & path)
    End If


    ErrorCode = vbNullString
End Function
```

```
Function AddPerm(path, account, access)
    ' Used to grant a user's rights to a folder or subfolders.
    On Error Resume Next
    strCommand = "subinacl /verbose /output=log.temp" _
        & " /subdirectories """ & path & """ /grant=""" _
        & account & """ =" & access

    ErrorCode = objWS.Run(strCommand, 0, TRUE)

    If ErrorCode <> 0 Then
        StdOut.Write("   " & account & ": " & access _
            & " [AddPerm Failed] on " & path)
    Else
        return = inStr(1, ParseTempFile("log.temp"), _
            "will not be processed")

        If Not return = 0 Then
            StdOut.Write("   " & account & ": " & access _
                & " [AddPerm Failed] on " & path)
        Else
            StdOut.Write("   " & account & ": " & access _
                & " [AddPerm OK] on " & path)
        End If
    End If

    ErrorCode = vbNullString
End Function

]]>
  </script>
</job>
</package>
```

The ProvisionWebFolders.ps1 Script

ProvisionWebFolders.ps1 is a PowerShell conversion of the ProvisionWebFolder.wsf script. A working copy is in the Scripts\Chapter 6\ProvisionWebFolders folder and is downloadable at www.samspublishing.com. You need to provide two parameters to run this script. First, TemplatePath should have its argument set to the source path of the template folder structure copied to new users' Web folders. Second, ImportFile should have its argument set to the name of the CSV import file used to define new users and their Web folder locations. Here's the command to run the ProvisionWebFolders.ps1 script, with sample output shown in Figure 6.2:

```
PS D:\Work> .\ProvisionWebFolders.ps1 .\template .\users.csv
```

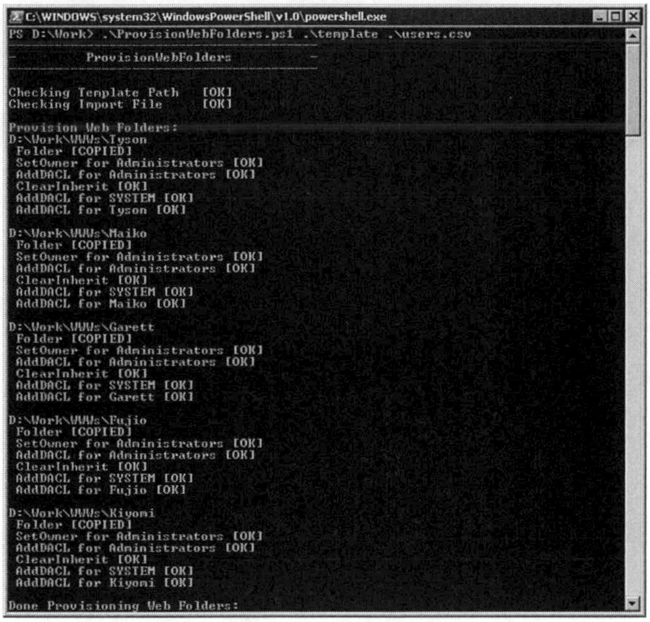

FIGURE 6.2   The ProvisionWebFolder.ps1 script being executed

The ProvisionWebFolders.ps1 script performs the following sequence of actions:

1. The script verifies that the template folder path exists.

2. Next, the script verifies that the import folder path exists.

3. The script import the CSV file into the $Targets variable.

4. For each user in $Targets, the script copies the template folder structure to the new user's Web folder.

5. Finally, the script sets permissions on each folder, such as the following:

   ▶ Administrators: Owner

   ▶ Administrators: FullControl

   ▶ System: FullControl

   ▶ NewUser: FullControl

The first code sample contains the header for the ProvisionWebFolder.ps1 script. In this header includes information about what the script does, when it was updated, and the script's author. Just after the header are the script's parameters:

```
###################################################
# ProvisionWebFolders.ps1
# Used to provision new user Web folders.
#
# Created: 9/12/2006
# Author: Tyson Kopczynski
###################################################
param([string] $TemplatePath = $(throw write-host `
    "Please specify the source template path of the folder structure to" `
    "be copied." -Foregroundcolor Red), [string] $ImportFile = $(throw `
    write-host "Please specify the import CSV filename." `
    -Foregroundcolor Red))
```

Notice how the throw keyword is being used in the param declaration to generate an error when a parameter does not have a defined argument. This technique is used force a parameter to be defined by stopping execution of the script and providing the script operator with information about the required parameter using the Write-Host cmdlet. When using the Write-Host cmdlet, you can use the Foregroundcolor parameter as shown in the previous code sample to control the color of output text. This feature is handy for focusing attention on details of the script status, as shown in Figure 6.3:

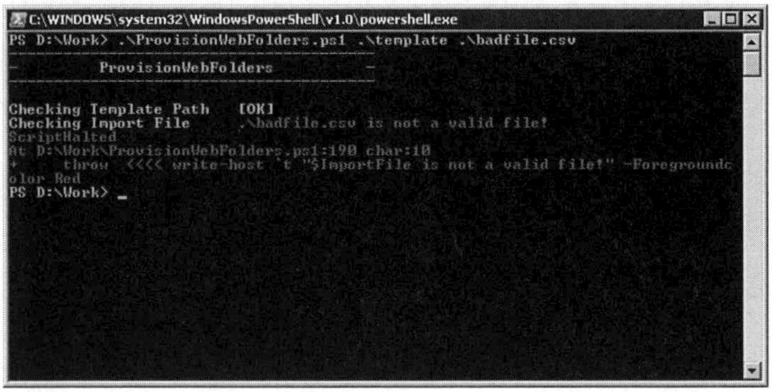

FIGURE 6.3   Green and red console output text being used to convey script status

Next, as seen in the following code sample, the script loads the file system management functions into its scope. Having reviewed these functions previously in this chapter, further explanation is not needed:

```
###################################################
# Functions
###################################################
#--------------------------------------------------
# Clear-Inherit
#--------------------------------------------------
# Usage:        Used to protect against inherited access rules
#               and remove all inherited explicitly defined rules.
# $Object:      The directory or file path. ("c:\myfolder" or
#               "c:\myfile.txt")

function Clear-Inherit{
    param ($Object)

    $SD = get-acl $Object
    $SD.SetAccessRuleProtection($True, $False)
    set-acl $Object $SD
    }


#--------------------------------------------------
# Set-Owner
#--------------------------------------------------
# Usage:        Used to set the owner on a folder or file.
# $Object:      The directory or file path. ("c:\myfolder" or
#               "c:\myfile.txt")
# $Identity:    User or Group name. ("Administrators" or
#               "mydomain\user1"

function Set-Owner{
    param ($Object,
        [System.Security.Principal.NTAccount]$Identity)

    # Get the item that will be changed
    $Item = get-item $Object

    # Set the owner
    $SD = $Item.GetAccessControl()
    $SD.SetOwner($Identity)
    $Item.SetAccessControl($SD)
    }
```

6

```
#----------------------------------------------------
# Add-ACE
#----------------------------------------------------
# Usage:        Grants rights to a folder or file.
# $Object:      The directory or file path.  ("c:\myfolder" or
#               "c:\myfile.txt")
# $Identity:    User or group name. ("Administrators" or
#               "mydomain\user1"
# $AccessMask:  The access rights to use when creating the access rule.
#               ("FullControl", "ReadAndExecute, Write", etc.)
# $Type:        Allow or deny access. ("Allow" or "Deny")

function Add-ACE{
    param ($Object,
    [System.Security.Principal.NTAccount]$Identity,
    [System.Security.AccessControl.FileSystemRights]$AccessMask,
    [System.Security.AccessControl.AccessControlType]$Type)

    $InheritanceFlags = `
        [System.Security.AccessControl.InheritanceFlags]`
        "ContainerInherit, ObjectInherit"
    $PropagationFlags = `
        [System.Security.AccessControl.PropagationFlags]"None"

    # Get the security descriptor for the object
    $SD = get-acl $Object

    # Add the AccessRule
    $Rule = new-object `
        System.Security.AccessControl.FileSystemAccessRule($Identity, `
        $AccessMask, $InheritanceFlags, $PropagationFlags, $Type)

    $SD.AddAccessRule($Rule)
    set-acl $Object $SD
    }
```

The next code sample contains the beginning of the script's automation portion. First the script checks to see if the string contained in the $TemplatePath variable is a valid folder path. Then the script checks to see if the string contained in the $ImportFile variable is a valid file path. To perform these tests, the if...then statements in code sample use of Test-Path cmdlet. This is a very handy cmdlet that can be used for verifying whether a folder or file (-pathType container or leaf) is valid. If any of these paths are invalid, the script execution is halted and information about the invalid paths is returned to script operator:

```
##################################################
# Main
##################################################
write-host "-----------------------------------------"
write-host "-           ProvisionWebFolders         -"
write-host "-----------------------------------------"
write-host
write-host "Checking Template Path" -NoNewLine

if (!(test-path $TemplatePath -pathType container)){
    throw write-host `t "$TemplatePath is not a valid directory!" `
        -Foregroundcolor Red
    }
else {
    write-host `t "[OK]" -Foregroundcolor Green
    }

write-host "Checking Import File" -NoNewLine

if (!(test-path $ImportFile -pathType leaf)){
    throw write-host `t "$ImportFile is not a valid file!" -Foregroundcolor Red
    }
else {
    write-host `t "[OK]" -Foregroundcolor Green
    }
```

In the next code sample, the rest of the variables that are used in the script are defined.
The first variable, $Owner, is used by the script to define the owner for each user's Web
folder structure, which in this case is the local Administrators group. Then the variable
$Targets is defined using the Import-Csv cmdlet. This cmdlet is used to read values from
the import CSV file ($ImportFile) into the $Targets variable, which is used to provision
new users' Web folders:

```
#--------------------
# Set Vars
#--------------------
$Owner = "Administrators"
$Targets = import-csv $ImportFile
```

In the following code sample, the script uses the path and username information from
the information contained in the $Target variable to construct the final destination path

using the Join-Path cmdlet. Then the script uses the Copy-Item cmdlet to copy the template folders to the destination path:

```
#--------------------
# Provision Web Folders
#--------------------
write-host
write-host "Provision Web Folders:"

foreach ($Target in $Targets){
    $Path = join-path $Target.DestPath $Target.UserName
    $UserName = $Target.UserName

    write-host $Path

    if (!(test-path $Path)){
        copy-item $TemplatePath -Destination $Path -Recurse `
        -ErrorVariable Err -ErrorAction SilentlyContinue

        if (!$Err){
            write-host " Folder " -NoNewLine
            write-host "[COPIED]" -Foregroundcolor Green

            # Used to stop loops
            $Err = $False
```

Next, the script uses the Set-Owner function to change ownership of user's Web folder structure to the local Administrators group:

```
.{
    trap{write-host "[ERROR] Failed to take ownership!" `
        -Foregroundcolor Red;
        $Script:Err = $True;
        Continue}

    # Set Owner
    write-host " SetOwner for $Owner " -NoNewLine

    Set-Owner $Path $Owner

    if ($Err -eq $False){
        $Items = get-childitem $Path -Recurse
        [void]($Items | foreach-object `
```

```
                    {Set-Owner $_.FullName $Owner})
        }
    else{
        # Stop the loop
        Continue
        }

    write-host "[OK]" -Foregroundcolor Green
}
```

You might be wondering why the code for Set-Owner is enclosed in a script block. The
dot (.) call operator preceding the script block tells PowerShell to run the script block
within the current scope. If the call operator isn't used, PowerShell doesn't run the script
block. The reason for creating an independent script block to handle the code for Set-
Owner is to ensure that the trap statement is scoped only to this block of code. This technique for controlling the trap's scope is used frequently in this book.

```
.{
    trap{write-host "[ERROR] Failed to add rights!" `
        -Foregroundcolor Red;
        $Script:Err = $True;
        Continue}

    # Add Administrators
    write-host " AddACE for Administrators " -NoNewLine

    Add-ACE $Path "Administrators" "FullControl" "Allow"

    if ($Err -eq $False){
        write-host "[OK]" -Foregroundcolor Green
        }
    else{
        # Stop the loop
        Continue
        }
    }

.{
    trap{write-host "[ERROR] Failed to clear inherited"`
        "permissions!" -Foregroundcolor Red;
        $Script:Err = $True;
        Continue}
```

6

```
            # Clear inherited permissions
            write-host " ClearInherit " -NoNewLine

            Clear-Inherit $Path

            if ($Err -eq $False){
                write-host "[OK]" -Foregroundcolor Green
                }
            else{
                # Stop the loop
                Continue
                }
        }
```

As mentioned previously, the `Clear-Inherit` function clears inherited permissions from the root folder, subfolders, and files as well as explicitly defined permissions on all subfolders and files. If the Administrators group didn't have explicitly defined rights on the root folder, the rest of the script wouldn't run because of a lack of rights.

NOTE

Explicitly defined permissions are permissions that are directly defined for a user on an object. Implicitly defined permissions are permissions that are either inherited or defined through membership of a group.

In the last code sample, the `SYSTEM` and the user are then granted `FullControl` to the user's Web folder and the script notifies the script operator of its completion:

```
        # Add SYSTEM
        write-host " AddACE for SYSTEM " -NoNewLine

        if ((Add-ACE $Path "SYSTEM" "FullControl" "Allow") -eq $True){
            write-host "[OK]" -Foregroundcolor Green
            }

        # Add User
        write-host " AddACE for $UserName " -NoNewLine

        if ((Add-ACE $Path $UserName "FullControl" "Allow") -eq $True){
            write-host "[OK]" -Foregroundcolor Green
            }
    }
```

```
        else {
            write-host " Folder " -NoNewLine
            write-host "Error:" $Err -Foregroundcolor Red
            }
        }
    else {
        write-host " Folder " -NoNewLine
        write-host "[EXISTS]" -Foregroundcolor Yellow
        }

    write-host
    }

write-host "Done Provisioning Web Folders:"
```

Summary

In summary, this chapter has focused on how to manage the Windows File System using both WSH and PowerShell. While both scripting interfaces provide methods to manage the file system, PowerShell's FileSystem provider allows for a more holistic data source-like approach when it comes to working with the file system. When developing future scripts or from working with the PowerShell console, you may find that the PowerShell approach allows greater freedom to access, review, and manipulate the file system.

In addition to helping you understand the differences between WSH and PowerShell when working with the Windows file system, this chapter also focused on explaining how to manage file system permissions using both scripting interfaces. You may have the opinion that trying to manage permissions using either scripting interfaces may seem like a daunting task. While permission management is seemingly difficult, you should have also hopefully come to the conclusion that the task is not impossible, as demonstrated in this chapter. Permission management via an automation script can be a very powerful tool. For example, you could create very powerful automation scripts that enforce file system permissions based on a defined policy, audit permissions on a file system for changes based on a baseline, or search for instances where a user or group have been granted rights.

CHAPTER 7

PowerShell and the Registry

Introduction

This chapter explains how PowerShell can be used to manage the Windows Registry. To do this, the chapter explores in-depth examples of managing the Registry using both Windows Script Host (WSH) and PowerShell. These examples are presented from both perspectives in an effort to give the reader a path to learn PowerShell based on existing Windows scripting knowledge. In addition, to the example-based comparisons, this chapter also presents a series of working Registry management functions that are based on a real-world situation. The goal is to give the reader a chance to learn how PowerShell scripting techniques can be applied to meet real-world Registry management automation needs.

Registry Management in WSH and PowerShell

The WSH object model has an object for working with running applications, launching new applications, creating shortcuts, creating popups, handling environmental variables, logging event messages, and even accessing or modifying the local Registry. This object, called WshShell, contains three methods for accessing and manipulating the Registry, described in the following list:

▶ RegDelete deletes a key or one of its values from the Registry.

▶ RegRead reads the value of a named value from the Registry.

▶ RegWrite creates new keys, adds another named value to an existing key, or changes the value of an existing named value.

Using the WshShell object and its Registry methods is simple. The WshShell object is a COM object and, like all COM objects, can be created by using the CreateObject() WSH method. After a WshShell object is created, you can use its Registry methods as you would any other method in WSH.

In PowerShell, you work with the Registry a little differently. As discussed in Chapter 3, "PowerShell: A More In-Depth Look," PowerShell has a built-in provider, Registry, for accessing and manipulating the Registry on a local machine. The Registry hives available in this provider are HKEY_LOCAL_MACHINE (HKLM) and HKEY_CURRENT_USER (HKCU). These hives are represented in a PowerShell session as two additional PSDrive objects named HKLM: and HKCU:.

> **NOTE**
>
> The WshShell object has access to not only the HKLM: and HKCU: hives, but also HKEY_CLASSES_ROOT (HKCR), HKEY_USERS, and HKEY_CURRENT_CONFIG. To access these additional Registry hives in PowerShell, you use the Set-Location cmdlet to change the location to the root of the Registry provider.

As you'll also recall from Chapter 3, accessing data through the Registry provider means PowerShell treats data in the HKLM: and HKCU: PSDrive objects like other hierarchical data stores. Therefore, accessing and manipulating data from these PSDrives requires using the PowerShell core cmdlets, as shown in this example:

```
PS C:\> set-location hkcu:
PS HKCU:\> get-childitem


    Hive: Microsoft.PowerShell.Core\Registry::HKEY_CURRENT_USER

SKC  VC Name                          Property
--   -- ----                          --------
  2   0 AppEvents                     {}
  2  32 Console                       {ColorTable00, ColorTable01, ColorTab...
 24   1 Control Panel                 {Opened}
  0   2 Environment                   {TEMP, TMP}
  1   6 Identities                    {Identity Ordinal, Migrated5, Last Us...
  4   0 Keyboard Layout               {}
  3   1 Printers                      {DeviceOld}
 32   1 Software                      {(default)}
  0   0 UNICODE Program Groups        {}
  2   0 Windows 3.1 Migration Status  {}
  0   1 SessionInformation            {ProgramCount}
  0   8 Volatile Environment          {LOGONSERVER, HOMESHARE, HOMEPATH, US...
```

```
PS HKCU:\> get-itemproperty 'Volatile Environment'


PSPath           : Microsoft.PowerShell.Core\Registry::HKEY_CURRENT_USER\Volatile
                   Environment
PSParentPath     : Microsoft.PowerShell.Core\Registry::HKEY_CURRENT_USER
PSChildName      : Volatile Environment
PSDrive          : HKCU
PSProvider       : Microsoft.PowerShell.Core\Registry
LOGONSERVER      : \\SOL
HOMESHARE        : \\taosage.internal\homes\tyson
HOMEPATH         : \
USERDNSDOMAIN    : TAOSAGE.INTERNAL
CLIENTNAME       :
SESSIONNAME      : Console
APPDATA          : C:\Documents and Settings\tyson\Application Data
HOMEDRIVE        : U:


PS HKCU:\>
```

By using the PowerShell core cmdlets, you can manipulate the local Registry as you see
fit, just as you would when using Registry methods of the WshShell object. The syntax
and methodology are slightly different, however. In WSH, you create an object and then
use the object's methods to perform the Registry task. In PowerShell, you access and
manipulate the Registry as you do with the file system. For example, to read a Registry
value in WSH, you use the RegRead method shown in the following example:

```
Dim objWS
Set objWS = CreateObject("WScript.Shell")

strKey = "HKEY_LOCAL_MACHINE\Software\Microsoft\Windows NT\CurrentVersion\"

WScript.Echo objWS.RegRead(strKey & "ProductName")
```

In PowerShell, you use the Get-ItemProperty cmdlet shown in the following example:

```
PS C:\> $Path = "HKLM:\Software\Microsoft\Windows NT\CurrentVersion"
PS C:\> $Key = get-itemproperty $Path
PS C:\> $Key.ProductName
Microsoft Windows XP
PS C:\>
```

To create or modify a Registry value in WSH, you use the `RegWrite` method shown in this example:

```
Dim objWS
Set objWS = CreateObject("WScript.Shell")

strKey = "HKEY_CURRENT_USER\Software\"

objWS.RegWrite strKey & "PSinfo", "PowerShell_Was_Here"

WScript.Echo objWS.RegRead(strKey & "PSinfo")
```

In PowerShell, you use the `Set-ItemProperty` cmdlet:

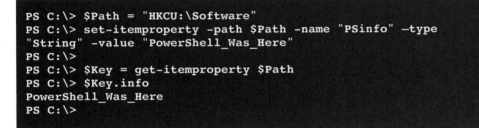

```
PS C:\> $Path = "HKCU:\Software"
PS C:\> set-itemproperty -path $Path -name "PSinfo" —type
"String" -value "PowerShell_Was_Here"
PS C:\>
PS C:\> $Key = get-itemproperty $Path
PS C:\> $Key.info
PowerShell_Was_Here
PS C:\>
```

Remember that the Windows Registry has different types of Registry values. You use the `Set-ItemProperty` cmdlet to define the `Type` parameter when creating or modifying Registry values. As a best practice, you should always define Registry values when using the `Set-ItemProperty` cmdlet. Otherwise, the cmdlet defines the Registry value with the default type, which is `String`. Other possible types are as follows:

- ▶ `ExpandString`
- ▶ `Binary`
- ▶ `DWord`
- ▶ `MultiString`
- ▶ `Qword`

NOTE

Depending on the Registry value you're creating or modifying, the data value you set the named value to needs to be in the correct format. So if the Registry value is type REG_BINARY, you use a binary value, such as $Bin = 101, 118, 105.

To delete a Registry value in WSH, you use the `RegDelete` method, as shown here:

```
Dim objWS
Set objWS = CreateObject("WScript.Shell")

strKey = "HKEY_CURRENT_USER\Software\"

objWS.RegDelete strKey & "PSinfo"
```

In PowerShell, you use the `Remove-ItemProperty` cmdlet:

```
PS C:\> $Path = "HKCU:\Software"
PS C:\> remove-itemproperty -path $Path -name "PSinfo"
PS C:\>
```

These examples give you an idea of how to work with the Registry. It's fairly simple as long as you understand how to use the core cmdlets and remember that working with the Registry is much like working with the Window file system.

However, there's no built-in cmdlet for accessing the Registry on a remote machine. This omission makes sense because by default, no PowerShell providers are available for accessing remote data stores. Until someone writes a provider you can use to manage the Registry remotely, you have to turn to an existing method, explained in the next section.

From VBScript to PowerShell

This section focuses on a VBScript script for reading and manipulating the Registry and the script's conversion to PowerShell. Companyabc.com was in the process of evaluating the IT department's efficiency. When reviewing the development of automation scripts, the evaluation team noticed a pattern of certain tasks being repeated in many scripts. These tasks included creating user accounts, setting account information, managing machines remotely, performing maintenance activities, and so forth.

The evaluation team concluded that consolidating repetitive code into a series of reusable library files would cut the time needed to develop scripts. This simple method creates a generic function or script for performing an often repeated task, such as generating a random password. When developing a script that requires this task, you don't need to write new code. In WSH and PowerShell, you simply include or dot source the library file you want in your script or console session.

The script examples in this section contain a series of functions for reading and modifying the Registry on a local host or remote machine that were developed for companyabc.com. To use these functions, scripters can simply copy them into a script or call them from a library file that has been included or dot sourced into the script.

In addition to reducing the time to create scripts, using reusable code stored in a library file makes your code more standardized and interchangeable. In fact, Jeffrey Snover, the PowerShell architect, has often recommended following this best practice for scripting.

The LibraryRegistry.vbs Script

LibraryRegistry.vbs is a VBScript file for reading or modifying the Registry on the local host or a remote machine. A working copy is in the Scripts\Chapter 7\LibraryRegistry folder and is downloadable at www.samspublishing.com. To use this file in another script, you must include it in the calling script. The calling script then has access to the functions, routines, constants, and so on defined in the included file.

VBScript has two methods for including a script file in another script file. The first method works only with VBScript (.vbs) files and uses the VBScript ExecuteGlobal statement. This statement takes a single string value and runs it as a VBScript statement in a script's global namespace. Then the script can access the contents of the string value. The following code shows this process:

```
' Method to include VBScript files
Sub Include(strFileName)
    On Error Resume Next

    Dim objFSO, objFile, strScript

    Set objFSO = CreateObject("Scripting.FileSystemObject")

    If objFSO.FileExists(strFileName) Then
        Set objFile = objFSO.OpenTextFile(strFileName)
        strScript = objFile.ReadAll
        objFile.Close

        ExecuteGlobal strScript
    End If

    Set objFSO = Nothing
    Set objFile = Nothing
End Sub
```

This method has several disadvantages, however. First, you run the risk of overwriting existing global variables and functions at runtime. Second, there's no good way to debug the contents of the string value you supply to ExecuteGlobal. After all, the value is just a string that happens to run. Third, VBScript doesn't have a valid include statement, so this method is actually just a workaround.

For these reasons, using the `ExecuteGlobal` statement in a VBScript file isn't the preferred method for including files in a script file. The most reliable, robust method for including external code in a script is using a WSF file because the format supports `include` statements, as shown in this example:

```
<job>
    <script src="LibrarySuperFunctions.js" language="JScript" />
    <script language="vbscript">

strEvent = "Vaction Time!"

strDate = GetCalendarDate(strEvent)
WScript.Echo strDate

    </script>
</job>
```

As this example shows, a VBScript job in a WSF file can include a JScript file. The reverse is possible, too; a JScript job can include a VBScript file. You can also include both types of files in a script or have a single WSF file performing multiple jobs that use different languages (engines) for each job. The point is that regardless of the method you choose, after you have included a script file, you can use its functions, constants, routines, and so on in your script.

Each function in the `LibraryRegistry.vbs` script uses the WMI `StdRegProv` class, located in the WMI `root\default` namespace. This class contains methods for reading and manipulating Registry keys and values to perform the following tasks:

▶ Verify that a user has the specified permissions.

▶ Create, enumerate, and delete Registry keys.

▶ Create, enumerate, and delete Registry values.

▶ Get or update a security descriptor for a Registry key (supported only in Vista or Longhorn).

The remainder of this section gives code examples to illustrate the functions in `LibraryRegistry.vbs`.

The `ReadRegValue` function:

```
'-------------------
' ReadRegValue
'-------------------
Function ReadRegValue(strComputer, strKeyPath, strValueName, strType)
    On Error Resume Next

    const HKEY_LOCAL_MACHINE = &H80000002

    Set objReg = GetObject("winmgmts:{impersonationLevel=impersonate}!\\" _
        & strComputer & "\root\default:StdRegProv")

    If strType = "BIN" Then
        objReg.GetBinaryValue HKEY_LOCAL_MACHINE, strKeyPath,_
            strValueName, arrValue

        ReadRegValue = arrValue
    End If
    If strType = "DWORD" Then
        objReg.GetDWORDValue HKEY_LOCAL_MACHINE, strKeyPath,_
            strValueName, strValue

        ReadRegValue = strValue
    End If
    If strType = "EXP" Then
        objReg.GetExpandedStringValue HKEY_LOCAL_MACHINE, strKeyPath,_
            strValueName, strValue

        ReadRegValue = strValue
    End If
    If strType = "MULTI" Then
        objReg.GetMultiStringValue HKEY_LOCAL_MACHINE, strKeyPath,_
            strValueName, arrValue

        ReadRegValue = arrValue
    End If
    If strType = "STR" Then
        objReg.GetStringValue HKEY_LOCAL_MACHINE, strKeyPath,_
            strValueName, strValue

        ReadRegValue = strValue
    End If
End Function
```

The `ReadRegValue` function retrieves a Registry data value for named values under the `HKEY_LOCAL_MACHINE` hive. This function requires defining the following parameters:

- `strComputer`—The name or IP address of the computer to retrieve Registry information from; `"."` can be used to denote the local host

- `strKeyPath`—The key path where the Registry value is located

- `strValueName`—The name of the Registry value you're trying to retrieve data from

- `strType`—A defined string representing the type of Registry value from which data is being retrieved, such as `BIN` (`REG_BINARY`), `DWORD` (`REG_DWORD`), `EXP` (`REG_EXPAND_SZ`), `MULTI` (`REG_MULTI_SZ`), and `STR` (`REG_SZ`)

Based on the `strType` value, the `ReadRegValue` function uses the appropriate `StdRegProv` method to retrieve the specified value's data from the Registry. The data returned from `ReadRegValue` can be in the form of a string, an integer, or an array. The return value needs to be handled according to the type of Registry value you're reading. For example, if you retrieve data from a `REG_BINARY` value, the data returned from `ReadRegValue` is in an array containing binary values. To read the binary values, you need to step through the array, as shown here:

```
Set StdOut = WScript.StdOut
strServer = "serverxyz.companyabc.com"

binValue = ReadRegValue(strServer, "SOFTWARE\Turtle_Worm", "binValue", "BIN")

StdOut.WriteLine "BIN Value:"
For i = lBound(binValue) to uBound(binValue)
    StdOut.WriteLine binValue(i)
Next
```

The `CreateRegKey` function:

```
Function CreateRegKey(strComputer, strKeyPath)
    On Error Resume Next

    const HKEY_LOCAL_MACHINE = &H80000002

    Set objReg = GetObject("winmgmts:{impersonationLevel=impersonate}!\\" &_
        strComputer & "\root\default:StdRegProv")

    objReg.CreateKey HKEY_LOCAL_MACHINE, strKeyPath

End Function
```

7

The `CreateRegKey` function creates a Registry key under the `HKEY_LOCAL_MACHINE` hive. This function requires defining the following parameters:

▶ `strComputer`—The name or IP address of the computer to create the key on; "." can be used to denote the local host

▶ `strKeyPath`—The key path for the new Registry key

Here's an example of using this function:

```
strServer = "serverxyz.companyabc.com"

CreateRegKey strServer, "SOFTWARE\Turtle_Worm"
```

The `CreateRegValue` function:

```
Function CreateRegValue(strComputer, strKeyPath,_
                        strValueName, strvalue, strType)
    On Error Resume Next

    const HKEY_LOCAL_MACHINE = &H80000002

    Set objReg = GetObject("winmgmts:{impersonationLevel=impersonate}!\\" &_
        strComputer & "\root\default:StdRegProv")

    If strType = "BIN" Then
        objReg.SetBinaryValue HKEY_LOCAL_MACHINE, strKeyPath,_
            strValueName, strValue
    End If
    If strType = "DWORD" Then
        objReg.SetDWORDValue HKEY_LOCAL_MACHINE, strKeyPath,_
            strValueName, strValue
    End If
    If strType = "EXP" Then
        objReg.SetExpandedStringValue HKEY_LOCAL_MACHINE, strKeyPath,_
            strValueName, strValue
    End If
    If strType = "MULTI" Then
        objReg.SetMultiStringValue HKEY_LOCAL_MACHINE, strKeyPath,_
            strValueName, strValue
    End If
```

```
     If strType = "STR" Then
         objReg.SetStringValue HKEY_LOCAL_MACHINE, strKeyPath,_
             strValueName, strValue
     End If
End Function
```

The `CreateRegValue` function creates or modifies a Registry value under the `HKEY_LOCAL_MACHINE` hive. This function requires defining the following parameters:

- `strComputer`—The name or IP address of the computer to create or change a Registry value on; `"."` can be used to denote the local host

- `strKeyPath`—The key path where the Registry value is located

- `strValueName`—The name of the Registry value you're trying to create or change

- `strValue`—The value to which to set the Registry value

- `strType`—A defined string representing the type of Registry value being created or changed, such as `BIN (REG_BINARY)`, `DWORD (REG_DWORD)`, `EXP (REG_EXPAND_SZ)`, `MULTI (REG_MULTI_SZ)`, and `STR (REG_SZ)`

The value you supply for the `strValue` parameter depends on the type of Registry value you're creating or modifying. If you're working with a `REG_BINARY` value, the value provided to `CreateRegValue` must be an array containing binary values. For `REG_MULTI_SZ`, the value must be an array containing string values. With `REG_SZ` and `REG_EXPAND_SZ`, the values must be in the form of a string. However, with `REG_EXPAND_SZ`, the value must include a valid environment variable, or the `GetExpandedStringValue` method can't expand the string when the value is retrieved. Last, when creating or modifying `REG_DWORD`, the value provided to `CreateRegValue` must be a valid `DWORD` value.

Here's an example of using this function:

```
Set StdOut = WScript.StdOut
strServer = "serverxyz.companyabc.com"

Multi = Array("PowerShell", "is", "fun!")
CreateRegValue strServer, "SOFTWARE\Turtle_Worm", "multiValue", Multi,_
    "MULTI"
```

The `DeleteRegKey` function:

```
Function DeleteRegKey(strComputer, strKeyPath)
    On Error Resume Next

    const HKEY_LOCAL_MACHINE = &H80000002

    Set objReg = GetObject("winmgmts:{impersonationLevel=impersonate}!\\" &_
        strComputer & "\root\default:StdRegProv")

    objReg.DeleteKey HKEY_LOCAL_MACHINE, strKeyPath

End Function
```

The `DeleteRegKey` function deletes a Registry key from the `HKEY_LOCAL_MACHINE` hive. This function requires defining the following parameters:

- ▶ strComputer—The name or IP address of the computer to delete the key from; "." can be used to denote the local host

- ▶ strKeyPath—The key path for the Registry key to be deleted

> **NOTE**
>
> Deleting a key deletes all subkeys and their values.

Here's an example of using this function:

```
Set StdOut = WScript.StdOut
strServer = "serverxyz.companyabc.com"

DeleteRegKey strServer, "SOFTWARE\Turtle_Worm"
```

The `DeleteRegValue` value:

```
Function DeleteRegValue(strComputer, strKeyPath, strValueName)
    On Error Resume Next

    const HKEY_LOCAL_MACHINE = &H80000002
```

```
      Set objReg = GetObject("winmgmts:{impersonationLevel=impersonate}!\\" &_
          strComputer & "\root\default:StdRegProv")

      objReg.DeleteValue HKEY_LOCAL_MACHINE, strKeyPath, strValueName

End Function
```

The `DeleteRegValue` function deletes a Registry value from the `HKEY_LOCAL_MACHINE` hive. This function requires defining the following parameters:

- ▶ `strComputer`—The name or IP address of the computer to create the key on; "." can be used to denote the local host

- ▶ `strKeyPath`—The key path where the Registry value resides

- ▶ `strValueName`—The name of the Registry value being deleted

Here's an example of using this function:

```
Set StdOut = WScript.StdOut
strServer = "server1000"

DeleteRegValue strServer, "SOFTWARE\Turtle_Worm", "binValue"
```

The `LibraryRegistry.ps1` Script

`LibraryRegistry.ps1` is a PowerShell conversion of the `LibraryRegistry.vbs` VBScript file. A working copy is in the `Scripts\Chapter 7\LibraryRegistry` folder and is downloadable at www.samspublishing.com. Before using this library file in a PowerShell console session, you must dot source it as discussed in Chapter 3. The dot sourcing format is a period followed by a space and then the filename, as in this example: `.\myscript.ps1`. To dot source `LibraryRegistry.ps1` from a PowerShell console session, use the following command:

```
. "D:\Scripts\LibraryRegistry.ps1"PS C:\>
```

However, dot sourcing a script file every time you want to use its set of functions tends to be more work than it should be. When you dot source a script file, the contents are loaded into your current PowerShell console session's global scope. If you close that session and open a new session, everything that was in the global scope is discarded, forcing you to dot source the script file every time you start a new session.

To avoid this problem, you can use a PowerShell profile to control the configuration of your PowerShell console. By using a PowerShell profile, such as `Profile.ps1`, and dot sourcing your script files in a profile file, you have everything you need already loaded in the global scope every time you start a new console session. Here's an example of a Profile.ps1 file:

```
. "D:\Scripts\LibraryRegistry.ps1"


set-location C:\
cls

# Welcome Message
"Welcome to back to more reg fun: " + $ENV:UserName
```

> **NOTE**
>
> LibraryRegistry.ps1 can also be dot sourced in a script file. Dot sourcing a .ps1 script file as such tells PowerShell to load the script into the calling script's scope. Remember that a script's parent scope can be a PowerShell session or another script.

After a new PowerShell session is loaded with the customized Profile.ps1, the console prompt looks like this:

```
Welcome back to more reg fun: script_master_snover
PS C:\>
```

By retrieving information from the Function PSDrive object, as shown in the following example, you can determine whether the Registry functions defined in LibraryRegistry.ps1 have been loaded into the current PowerShell session:

```
PS C:\> get-childitem Function:

CommandType     Name            Definition
-----------     ----            ----------
Function        prompt          'PS ' + $(Get-Location) + $(...
Function        TabExpansion    ...
Function        Clear-Host      $spaceType = [System.Managem...
Function        more            param([string[]]$paths);  if...
Function        help            param([string]$Name,[string[...
Function        man             param([string]$Name,[string[...
Function        mkdir           param([string[]]$paths); New...
Function        md              param([string[]]$paths); New...
Function        A:              Set-Location A:
```

```
Function        B:                          Set-Location B:
Function        C:                          Set-Location C:

...

Function        W:                          Set-Location W:
Function        X:                          Set-Location X:
Function        Y:                          Set-Location Y:
Function        Z:                          Set-Location Z:
Function        Get-RegValue                param($Computer, $KeyPath, $...
Function        Set-RegKey                  param($Computer, $KeyPath) $...
Function        Set-RegValue                param($Computer, $KeyPath, $...
Function        Remove-RegKey               param($Computer, $KeyPath) $...
Function        Remove-RegValue             param($Computer, $KeyPath, $...


PS C:\>
```

Notice in the preceding example there are five different Reg functions that can be used in the current PowerShell session to read and manipulate subkeys under the HKEY_LOCAL_ MACHINE hive for the local host or remote machines. The remainder of this section gives you more information about these functions.

The Get-RegValue function:

```
#----------------------------------------------------
# Get-RegValue
#----------------------------------------------------
# Usage:        Used to read an HKLM Registry value
#               on a local or remote machine.
# $Computer:    The name of the computer.
# $KeyPath:     The Registry key path.
#               ("SYSTEM\CurrentControlSet\Control")
# $ValueName:   The 1 value name. ("CurrentUser")
# $Type:        The Registry value type. ("BIN", "DWORD",
#               "EXP", "MULTI", or "STR")

function Get-RegValue{
    param ($Computer, $KeyPath, $ValueName, $Type)

    $HKEY_LOCAL_MACHINE = 2147483650


    trap{write-host "[ERROR] $_" -Foregroundcolor Red; Continue}
```

```
$Reg = get-wmiobject -Namespace Root\Default -computerName `
    $Computer -List ¦ where-object `
    {$_.Name -eq "StdRegProv"}


if ($Type -eq "BIN"){
    return $Reg.GetBinaryValue($HKEY_LOCAL_MACHINE, $KeyPath, `
        $ValueName)
    }
elseif ($Type -eq "DWORD"){
    return $Reg.GetDWORDValue($HKEY_LOCAL_MACHINE, $KeyPath, `
        $ValueName)
    }
elseif ($Type -eq "EXP"){
    return $Reg.GetExpandedStringValue($HKEY_LOCAL_MACHINE, `
        $KeyPath, $ValueName)
    }
elseif ($Type -eq "MULTI"){
    return $Reg.GetMultiStringValue($HKEY_LOCAL_MACHINE, `
        $KeyPath, $ValueName)
    }
elseif ($Type -eq "STR"){
    return $Reg.GetStringValue($HKEY_LOCAL_MACHINE, `
        $KeyPath, $ValueName)
    }
}
```

The Get-RegValue function retrieves a Registry value for named values under the HKEY_LOCAL_MACHINE hive. This function requires defining the following parameters:

- $Computer—The name or IP address of the computer to retrieve Registry information from; "." can be used to denote the local host

- $KeyPath—The key path where the Registry value is located

- $ValueName—The name of the Registry value you're trying to retrieve data from

- $Type—A defined string representing the type of Registry value from which data is being retrieved, such as BIN (REG_BINARY), DWORD (REG_DWORD), EXP (REG_EXPAND_SZ), MULTI (REG_MULTI_SZ), and STR (REG_SZ)

The following example shows how to use this function:

```
PS C:\> get-regvalue "Arus" "SOFTWARE\Voltron" "BlueLion" "BIN"
```

The Set-RegKey function:

```
#--------------------------------------------------
# Set-RegKey
#--------------------------------------------------
# Usage:        Used to create/set an HKLM Registry key
#               on a local or remote machine.
# $Computer:    The name of the computer.
# $KeyPath:     The Registry key path.
#               ("SYSTEM\CurrentControlSet\Control")

function Set-RegKey{
    param ($Computer, $KeyPath)

    $HKEY_LOCAL_MACHINE = 2147483650

    trap{write-host "[ERROR] $_" -Foregroundcolor Red; Continue}

    $Reg = get-wmiobject -Namespace Root\Default -computerName `
        $Computer -List ¦ where-object `
        {$_.Name -eq "StdRegProv"}

    return $Reg.CreateKey($HKEY_LOCAL_MACHINE, $KeyPath)
    }
```

The Set-RegKey function creates a Registry key under the HKEY_LOCAL_MACHINE hive. This function requires defining the following parameters:

- $Computer—The name or IP address of the computer to create the key on; "." can be used to denote the local host

- $KeyPath—The key path for the new Registry key

Here's an example of using this function:

```
PS C:\> set-regkey "Arus" "SOFTWARE\Voltron"
```

The Set-RegValue function:

```
#--------------------------------------------------
# Set-RegValue
#--------------------------------------------------
# Usage:        Used to create/set an HKLM Registry value
```

```
#                 on a local or remote machine.
# $Computer:      The name of the computer.
# $KeyPath:       The Registry key path.
#                 ("SYSTEM\CurrentControlSet\Control")
# $ValueName:     The Registry value name. ("CurrentUser")
# $Value:         The Registry value. ("value1", Array, Integer)
# $Type:          The Registry value type. ("BIN", "DWORD",
#                 "EXP", "MULTI", or "STR")

function Set-RegValue{
    param ($Computer, $KeyPath, $ValueName, $Value, $Type)

    $HKEY_LOCAL_MACHINE = 2147483650

    trap{write-host "[ERROR] $_" -Foregroundcolor Red; Continue}

    $Reg = get-wmiobject -Namespace Root\Default -computerName `
        $Computer -List ¦ where-object `
        {$_.Name -eq "StdRegProv"}

    if ($Type -eq "BIN"){
        return $Reg.SetBinaryValue($HKEY_LOCAL_MACHINE, $KeyPath, `
            $ValueName, $Value)
        }
    elseif ($Type -eq "DWORD"){
        return $Reg.SetDWORDValue($HKEY_LOCAL_MACHINE, $KeyPath, `
            $ValueName, $Value)
        }
    elseif ($Type -eq "EXP"){
        return $Reg.SetExpandedStringValue($HKEY_LOCAL_MACHINE, `
            $KeyPath, $ValueName, $Value)
        }
    elseif ($Type -eq "MULTI"){
        return $Reg.SetMultiStringValue($HKEY_LOCAL_MACHINE, `
            $KeyPath, $ValueName, $Value)
        }
    elseif ($Type -eq "STR"){
        return $Reg.SetStringValue($HKEY_LOCAL_MACHINE, `
            $KeyPath, $ValueName, $Value)
        }
    }
```

The `Set-RegValue` function creates or changes a Registry value under the `HKEY_LOCAL_MACHINE` hive. This function requires defining the following parameters:

- ▶ `$Computer`—The name or IP address of the computer on which to create or change a Registry value; `"."` can be used to denote the local host
- ▶ `$KeyPath`—The key path where the Registry value is located
- ▶ `$ValueName`—The name of the Registry value you're trying to create or change
- ▶ `$Value`—The data to which to set the Registry value
- ▶ `$Type`—A defined string representing the type of Registry value being created or changed, such as `BIN` (`REG_BINARY`), `DWORD` (`REG_DWORD`), `EXP` (`REG_EXPAND_SZ`), `MULTI` (`REG_MULTI_SZ`), and `STR` (`REG_SZ`)

The following example shows how to use this function:

```
PS C:\> $Multi = "PowerShell", "is", "fun!"
PS C:\> set-regvalue "Arus" "SOFTWARE\Voltron" "Lion_Statement" $Multi "MULTI"
```

The `Remove-RegKey` function:

```
#-----------------------------------------------------
# Remove-RegKey
#-----------------------------------------------------
# Usage:        Used to delete an HKLM Registry key
#               on a local or remote machine.
# $Computer:    The name of the computer.
# $KeyPath:     The Registry key path.
#               ("SYSTEM\CurrentControlSet\Control")

function Remove-RegKey{
    param ($Computer, $KeyPath)

    $HKEY_LOCAL_MACHINE = 2147483650

    trap{write-host "[ERROR] $_" -Foregroundcolor Red; Continue}

    $Reg = get-wmiobject -Namespace Root\Default -computerName `
        $Computer -List ¦ where-object `
        {$_.Name -eq "StdRegProv"}

    return $Reg.DeleteKey($HKEY_LOCAL_MACHINE, $KeyPath)
    }
```

The `Remove-RegKey` function deletes a Registry key from the `HKEY_LOCAL_MACHINE` hive. This function requires defining the following parameters:

- ▶ `$Computer`—The name or IP address of the computer where you're deleting the key; `"."` can be used to denote the local host

- ▶ `$KeyPath`—The key path for the Registry key to delete

An example of using this function is shown here:

```
PS C:\> remove-regkey "Arus" "SOFTWARE\Voltron"
```

The `Remove-RegValue` function:

```
#-------------------------------------------------
# Remove-RegValue
#-------------------------------------------------
# Usage:        Used to delete an HKLM Registry value
#               on a local or remote machine.
# $Computer:    The name of the computer.
# $KeyPath:     The Registry key path.
#               ("SYSTEM\CurrentControlSet\Control")
# $ValueName:   The Registry value name. ("CurrentUser")

function Remove-RegValue{
    param ($Computer, $KeyPath, $ValueName)

    $HKEY_LOCAL_MACHINE = 2147483650

    trap{write-host "[ERROR] $_" -Foregroundcolor Red; Continue}

    $Reg = get-wmiobject -Namespace Root\Default -computerName `
        $Computer -List ¦ where-object `
        {$_.Name -eq "StdRegProv"}

    return $Reg.DeleteValue($HKEY_LOCAL_MACHINE, $KeyPath, $ValueName)
    }
```

The `Remove-RegValue` function deletes a Registry value from the `HKEY_LOCAL_MACHINE` hive. You must define the following parameters:

- ▶ `$Computer`—The name or IP address of the computer where you're creating the key; `"."` can be used to denote the local host

▶ $KeyPath—The key path where the Registry value resides

▶ $ValueName—The name of the Registry value being deleted

Here's an example of using this function:

```
PS C:\> remove-regvalue "Arus" "SOFTWARE\Voltron" "Lion_Statement"
```

Using the Library

Now that you understand the Registry functions in the LibraryRegistry.ps1 script, you can practice using these functions. The first step is to create a Registry key called Turtle_Worm under the HKLM\Software key on an Active Directory domain controller named DC1. To do this, you use the following command:

```
PS C:\> set-regkey "DC1" "SOFTWARE\Turtle_Worm"


__GENUS             : 2
__CLASS             : __PARAMETERS
__SUPERCLASS        :
__DYNASTY           : __PARAMETERS
__RELPATH           :
__PROPERTY_COUNT    : 1
__DERIVATION        : {}
__SERVER            :
__NAMESPACE         :
__PATH              :
ReturnValue         : 0


PS C:\>
```

The command returns a WMI object that contains no information. If any error occurred, the trap in the function would write the error information to the console, as shown in this example:

```
PS C:\> set-regkey "Pinky" "SOFTWARE\Turtle_Worm"
[ERROR] The RPC server is unavailable. (Exception from HRESULT: 0x800706BA)
PS C:\>
```

Next, you create values under the Turtle_Worm Registry key with the following set of commands:

```
PS C:\> $Bin = 101, 118, 105, 108, 95, 116, 117, 114, 116, 108, 101
PS C:\> set-regvalue "DC1" "SOFTWARE\Turtle_Worm" "binValue" $Bin
"BIN"


__GENUS              : 2
__CLASS              : __PARAMETERS
__SUPERCLASS         :
__DYNASTY            : __PARAMETERS
__RELPATH            :
__PROPERTY_COUNT     : 1
__DERIVATION         : {}
__SERVER             :
__NAMESPACE          :
__PATH               :
ReturnValue          : 0


PS C:\> $Null = set-regvalue "DC1" "SOFTWARE\Turtle_Worm" "dwordValue"
"1" "DWORD"
PS C:\> $Null = set-regvalue "DC1" "SOFTWARE\Turtle_Worm" "expValue"
"%SystemRoot%\system32\Turtle_Hacker.dll" "EXP"
PS C:\> $Multi = "PowerShell", "is", "fun!"
PS C:\> $Null = set-regvalue "DC1" "SOFTWARE\Turtle_Worm" "multiValue"
$Multi "MULTI"
PS C:\> $Null = set-regvalue "DC1" "SOFTWARE\Turtle_Worm" "strValue"
"Reg work done!" "STR"
PS C:\>
```

These steps simulate creating a Registry key and its values. Next, you use the Registry library functions to determine whether a set of values exists. To do this, use the Get-RegValue function:

```
PS C:\> get-regvalue "DC1" "SOFTWARE\Turtle_Worm" "binValue" "BIN"


__GENUS              : 2
__CLASS              : __PARAMETERS
__SUPERCLASS         :
__DYNASTY            : __PARAMETERS
__RELPATH            :
__PROPERTY_COUNT     : 2
__DERIVATION         : {}
__SERVER             :
__NAMESPACE          :
__PATH               :
```

```
ReturnValue         : 0
uValue              : {101, 118, 105, 108...}


PS C:\> get-regvalue "DC1" "SOFTWARE\Turtle_Worm" "dwordValue" "DWORD"


__GENUS             : 2
__CLASS             : __PARAMETERS
__SUPERCLASS        :
__DYNASTY           : __PARAMETERS
__RELPATH           :
__PROPERTY_COUNT    : 2
__DERIVATION        : {}
__SERVER            :
__NAMESPACE         :
__PATH              :
ReturnValue         : 0
uValue              : 1


PS C:\> get-regvalue "DC1" "SOFTWARE\Turtle_Worm" "expValue" "EXP"


__GENUS             : 2
__CLASS             : __PARAMETERS
__SUPERCLASS        :
__DYNASTY           : __PARAMETERS
__RELPATH           :
__PROPERTY_COUNT    : 2
__DERIVATION        : {}
__SERVER            :
__NAMESPACE         :
__PATH              :
ReturnValue         : 0
sValue              : C:\WINDOWS\system32\Turtle_Hacker.dll


PS C:\> get-regvalue "DC1" "SOFTWARE\Turtle_Worm" "multiValue" "MULTI"


__GENUS             : 2
__CLASS             : __PARAMETERS
__SUPERCLASS        :
__DYNASTY           : __PARAMETERS
__RELPATH           :
__PROPERTY_COUNT    : 2
__DERIVATION        : {}
__SERVER            :
__NAMESPACE         :
```

```
__PATH                :
ReturnValue           : 0
sValue                : {PowerShell, is, fun!}



PS C:\> get-regvalue "DC1" "SOFTWARE\Turtle_Worm" "strValue" "STR"


__GENUS               : 2
__CLASS               : __PARAMETERS
__SUPERCLASS          :
__DYNASTY             : __PARAMETERS
__RELPATH             :
__PROPERTY_COUNT : 2
__DERIVATION          : {}
__SERVER              :
__NAMESPACE           :
__PATH                :
ReturnValue           : 0
sValue                : Reg work done!



PS C:\>
```

As you can see from the WMI object returned, if a value exists, its information is returned
as an sValue or uValue property. If the value or key doesn't exist, the ReturnValue property is the integer 2. If the ReturnValue property is set to the integer 0, it indicates that
the WMI method was completed successfully.

Now that you have verified that values under the Turtle_Worm Registry key exist on DC1,
it's time to delete the Turtle_Worm Registry key and its values. There are two methods to
perform this task. You can delete each value by using the Remove-RegValue function, as
shown in the following example:

```
PS C:\> remove-regvalue "DC1" "SOFTWARE\Turtle_Worm" "binValue"


__GENUS               : 2
__CLASS               : __PARAMETERS
__SUPERCLASS          :
__DYNASTY             : __PARAMETERS
__RELPATH             :
__PROPERTY_COUNT : 1
__DERIVATION          : {}
__SERVER              :
__NAMESPACE           :
__PATH                :
```

```
ReturnValue         : 0


PS C:\>
```

The other method is using the `Remove-RegKey` function to delete the `Turtle_Worm` Registry key, which deletes all its subkeys and their values, as shown here:

```
PS C:\> remove-regkey "sol" "SOFTWARE\Turtle_Worm"


__GENUS             : 2
__CLASS             : __PARAMETERS
__SUPERCLASS        :
__DYNASTY           : __PARAMETERS
__RELPATH           :
__PROPERTY_COUNT    : 1
__DERIVATION        : {}
__SERVER            :
__NAMESPACE         :
__PATH              :
ReturnValue         : 0


PS C:\>
```

Summary

In closing, this chapter has focused on how to manage the Windows Registry using both WSH and PowerShell. While both scripting interfaces provide methods to manage the Registry, PowerShell's method tends to be more robust because it treats the Registry as a hierarchical data store. The only shortcoming in the current implementation is that PowerShell doesn't have a built-in method for managing the Registry on a remote machine (which WSH also suffers from). In this case, as reviewed in this chapter, PowerShell in conjunction with WMI can be used to remotely manage the Registry on a machine. Using both WMI and PowerShell, you should be able to accomplish any future Registry automation tasks that are required of you.

How to use reusable code and library files were also introduced in this chapter. As explained in Chapter 5, "PowerShell Scripting Best Practices," reusing code is a very important practice that can reduce the amount of time it takes to develop a script. This chapter further expanded the concept of reusable code by showing you how to implement it in the form of a library file based on a real-world example.

# CHAPTER 8

PowerShell and WMI

Introduction

This chapter shows how to use PowerShell to manage systems with Windows Management Instrumentation (WMI) and compares the methods Windows Script Host (WSH) and PowerShell use for WMI tasks. You also examine some scripting examples that use WSH to perform WMI tasks and then see how PowerShell can be used for those tasks. Finally, you look at an example of converting a VBScript script to PowerShell to perform an automation task by using WMI. The goal is to give the reader a chance to learn how PowerShell scripting techniques can be applied to complete real-world automation needs.

Comparing WMI Usage Between WSH and PowerShell

To use WMI via scripting, you use a set of objects in the Scripting API for WMI with the WSH methods `CreateObject()` and `GetObject()` (or another scripting language's methods for creating or connecting to COM objects). In this way, you can connect to a WMI object that might be a WMI class or an instance of a WMI class.

There are two methods to connect to a WMI object. The first is creating a `SWbemServices` object with the corresponding `CreateObject()` method and then connect to a WMI object by specifying that object's path. For the purpose of this discussion, however, you should focus on the second method. This method uses a `"winmgmts:"` **moniker string** (a standard COM mechanism for encapsulating the location and binding of another COM object). These methods are similar, but the `SWbemServices` object method is often chosen for error handling and authentication reasons, and the moniker string is usually chosen for convenience because a connection can be made with a single statement.

Using WMI in WSH

The following VBScript example uses a moniker string, which connects to a remote machine and then returns the amount of installed RAM:

```
On Error Resume Next

Dim objWMIService, objComputer, colItems
Dim strComputerName

strComputerName = "Jupiter"

Set objWMIService = GetObject("winmgmts:\\" & strComputerName _
        & "\root\cimv2")

Set colItems = objWMIService.ExecQuery _
    ("Select * from Win32_ComputerSystem")

For Each objItem in colItems
    WScript.Echo "Total RAM is: " _
        & FormatNumber((objItem.TotalPhysicalMemory \ 1024) _
        \ 1000, 0, 0, 0, -1) & " MB"
Next
```

Saving the script as getmemory.vbs and then running it by using cscript produces the following results:

```
C:\>cscript getmemory.vbs
Microsoft (R) Windows Script Host Version 5.6
Copyright (C) Microsoft Corporation 1996-2001. All rights reserved.

Total RAM is: 774 MB
C:\>
```

The following sections walk through this script to show you how it gets the installed memory information from the remote machine Jupiter.

Step One

First, you connect to the WMI service object under the root\cimv2 namespace on Jupiter, as shown here:

```
Set objWMIService = GetObject("winmgmts:\\" & strComputerName _
     & "\root\cimv2")
```

Step Two

Next, you use the `ExecQuery()` method of the WMI service object with the WMI Query Language (WQL) to create an object bound to an instance of the `Win32_ComputerSytem` class, as shown in this example:

```
Set colItems = objWMIService.ExecQuery _
    ("Select * from Win32_ComputerSystem")
```

Step Three

Finally, using the `colItems` variable and a `for` loop, you step through the newly created object collection and retrieve memory information from the `TotalPhysicalMemory` property. After formatting the numeric value with the `FormatNumber` function, you write the amount of memory (in megabytes) installed on the remote machine to the cmd command prompt, as shown in the following code:

```
For Each objItem in colItems
    WScript.Echo "Total RAM is: " _
        & FormatNumber((objItem.TotalPhysicalMemory / 1024) _
        / 1000, 0, 0, 0, -1) & " MB"
Next
```

Using WMI in PowerShell

Using WMI in PowerShell has similar conceptual logic as in WSH. The main difference is that the PowerShell methods are based on WMI .NET instead of the WMI Scripting API. You have three methods for using WMI in PowerShell: WMI .NET (which is the .NET `System.Management` and `System.Management.Instrumentation` namespaces), the `Get-WmiObject` cmdlet, or the PowerShell WMI type accelerators: `[WMI]`, `[WMIClass]`, and `[WMISearcher]`.

The first method, using the `System.Management` and `System.Management.Instrumentation` namespaces, isn't discussed in this chapter because it's not as practical as the other methods. It should be only a fallback method in case PowerShell isn't correctly encapsulating an object within a `PSObject` object when using the other two methods.

The second method, the `Get-WmiObject` cmdlet, retrieves WMI objects and gathers information about WMI classes. This cmdlet is fairly simple. For example, getting an instance of the local `Win32_ComputerSystem` class just requires the name of the class, as shown here:

```
PS C:\> get-wmiobject "Win32_ComputerSystem"

Domain              : companyabc.com
Manufacturer        : Hewlett-Packard
Model               : Pavilion dv8000 (ES184AV)
Name                : Wii
PrimaryOwnerName    : Damon Cortesi
TotalPhysicalMemory : 2145566720


PS C:\>
```

The next example, which is more robust, connects to the remote machine named Jupiter
and gets an instance of the Win32_Service class in which the instance's name equals
Virtual Server. The result is an object containing information about the Virtual Server
service on Jupiter:

```
PS C:\> get-wmiobject -class "Win32_Service" -computerName
"Jupiter" -filter "Name='Virtual Server'"

ExitCode  : 0
Name      : Virtual Server
ProcessId : 656
StartMode : Auto
State     : Running
Status    : OK


PS C:\>
```

The following command returns the same information as the previous one but makes use
of a WQL query:

```
PS C:\> get-wmiobject -computerName "Jupiter" -query "Select * From
Win32_Service Where Name='Virtual Server'"

ExitCode  : 0
Name      : Virtual Server
ProcessId : 656
StartMode : Auto
State     : Running
Status    : OK


PS C:\>
```

Finally, here's an example of using Get-WmiObject to gather information about a WMI class:

```
PS C:\> get-wmiobject -namespace "root/cimv2" -list | where
{$_.Name -eq "Win32_Product"} | format-list *


Name                 : Win32_Product
__GENUS              : 1
__CLASS              : Win32_Product
__SUPERCLASS         : CIM_Product
__DYNASTY            : CIM_Product
__RELPATH            : Win32_Product
__PROPERTY_COUNT     : 12
__DERIVATION         : {CIM_Product}
__SERVER             : PLANX
__NAMESPACE          : ROOT\cimv2
__PATH               : \\PLANX\ROOT\cimv2:Win32_Product


PS C:\>
```

Although using Get-WmiObject is simple, using it almost always requires typing a long command string. This drawback brings you to the third method for using WMI in PowerShell: the WMI type accelerators. The following section explains what a type accelerator is and how to use the PowerShell WMI type accelerators.

Type Accelerators

Type accelerators have been used in previous chapters but haven't been fully explained yet. A **type accelerator** is simply an alias for specifying a .NET type. Without a type accelerator, defining a variable type requires entering a fully qualified class name, as shown here:

```
PS C:\> $User = [System.DirectoryServices.DirectoryEntry]"LDAP://CN=Fujio
Saitoh,OU=Accounts,OU=Managed Objects,DC=companyabc,DC=com"
PS C:\> $User

distinguishedName
-----------------
{CN=Fujio Saitoh,OU=Accounts,OU=Managed Objects,DC=companyabc,DC=com}


PS C:\>
```

8

Instead of typing the entire class name, you just use the [ADSI] type accelerator to define the variable type, as in the following example:

```
PS C:\> $User = [ADSI]"LDAP://CN=Fujio Saitoh,OU=Accounts,OU=Managed
Objects,DC=companyabc,DC=com"
PS C:\> $User

distinguishedName
-----------------
{CN=Fujio Saitoh,OU=Accounts,OU=Managed Objects,DC=companyabc,DC=com}


PS C:\>
```

The PowerShell team has included type accelerators in PowerShell, mainly to cut down on the amount of typing to define an object type. However, for some reason, type accelerators aren't covered in the PowerShell documentation, even though the [WMI], [ADSI], and other common type accelerators are referenced on many Web blogs.

Regardless of the lack of documentation, type accelerators are a fairly useful feature of PowerShell. Table 8.1 lists commonly used type accelerators.

TABLE 8.1   Type Accelerators in PowerShell

Type Accelerator Name	Type
[int]	typeof(int)
[int[]]	typeof(int[])
[long]	typeof(long)
[long[]]	typeof(long[])
[string]	typeof(string)
[string[]]	typeof(string[])
[char]	typeof(char)
[char[]]	typeof(char[])
[bool]	typeof(bool)
[bool[]]	typeof(bool[])
[byte]	typeof(byte)
[double]	typeof(double)
[decimal]	typeof(decimal)
[float]	typeof(float)
[single]	typeof(float)
[regex]	typeof(System.Text.RegularExpressions.Regex)
[array]	typeof(System.Array)
[xml]	typeof(System.Xml.XmlDocument)
[scriptblock]	typeof(System.Management.Automation.ScriptBlock)

Type Accelerator Name	Type
[switch]	typeof(System.Management.Automation.SwitchParameter)
[hashtable]	typeof(System.Collections.Hashtable)
[type]	typeof(System.Type)
[ref]	typeof(System.Management.Automation.PSReference)
[psobject]	typeof(System.Management.Automation.PSObject)
[wmi]	typeof(System.Management.ManagementObject)
[wmisearcher]	typeof(System.Management.ManagementObjectSearcher)
[wmiclass]	typeof(System.Management.ManagementClass)
[adsi]	typeof(System.DirectoryServices.DirectoryEntry)

How to use the PowerShell WMI type accelerators is explained in the following sections.

[WMI] Type Accelerator

This type accelerator for the ManagementObject class takes a WMI object path as a string and gets a WMI object bound to an instance of the specified WMI class, as shown in this example:

```
PS C:\> $CompInfo = [WMI]'\\.\root\cimv2:Win32_ComputerSystem.Name="PLANX"'
PS C:\> $CompInfo


Domain               : companyabc.com
Manufacturer         : Hewlett-Packard
Model                : Pavilion dv8000 (ES184AV)
Name                 : PLANX
PrimaryOwnerName     : Frank Miller
TotalPhysicalMemory  : 2145566720



PS C:\>
```

8

NOTE

To bind to an instance of a WMI object directly, you must include the key property in the WMI object path. For the preceding example, the key property is Name.

[WMIClass] Type Accelerator

This type accelerator for the ManagementClass class takes a WMI object path as a string and gets a WMI object bound to the specified WMI class, as shown in the following example:

```
PS C:\> $CompClass = [WMICLASS]"\\.\root\cimv2:Win32_ComputerSystem"
PS C:\> $CompClass


Win32_ComputerSystem

PS C:\> $CompClass | format-list *


Name                : Win32_ComputerSystem
__GENUS             : 1
__CLASS             : Win32_ComputerSystem
__SUPERCLASS        : CIM_UnitaryComputerSystem
__DYNASTY           : CIM_ManagedSystemElement
__RELPATH           : Win32_ComputerSystem
__PROPERTY_COUNT    : 54
__DERIVATION        : {CIM_UnitaryComputerSystem, CIM_ComputerSystem,
CIM_System,

                      CIM_LogicalElement...}
__SERVER            : PLANX
__NAMESPACE         : ROOT\cimv2
__PATH              : \\PLANX\ROOT\cimv2:Win32_ComputerSystem


PS C:\>
```

[WMISearcher] Type Accelerator

This type accelerator for the ManagementObjectSearcher class takes a WQL string and creates a WMI searcher object. After the searcher object is created, you use the Get() method to get a WMI object bound to an instance of the specified WMI class, as shown here:

```
PS C:\> $CompInfo = [WMISearcher]"Select * From Win32_ComputerSystem"
PS C:\> $CompInfo.Get()


Domain              : companyabc.com
Manufacturer        : Hewlett-Packard
Model               : Pavilion dv8000 (ES184AV)
Name                : PLANX
PrimaryOwnerName    : Miro
TotalPhysicalMemory : 2145566720


PS C:\>
```

From VBScript to PowerShell

This next section explains the conversion of a VBScript script into a PowerShell script. The sample script is used to monitor virtual machines on a Microsoft Virtual Server 2005 host.

Before this script was developed, companyabc.com was in the process of switching most of its hardware application servers to virtual machines. As part of this switch, the company wanted a simple yet effective method for monitoring the virtual machines each Microsoft Virtual Server hosted. However, an effective monitoring platform, such as Microsoft Operations Manager (MOM), wasn't in place. The IT department suggested an automation script to meet the company's short-term monitoring needs, so one was developed that administrators could use to manage Virtual Server systems.

The MonitorMSVS.wsf Script

MonitorMSVS.wsf is a VBScript WSF file developed to meet companyabc.com's virtual machine monitoring needs. A working copy is in the Scripts\Chapter 8\MonitorMSVS folder and is downloadable at www.samspublishing.com. Running this script requires defining the servername parameter, which should have its argument set to the name of the Virtual Server system hosting the virtual machines to be monitored. Here's the command to run MonitorMSVS.wsf, with an example of the output shown in Figure 8.1:

```
D:\Scripts>cscript MonitorMSVS.wsf /servername:vsserver01
```

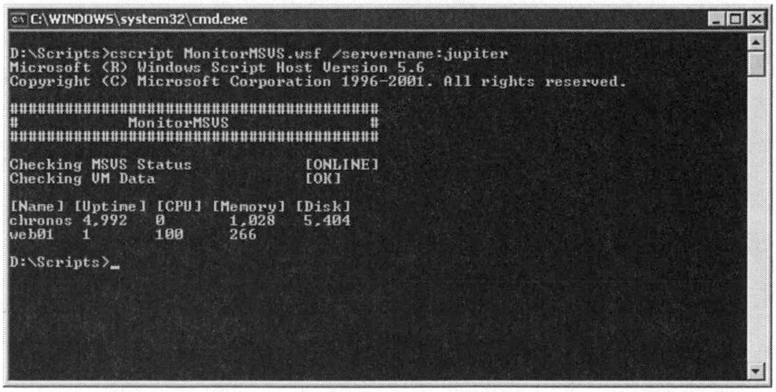

FIGURE 8.1   The MonitorMSVS.wsf script being executed

The MonitorMSVS.wsf script performs the following sequence of actions:

1. The script pings the specified Microsoft Virtual Server (MSVS) to verify that the server is operational.

2. Next, the script connects to the MSVS host by using a moniker string and, therefore, creating a WMI service object.

3. Next, the script calls the ExecQuery() method of the WMI service object, passing it a WQL query requesting a collection of instances of the VirtualMachine class.

4. Finally, for each currently active virtual machine (present in the collection), the script writes to the cmd command prompt the current values for the Uptime, CpuUtilization, PhysicalMemoryAllocated, and DiskSpaceUsed properties.

The first code sample consists of the initial XML elements for a WSF. These elements are used to define the allowed parameters, the script's description, examples on the script's operation, and the scripting language being used:

```
<?xml version="1.0" ?>
<package>
<job id="MonitorMSVS">
    <runtime>
        <description>
*************************************************************
This script is used to monitor Microsoft Virtual Server 2005.
*************************************************************
        </description>
        <named name="servername" helpstring="The name of the MSVS host to monitor."
type="string" required="1" />
        <example>
Example:
cscript MonitorMSVS.wsf /servername:"vms01.companyabc.com"
        </example>
    </runtime>
<script language="VBScript">
<![CDATA[
```

Next, the script checks to see if an argument has been defined for the required parameter servername. If an argument is not present, the script returns the script usage information (defined in the previous code snippet) to the console and quits. If an argument is defined, the script then sets up the script environment by defining the variables that will be used throughout the rest of the script:

```
On Error Resume Next

'=====================================================================
' Check required args
'=====================================================================
If WScript.Arguments.Named.Exists("servername") = FALSE Then
    WScript.Arguments.ShowUsage()
```

```
    WScript.Quit
End If


'=====================================================================
' Set up job env
'=====================================================================
Dim StdOut
Dim strServerName

Set StdOut = WScript.StdOut

strServerName = WScript.Arguments.Named("servername")
```

The next code snippet is the beginning of the actual automation portion of the script. First, the script writes the script header to the console, then checks to see if the specified MSVS host in the `servername` variable is operational by pinging it using the `Ping` function. If the MSVS host is operational, the script continues; otherwise, script execution is stopped and an appropriate status message is displayed to the script operator:

```
'=====================================================================
' Start Job
'=====================================================================
Mess "####################################"
Mess "#             MonitorMSVS          #"
Mess "####################################"
Mess vbNullString

StatStart "Checking MSVS Status"

If Ping(strServerName) = 0 Then
    StdOut.Write(vbTab & vbTab)
    StdOut.WriteLine("[OFFLINE]")
    WScript.Quit()
Else
    StdOut.Write(vbTab & vbTab)
    StdOut.WriteLine("[ONLINE]")
End If
```

The next task is to connect to the MSVS host using WMI and retrieve performance information about its virtual machines. Once the information has been retrieved, it then needs to be converted into a readable format before being written to the console, as shown in the following code snippet:

```
'-------------------
' Get VM data
'-------------------
StatStart "Checking VM Data"
    Set objWMIService = GetObject("winmgmts:\\" & strServerName _
        & "\root\vm\virtualserver")
    Set colItems = objWMIService.ExecQuery("SELECT * FROM VirtualMachine")

    Xerror
StatDone
StdOut.WriteLine(vbNullString)


' Header Info
StdOut.WriteLine("[Name] [Uptime] [CPU] [Memory] [Disk]")

For Each objItem In colItems
    StdOut.Write(objItem.Name & vbTab)
    StdOut.Write(FormatNumber(objItem.Uptime / 60, 0, 0, 0, -1) & vbTab)
    StdOut.Write(FormatNumber(objItem.CpuUtilization, 0) & vbTab)
    StdOut.Write(FormatNumber((objItem.PhysicalMemoryAllocated _
            / 1024) / 1000, 0, 0, 0, -1) & vbTab)
    StdOut.Write(FormatNumber((objItem.DiskSpaceUsed / 1024) _
            / 1000, 0, 0, 0, -1))
    StdOut.WriteLine(vbNullString)
Next
```

To make the values returned from the Uptime, CpuUtilization, PhysicalMemoryAllocated, and DiskSpaceUsed properties more readable, the script uses the FormatNumber function. This VBScript function controls the formatting of a numeric value and can be used to specify formatting such as the following:

▶ How many places to the right of the decimal are displayed

▶ Whether a leading zero is displayed for fractional values

▶ Whether to place negative values in parentheses

▶ Whether numbers are grouped by using the group delimiter specified in Control Panel

MonitorMSVS.wsf uses the FormatNumber function to format numeric values so that zero decimal places are shown and values are grouped by using the delimiter specified in a machine's regional settings. Last, those values are also converted into units that make more sense, as in these examples:

▶ Uptime is converted from seconds to minutes.

▶ PhysicalMemoryAllocated is converted from bytes to megabytes.

▶ DiskSpaceUsed is converted from bytes to megabytes.

The next code snippet consists of all the Subs that are used throughout the script:

```
'=======================================================================
' Subs
'=======================================================================
'--------------------
' General Message Sub
'--------------------
Sub Mess(Message)
    ' Write to console
    StdOut.WriteLine(Message)
End Sub


'--------------------
' General Start Message Sub
'--------------------
Sub StatStart(Message)
    ' Write to console
    StdOut.Write(Message)
End Sub


'--------------------
' General Finish Message Sub
'--------------------
Sub StatDone
    ' Write to console
    StdOut.Write(vbTab & vbTab)
    StdOut.WriteLine("[OK]")
End Sub


'--------------------
' General Xerror Sub
'--------------------
Sub Xerror
    If Err.Number <> 0 Then
        ' Write to console
        StdOut.WriteLine(" Critical Error: " & CStr(Err.Number) _
            & " " & Err.Description)

        WScript.Quit()
    End If
End Sub
```

8

Part of the logic in the MonitorMSVS.wsf script is to verify that the specified MSVS host is operational before continuing. This check is performed with an ICMP ping, as shown in the following example:

```
'========================================================================
' Functions
'========================================================================
'.....................
' Ping A Machine
'.....................
' This function is used to test if a machine is on the network.
Function Ping(Machine)
    On Error Resume Next

    Set colItems = GetObject("winmgmts:{impersonationLevel=impersonate}")._
        ExecQuery("select * from Win32_PingStatus where address = '"_
        & Machine & "'")

    For Each colItem in colItems
        If IsNull(colItem.StatusCode) or colItem.StatusCode <> 0 Then
            Ping = 0
        Else
            Ping = 1
        End If
    Next
End Function
```

To carry out the ICMP ping, the script uses a function aptly named Ping that performs the following sequence of actions:

1. The Ping function calls the ExecQuery() method of the WMI service object.

2. Ping passes ExecQuery() a WQL query requesting all properties from the instance of the Win32_PingStatus class, in which the address is that of the host you're trying to ping.

3. The resulting collection of instances (in this case, one instance, which is just an object) is assigned to the colItems variable.

4. The ping's results are collected from colItems and returned to the script so that it can determine whether to continue or stop.

Using an ICMP ping reduces the time the script would take to fail if the server requested a WMI query it wasn't capable of performing. This advanced error-handling technique can predict when the script might fail and includes logic to prevent the failure from happening. Also, a WMI method is used instead of ping.exe because the results returned from WMI are easier to work with than the text-based results ping.exe returns.

The last code snippet consists of closing XML elements for the script:

```
]]>
  </script>
</job>
</package>
```

The MonitorMSVS.ps1 Script

MonitorMSVS.ps1 is a PowerShell conversion of the MonitorMSVS.wsf script. A working copy is in the Scripts\Chapter 8\MonitorMSVS folder and is downloadable at www.samspublishing.com. Running this script requires defining the ServerName parameter, which should have its argument set to the name of the Virtual Server system hosting the virtual machines to be monitored. Here's the command to run MonitorMSVS.ps1, with an example of the output shown in Figure 8.2:

```
PS D:\Scripts> .\MonitorMSVS.ps1 -ServerName Jupiter
```

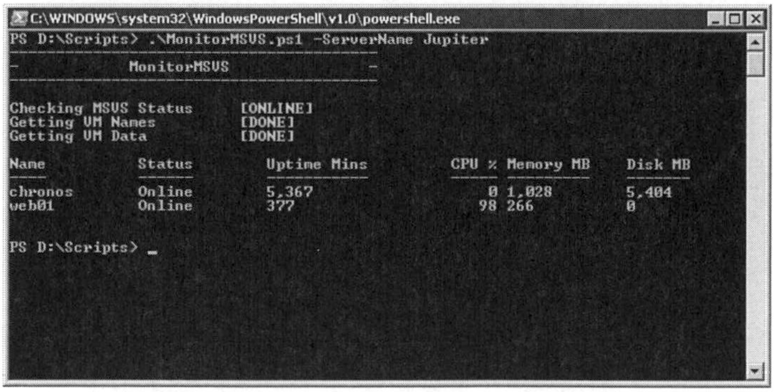

FIGURE 8.2   The MonitorMSVS.ps1 script being executed

NOTE

In the command to run the MonitorMSVS.ps1 script, the ServerName parameter is named in the command string, whereas in the example from Chapter 6, "Powershell and the File System," the script's parameters aren't named in the command string. In PowerShell, you can name or partially name parameters when running a script, as shown here:

```
.\MonitorMSVS.ps1 -S Jupiter
```

If you define the arguments in an order matching how parameters are defined in the script, the parameters don't need to be named at all when running a script, as shown here:

```
.\MonitorMSVS.ps1 Jupiter
```

The `MonitorMSVS.ps1` script performs the following sequence of actions:

1. The script pings the specified Microsoft Virtual Server (MSVS) to verify that the server is operational.

2. Next, the script connects to the Microsoft Virtual Server Administration Web site and retrieves a list of virtual machines on that MSVS host. The list of virtual machines is defined as the `$Servers` variable.

3. The script uses the `Get-WmiObject` cmdlet to retrieve a collection of instances of the `VirtualMachine` class, which is defined as the `$VirtualMachines` variable.

4. For each virtual machine object in the `$Servers` variable, the script adds the virtual machine's current status as another member of that object. If the virtual machine is online (present in the `$VirtualMachines` collection), the script also adds current values for the `Uptime`, `CpuUtilization`, `PhysicalMemoryAllocated`, and `DiskSpaceUsed` properties as members of the virtual machine object.

5. Finally, the script returns the information to the PowerShell console by using the `Format-Table` cmdlet.

The first code snippet contains the header for the `MonitorMSVS.ps1` script. This header includes information about what the script does, when it was updated, and the script's author. Just after the header is the script's only parameter ($ServerName):

```
################################################
# MonitorMSVS.ps1
# Used to monitor Microsoft Virtual Server 2005.
#
# Created: 12/01/2006
# Author: Tyson Kopczynski
################################################
param([string] $ServerName = $(throw write-host `
    "Please specify the name of the MSVS host to monitor!" `
    -Foregroundcolor Red))
```

The next code snippet contains the beginning of the script's automation portion. First, the variable $URL is defined as the URL for the MSVS host's Virtual Server Administration Website. Then, like the `MonitorMSVS.wsf` script, `MonitorMSVS.ps1` uses an ICMP ping to verify that the specified MSVS host is operational before continuing. However, the

`MonitorMSVS.ps1` script uses the .NET `Net.NetworkInformation.Ping` class instead of WMI to conduct the ping. Either method, including `ping.exe`, could have been used, but `Net.NetworkInformation.Ping` requires less work and less code. The choice of a method doesn't matter, however, as long as you try to predict where the script will fail and handle that failure accordingly:

```
###############################################
# Main
###############################################
$URL = "http://$($ServerName):1024/VirtualServer/VSWebApp.exe?view=1"


#--------------------
# Begin Script
#--------------------
write-host "------------------------------------------"
write-host "-              MonitorMSVS              -"
write-host "------------------------------------------"
write-host
write-host "Checking MSVS Status" -NoNewLine


.{
    trap{write-host `t "[ERROR]" -Foregroundcolor Red;
        throw write-host $_ -Foregroundcolor Red;
        Break}

    $Ping = new-object Net.NetworkInformation.Ping
    $Result = $Ping.Send($ServerName)

    if ($Result.Status -eq "Success"){
        write-host `t "[ONLINE]" -Foregroundcolor Green
        }
    else{
        write-host `t "[OFFLINE]" -Foregroundcolor Red
        write-host
        Break
        }
}
```

If the MSVS host is operational, script writes to the console that the host is "ONLINE" and continues execution of the script. Conversely, if the MSVS host is not operational, then the script writes to the console that the host is "OFFLINE" and halts execution of the script.

Once the operational status of the MSVS host has been verified, the next step is to connect to host and retrieve a list of virtual machines that are hosted. The following code

snippet completes this task by improving the logic from the original `MonitorMSVS.wsf`
script and showcasing one of PowerShell's more impressive capabilities:

```
#--------------------
# Get list of VMs
#--------------------
$Webclient = new-object Net.WebClient
$Webclient.UseDefaultCredentials = $True

write-host "Getting VM Names" -NoNewLine

.{
    trap{write-host `t "[ERROR]" -Foregroundcolor Red;
        throw write-host $_ -Foregroundcolor Red;
        Break}

    $Data = $Webclient.DownloadString("$URL")

    write-host `t "[DONE]" -Foregroundcolor Green
}

# This Regex gets a list of server entries from the data returned
$Servers = [Regex]::Matches($Data, '(?<=&amp;vm=)[^"\r\n]*(?=" )')

# There are many duplicates so you need to group them
# Plus, this gives you a better name for your property
$Servers = $Servers ¦ group Value ¦ select Name
```

The `MonitorMSVS.wsf` script had a major flaw: The WMI query returned information only
about virtual machines that were online at the time of the query. If a virtual machine
happens to be off when the `MonitorMSVS.wsf` script runs, there's no way to display that
fact to users. A list of all virtual machines and their current status is helpful information
for a script used as a monitoring tool.

To gain access to this information, the script must create a list of all virtual machines on
the MSVS host. Such a list exists on the Microsoft Virtual Server Administration Web site.
To access it, the script uses the .NET `Net.WebClient` class to connect to the Microsoft
Virtual Server Administration Web site remotely and download the HTML content from
the Master Status Page.

NOTE

Because PowerShell can use the .NET Framework, it can access Web services as sources for external data or as applications. For example, you can use PowerShell to post and read blogs, check the availability of the Wii on bestbuy.com, or perform an automation task based on data or applications provided by your enterprise's Web services. The possibilities are endless.

In the HTML content that is downloaded, the names of each virtual machine are embedded and repeated several times. To build the list, the script uses the regular expression type accelerator, [Regex], to strip each virtual machine name out of the HTML content and into the $Servers variable. The resulting list in the $Servers variable then contains each virtual machine's name, which is repeated several times. To shorten the list so that each virtual machine is listed only once, the script uses the Group-Object cmdlet. The final list, which contains the names of all virtual machines on the specified MSVS host, is then redefined in the $Servers variable.

Next, the script retrieves the virtual machines' performance information from instances of the WMI VirtualMachine class by using the Get-WmiObject cmdlet. The next step is to merge the two resulting data sets: the virtual machine information ($VirtualMachines) and the list of virtual machines ($Servers). To do this, the script steps through each virtual machine object in the $Servers variable. If the virtual machine name is in both object collections, the Add-Member cmdlet is used to extend the virtual machine object in the $Servers variable so that it includes the performance information in the $VirtualMachines variable.

This object extension adds an Online status indicator and related property information from $VirtualMachines. If the virtual machine is offline (not in both collections), the script only extends the object to include an Offline status indicator. The concept of changing an object dynamically was introduced in Chapter 3, "Powershell: A More In-Depth Look," but this example illustrates the power of this feature used in an automation script. The following example shows the code for this process:

```
#--------------------
# Get VM data
#--------------------
write-host "Getting VM Data" -NoNewLine

.{
    trap{write-host `t`t "[ERROR]" -Foregroundcolor Red;
        throw write-host $_ -Foregroundcolor Red;
        Break}

    $VSMachines = get-wmiobject -namespace "root/vm/virtualserver" `
        -class VirtualMachine -computername $ServerName
```

8

```
        -ErrorAction Stop

    write-host `t`t "[DONE]" -Foregroundcolor Green
}

foreach ($Server in $Servers){
    &{
        $VSMachine = $VSMachines ¦ where {$_.Name -eq $Server.Name}

        if($VSMachine){
            $Uptime = $VSMachine.Uptime / 60
            $Memory = ($VSMachine.PhysicalMemoryAllocated / 1024) / 1000
            $Disk = ($VSMachine.DiskSpaceUsed / 1024) /1000

            add-member -inputObject $Server -membertype noteProperty `
                -name "Status" -value "Online"
            add-member -inputObject $Server -membertype noteProperty `
                -name "Uptime" -value $Uptime
            add-member -inputObject $Server -membertype noteProperty `
                -name "CPU" -value $VSMachine.CpuUtilization
            add-member -inputObject $Server -membertype noteProperty `
                -name "Memory" -value $Memory
            add-member -inputObject $Server -membertype noteProperty `
                -name "Disk" -value $Disk
        }
        else{
            add-member -inputObject $Server -membertype noteProperty `
                -name "Status" -value "Offline"
        }
    }
}
```

The last step is writing information in the $Servers variable to the PowerShell console with the Format-Table cmdlet. This cmdlet can add calculated properties; in this case, it's used to change the labels of properties coming from $Servers. The format operator (-f) controls the formatting of these properties, as shown in the next code snippet:

NOTE

For more information on the -f operator, refer to the Format method of the .NET System.String class at http://msdn2.microsoft.com/en-us/library/system.string. format.aspx.

```
$Servers ¦ format-table Name, Status `
    ,@{label="Uptime Mins"; expression={"{0:N0}" -f $_.Uptime}} `
    ,@{label="CPU %"; expression={$_.CPU}} `
    ,@{label="Memory MB"; expression={"{0:N0}" -f $_.Memory}} `
    ,@{label="Disk MB"; expression={"{0:N0}" -f $_.Disk}} `
    -wrap
```

Summary

In summary, this chapter has focused on how to utilize WMI in conjunction with WSH and PowerShell to complete automation tasks. The examples and scripts shown in this chapter are by no means inclusive to what automation tasks can be completed using WMI. Furthermore, this chapter has shown you just how easy using WMI with PowerShell is. Armed with this knowledge, the limits to what you can accomplish using the two of these technologies should be fairly unbounded.

During the review of the real-world automation scripts, this chapter also unveiled a very powerful PowerShell feature. As discussed, a side effect of PowerShell's relationship with the .NET Framework is the ability to interact with and retrieve data from Web-based services. The resulting feature was used in the MonitorMSVS.ps1 script to gain access to Microsoft Virtual Server information that previously using VBScript would be more difficult to access and process. It really can't be stressed enough that the example shown in this chapter only scratched the surface in what can be done using this feature.

8

PowerShell and Active Directory

Introduction

This chapter explains Active Directory Services Interfaces (ADSI) and describes the approaches Windows Script Host (WSH) and PowerShell take for Active Directory management tasks. To understand these concepts, you review some examples that compare using WSH and PowerShell for Active Directory management tasks. Finally, you see a VBScript-to-PowerShell example that uses ADSI to perform an Active Directory automation task. The goal is to give the reader a chance to learn how PowerShell scripting techniques can be applied to complete real-world automation needs.

Comparing ADSI Usage Between WSH and PowerShell

Before learning how to use PowerShell to manage Active Directory, you need to know that **ADSI** is the primary programming interface for managing Active Directory. Any Active Directory management tool typically uses ADSI to interact with Active Directory. Similarly, when managing Active Directory through a script, you usually use ADSI.

To use ADSI as a component in your scripts, you need to understand several key concepts. First, ADSI consists of a series of providers: Lightweight Directory Access Protocol (LDAP), Novell Directory Services (NDS), Novell NetWare 3.x (NWCOMPAT), and Windows NT (WinNT). These providers allow external programs and scripts to manage a variety of network-based directories and data repositories, such as Active Directory, Novell NetWare 4.x NDS, and NetWare 3.x Bindery, and any LDAP-compliant directory service infrastructure (LDAP V2 and up). However, additional ADSI providers can be developed to support other types of data repositories. For example, Microsoft has an Internet Information Services (IIS) ADSI provider for managing IIS.

Second, an ADSI provider implements a group of COM objects to manage network directories and data repositories. For example, an administrator can use the ADSI WinNT provider to bind to and manage Windows domain resources because it includes objects for users, computers, groups, and domains, among others. Objects made available by an ADSI provider typically reside in the target resource you want to manage. By accessing the applicable ADSI provider, a program or script can bind to an object and manage it with a set of methods and properties defined for that object.

Third, ADSI provides an abstraction layer so that you can manage objects across different directory services and data repositories. This abstraction layer, called the IADs interface, defines a set of properties and methods as the foundation for all ADSI objects. For example, an ADSI object accessed through the IADs interface has the following features:

- An object can be identified by name, class, or ADsPath.

- An object's container can manage that object's creation and deletion.

- An object's schema definition can be retrieved.

- An object's attributes can be loaded into the ADSI property cache and changes to those attributes can be committed to the original data source.

- Object attributes loaded into the ADSI property cache can be modified.

Fourth, ADSI provides an additional interface (IADsContainer) for objects that are considered containers (such as organizational units, or OUs). When bound to a container object, this interface provides a set of common methods for creating, deleting, moving, enumerating, and managing child objects.

Fifth, ADSI maintains a client-side property cache for each ADSI object you bind to or create. Maintaining this local cache of object information improves the performance of reading from and writing to a data source because a program or script needs to access the data source less often. What's important to understand about the property cache is that object information it contains must be committed to the original data source. If new objects or object changes aren't committed to the original data source, those changes will not be reflected.

Now that you have a better understanding of using ADSI to interact with objects in Active Directory, you can compare ADSI use in WSH and PowerShell in the following sections.

Using ADSI in WSH

WSH has two methods for using ADSI. The first one is using a method (such as WSH's `GetObject()`) or function (such as VBScript's `GetObject()`) to connect (bind to) an Active Directory object. In doing so, you use ADSI's LDAP or WinNT provider while specifying the object's ADSI path, as shown in these two examples:

```
Set objUser = GetObject("LDAP://CN=Garett Kopczynski,OU=Accounts,OU=Managed
Objects,DC=companyabc,DC=com")
```

```
Set objUser = GetObject("WinNT://companyabc.com/garett")
```

The other WSH method for interacting with ADSI is ActiveX Data Objects (ADO). ADO allows applications or scripts to access data from different data sources by using a series of underlying Object Linking and Embedding Database (OLE DB) providers. One of these providers is an ADSI OLE DB (ADODB) provider that enables you to use ADO and its support for Structured Query Language (SQL) or LDAP to perform rapid searches in Active Directory. In the following example, you find a user account in Active Directory by using LDAP:

```
Set objConnection = CreateObject("ADODB.Connection")
Set objCommand = CreateObject("ADODB.Command")
objConnection.Provider = "ADsDSOObject"
objConnection.Open("Active Directory Provider")
objCommand.ActiveConnection = objConnection
objCommand.Properties("Page Size") = 1000
objCommand.CommandText = _
        "<LDAP://companyabc.com>;(&(objectCategory=user)" _
        & "(sAMAccountName=tyson));sAMAccountName,distinguishedName;subtree"
Set objRecordSet = objCommand.Execute
```

If the user exists, the resulting ADO recordset consists of the user's `sAMAccountName` and `distinguishedName`. This example shows just the tip of the iceberg, however. By using SQL or LDAP, you can build more powerful searches to retrieve complex filtered sets of information about Active Directory objects. Using ADO can make your Active Directory scripts more powerful. However, all this power has a catch. The ADSI OLE DB provider allows just read-only access to Active Directory, so to interact with objects, you still need to use ADSI.

6

Using ADSI with PowerShell

PowerShell also has two methods for working with Active Directory. The first (and easiest) method is using the built-in [ADSI] type accelerator. It's similar to the [WMI] type accelerator, in that you specify the object path to which you're connecting. The difference is that an object path must be in the form of an ADSI path, as shown in this example:

```
PS C:\> $User = [ADSI]"LDAP://CN=Garett
Kopczynski,OU=Accounts,OU=Managed Objects,DC=companyabc,DC=com"
```

This example uses an LDAP ADSI path. However, other providers as well as the [ADSI] type accelerator are available to ADSI. As discussed in Chapter 8, "PowerShell and WMI," PowerShell's [ADSI] type accelerator is a type shortcut for the .NET System.DirectoryServices.DirectoryEntry class, which can interface with these ADSI providers: IIS, LDAP, NDS, and WinNT. For example, if you want to access the same user account but with the ADSI WinNT provider, use the following command:

```
PS C:\> $User = [ADSI]"WinNT://companyabc.com/garett"
```

The second method is using the .NET System.DirectoryServices namespace via the New-Object cmdlet. When using this namespace, you can use two component classes to manage Active Directory. The first is System.DirectoryServices.DirectoryEntry, the same class used by the [ADSI] type accelerator. Its use is shown in the following example:

```
PS C:\> $User = new-object DirectoryServices.DirectoryEntry
("LDAP://CN=Garett Kopczynski,OU=Accounts,OU=Managed
Objects,DC=companyabc,DC=com")
```

The second is the System.DirectoryServices.DirectorySearcher class, which can be used to perform LDAP searches, as shown here:

```
PS C:\> $Searcher = new-object DirectoryServices.DirectorySearcher
PS C:\> $Searcher.Filter =
"(&(objectCategory=person)(objectClass=user)(samAccountName=garett))"
PS C:\> $User = $Searcher.FindOne().GetDirectoryEntry()
```

PowerShell's methods for using ADSI are similar to the WSH methods. Like WSH, PowerShell has a direct method involving the System.DirectoryServices.DirectoryEntry class or the [ADSI] type accelerator to connect to Active Directory objects and manage them. In addition, like WSH, PowerShell also has a second method involving the `System.DirectoryServices.DirectorySearcher` class to perform searches against Active Directory and retrieve read-only information about objects.

Therefore, managing Active Directory is much the same in PowerShell and WSH. Despite PowerShell using the .NET Framework to manage Active Directory, the `System.DirectoryServices.DirectoryEntry` and the `System.DirectoryServices.DirectorySearcher` classes are just .NET interfaces for ADSI. The differences between WSH and PowerShell are only in the specific functions and methods for managing Active Directory and their syntax. The next two sections examine these similarities by reviewing how to retrieve objection information and create an object using VBScript and PowerShell.

Retrieving Object Information

The following VBScript example binds to the specified user object by using the VBScript `GetObject()` method with an ADSI LDAP provider. The script then retrieves the user object's `Name`, `userPrincipalName`, `description`, and `physicalDeliveryOfficeName` attributes and echoes them back via a message box or to a cmd command prompt, as shown here:

```
Set objUser = GetObject("LDAP://CN=Garett Kopczynski,OU=Accounts,OU=Managed
Objects,DC=companyabc,DC=com")
WScript.Echo objUser.Name
WScript.Echo objUser.userPrincipalName
WScript.Echo objUser.description
WScript.Echo objUser.physicalDeliveryOfficeName
```

Saving the script as `getuserinfo.vbs` and then running it by using `cscript` produces the following results:

```
C:\>cscript getuserinfo.vbs
Microsoft (R) Windows Script Host Version 5.6
Copyright (C) Microsoft Corporation 1996-2001. All rights reserved.

CN=Garett Kopczynski
Garett@companyabc.com
Marketing Manager
Dallas

C:\>
```

To perform the same automation task in PowerShell, you use the `[ADSI]` type accelerator to bind to the specified user object. To retrieve the user object's attributes, you use the ADSI `Get()` method, as shown here:

```
PS C:\> $User = [ADSI]"LDAP://CN=Garett
Kopczynski,OU=Accounts,OU=Managed Objects,DC=companyabc,DC=com"
PS C:\> $User.Get("Name")
Garett Kopczynski
PS C:\>
```

After binding to the user object, you can access its attributes directly from PowerShell with any of the object formatting or manipulation cmdlets. For example, to access and display the same attributes as in the VBScript example, you use the Format-List cmdlet:

```
PS C:\> $User | format-list Name, userPrincipalName, description,
physicalDeliveryOfficeName


name                        : {Garett Kopczynski}
userPrincipalName           : {Garett@taosage.net}
description                 : {Marketing Manager}
physicalDeliveryOfficeName  : {Dallas}



PS C:\>
```

Creating an Object

The following VBScript example binds to the Accounts OU by using the VBScript GetObject() method with an ADSI LDAP provider. Next, the script uses the ADSI Create() method to create a user object named David Lightman in the Accounts OU, and then defines attributes for the new user object with the ADSI Put() method. Finally, the new user object is written to Active Directory by using the ADSI SetInfo() method, and a status message about the object creation is displayed via a message box or at a cmd command prompt, as shown here:

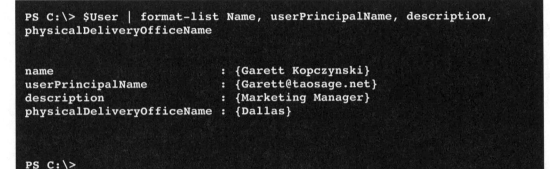

```
Set objOU = GetObject("LDAP://OU=Accounts,OU=Managed Objects,DC=companyabc,DC=com")
Set objUser = objOU.Create("user", "CN=David Lightman")
objUser.Put "sAMAccountName", "dlightman"
objUser.Put "sn", "Lightman"
objUser.Put "givenName", "David"
objUser.Put "userPrincipalName", "dlightman@norad.gov"
objUser.SetInfo
Wscript.Echo "User account " & objUser.Get("sAMAccountName") & " created."
```

Saving the script as `createuserinfo.vbs` and then running it by using `cscript` produces the following results:

```
C:\>cscript createuserinfo.vbs
Microsoft (R) Windows Script Host Version 5.6
Copyright (C) Microsoft Corporation 1996-2001. All rights reserved.

User account dlightman created.
C:\>
```

To perform the same automation task in PowerShell, you use the [ADSI] type accelerator. The resulting commands are similar in logic and syntax to the VBScript example. For example, to create the user object, you bind to the Accounts OU, and then create a new user object named David Lightman by using the ADSI `Create()` method. Next, you use the ADSI `Put()` method to define the user object's attributes and the ADSI `SetInfo()` method to write the user object to Active Directory. Last, to verify that the account was created, you bind to the new user object by using the [ADSI] type accelerator. This process is shown in the following code:

```
PS C:\> $OU = [ADSI]"LDAP://OU=Accounts,OU=Managed
Objects,DC=companyabc,DC=com"
PS C:\> $NewUser = $OU.Create("user", "CN=David Lightman")
PS C:\> $NewUser.Put("sAMAccountName", "dlightman")
PS C:\> $NewUser.Put("sn", "Lightman")
PS C:\> $NewUser.Put("givenName", "David")
PS C:\> $NewUser.Put("userPrincipalName", "dlightman@norad.gov")
PS C:\> $NewUser.SetInfo()
PS C:\> [ADSI]"LDAP://CN=David Lightman,OU=Accounts,OU=Managed
Objects,DC=companyabc,DC=com"

distinguishedName
-----------------
{CN=David Lightman,OU=Accounts,OU=Managed
Objects,DC=companyabc,DC=com}


PS C:\>
```

6

NOTE

If you try to use this example in your environment, you'll notice that the resulting user objects are disabled initially because the `userAccountControl` value defaults to 514, indicating that the account is disabled. To make this example work, you would need to define addition parameters, such as user password, account status, group memberships, and so on.

From VBScript to PowerShell

This section shows a VBScript script converted into a PowerShell script. The script determines whether a list of users are members of a specific group.

At the time this script was developed, companyabc.com was in the process of migrating users from the old retail management application to a new one. To streamline the process and limit interruptions in employee productivity, the migration was carried out in stages. Part of the process involved producing lists of users to be migrated from the old application. Each user on the list was migrated to the new application with a configuration based on Active Directory group membership.

However, manually verifying each user's group membership on a migration list was time consuming, and producing membership reports was daunting, with thousands of users and groups. companyabc.com needed a way to automate the group verification process so that migration could continue without interruptions. To meet this need, companyabc. com requested a script that could take a list of users being migrated and produce a report indicating group memberships for those users.

The IsGroupMember.wsf Script

IsGroupMember.wsf is a VBScript WSF file that was developed to handle companyabc. com's group verification process. A working copy is in the Scripts\Chapter 9\ IsGroupMember folder and is downloadable at www.samspublishing.com. To run this script, two parameters must be defined. The groupname parameter should have its argument set to the sAMAccountName of the group that user membership is verified against. The importfile parameter should have its argument set to the name of the CSV import file listing users who need to be verified. An optional parameter, exportfile, should have its argument set to the name of the export file where data by the script is stored.

> **NOTE**
>
> The CSV import file must contain only one column (sAMAccountName). To see an example, refer to the users.csv file in the Scripts\Chapter 9\IsGroupMember folder, which is downloadable at www.samspublishing.com.

Here's the command to run the IsGroupMember.wsf script, with an example of the output shown in Figure 9.1:

```
D:\Scripts>cscript IsGroupMember.wsf /groupname:
"TAO-D-RA-LS-LocalWorkstationPowerUsers"
/importfile:".\users.csv" /exportfile:"export.csv"
```

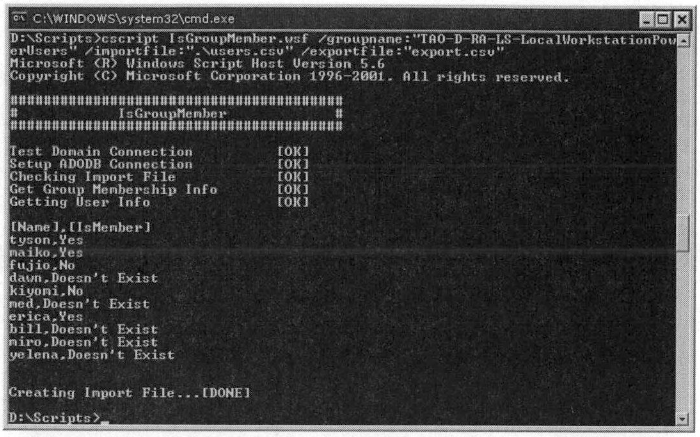

FIGURE 9.1   The `IsGroupMember.wsf` script being executed

The `IsGroupMember.wsf` script performs the following sequence of actions:

1. The script tests the connection to the current domain by retrieving its `DefaultNamingContext`, which is used later to query Active Directory. If this connection fails, the script halts.

2. The script creates an ADO connection object, which is used later to search Active Directory by using the ADSI OLE DB provider.

3. Next, the `ParseFile` function opens the specified CSV file and parses user information into the specified array (`arrUsers`). If this function fails because the specified file is invalid, the script halts.

4. The script queries Active Directory for the specified group by using the ADO object. If the group isn't valid, the script halts. If the group is valid, however, the script connects to the group by using ADSI, retrieves the group members, and adds them to the group `Dictionary` object (`dictGroup`).

5. Next, the script steps through users in the `arrUsers` array, connecting to each user object by using ADSI and retrieving the user's `distinguishedName`. Invalid users are added to the user `Dictionary` object (`dictUsers`) with the value `"Doesn't exist"`. If the user is valid, the script checks whether the user's `distinguishedName` exists in the `dictGroup` object. Users who are group members are added to the `dictUsers` object with the value `"Yes"`. Users who aren't group members are added to `dictUsers` with the value `"No"`.

6. Last, the script writes information in the `dictUsers` object to the cmd command prompt. If an export filename is specified, the same information is written to the export file.

The first code snippet consists of the initial XML elements for a WSF. These elements are used to define the allowed parameters, the script's description, examples on the script's operation, and the scripting language being used:

```
<?xml version="1.0" ?>
<package>
<job id="IsGroupMember">
    <runtime>
        <description>
**************************************************************
Used to check if users are members of a specified group.
**************************************************************
        </description>
        <named name="groupname" helpstring="The name of the group to check."
type="string" required="1" />
        <named name="importfile" helpstring="The import CSV file path/filename."
type="string" required="1" />
        <named name="exportfile" helpstring="The export CSV file." type="string"
required="0" />
        <example>
Example:
cscript ISGroupMember.wsf /groupname:"mygroup" /importfile:"users.csv"
        </example>
    </runtime>
<script language="VBScript">
<![CDATA[
```

Next, the script checks to see if arguments have been defined for the required parameters groupname and importfile. If the arguments are not present, the script returns the script usage information (defined in the previous code snippet) to the console and quits. If arguments are defined, the script then sets up the script environment by defining the variables that will be used throughout the rest of the script.

Because VBScript arrays are difficult to store and retrieve data from, this script makes use of the Windows Scripting Runtime Library's Dictionary object (dictGroup and dictUsers in the preceding code). The Dictionary object, unlike normal arrays, allows you to store data in key/value pairs. With this storage method, you can access data in the array by specifying the key, use the Dictionary object's methods and properties on data in the array, and add or remove data from the array dynamically without needing to resize it as shown in the next code snippet:

```
'On Error Resume Next


'=================================================================
' Check required args
'=================================================================
If WScript.Arguments.Named.Exists("groupname") = FALSE Then
    WScript.Arguments.ShowUsage()
    WScript.Quit
End If

If WScript.Arguments.Named.Exists("importfile") = FALSE Then
    WScript.Arguments.ShowUsage()
    WScript.Quit
End If


'=================================================================
' Set up job env
'=================================================================
Const ForReading = 1
Const ForWriting = 2
ReDim arrUsers(0)
Dim arrMemberOf
Dim StdOut
Dim FSO
Dim strGroupName, strImportFile, strExportFile
Dim strDNSDomain, dictGroup, dictUsers

Set StdOut = WScript.StdOut
Set FSO = CreateObject("Scripting.FileSystemObject")
Set dictGroup = CreateObject("Scripting.Dictionary")
Set dictUsers = CreateObject("Scripting.Dictionary")

strGroupName = WScript.Arguments.Named("groupname")
strImportFile = WScript.Arguments.Named("importfile")
strExportFile = WScript.Arguments.Named("exportfile")
```

The next code snippet is the beginning of the actual automation portion of the script. First, the script writes the script header to the console, binds to the RootDSE object, and retrieves the DefaultNamingContext. This is done for two reasons. First, the script is testing for a valid connection to an Active Directory domain. This test is performed because if the script cannot connect to an Active Directory domain at this point during its execution. Then the script will fail when it later tries to query information from Active Directory. As in Chapter 8, this is an advanced form of error handling by determining when a script might fail and including a method for preventing the failure.

Second, the script needs to get the current logon domain's name for use later in the script. Without this information, a script would have to be modified to ask users from which domain they want to get group membership information. In environments with multiple domains, you might want to add this feature to your scripts. However, for this example, you don't need it, so the script retrieves the domain's name from the RootDSE object and stores it in the strDNSDomain variable:

```
'====================================================================
' Start Job
'====================================================================
Mess "###################################"
Mess "#              IsGroupMember              #"
Mess "###################################"
Mess vbNullString


'...................
' Test connection to domain
'...................
StatStart "Test Domain Connection"
    Set objRootDSE = GetObject("LDAP://RootDSE")
    strDNSDomain = objRootDSE.Get("DefaultNamingContext")

    Xerror
StatDone
```

In the following code example, an ADO object (objConnection) is created, which will be used later in the script. Then the ParseFile function is used to import the user information from the CSV file into the arrUsers array:

```
'...................
' Set up ADODB connection
'...................
StatStart "Set up ADODB Connection"
    Dim objConnection
    Dim objCommand
    Dim objRecordSet

    Set objConnection = CreateObject("ADODB.Connection")
    Set objCommand = CreateObject("ADODB.Command")
```

```
     objConnection.Provider = "ADsDSOObject"
     objConnection.Open("Active Directory Provider")
     objCommand.ActiveConnection = objConnection
     objCommand.Properties("Page Size") = 1000


     Xerror
StatDone


'-------------------
' Check CSV Import File
'-------------------
StatStart "Checking Import File"
     ParseFile strImportFile, arrUsers
StatDone
```

Next, the script uses the ADO object created in the previous code example to perform an LDAP search for the specified group in the current Active Directory domain. Based on information from this search, the script determines whether the group exists and its distinguishedName. Next, the script uses distinguishedName to bind directly to the group object in Active Directory and retrieve the group's members. The members are then placed in the arrMemberOf array. This array is then stepped through with a For loop, adding each group member to the dictGroup object with a placeholder value of "Something" (which can be anything as long as the key/value pair is completed):

```
'-------------------
' Get Group Membership Info
'-------------------
StatStart "Get Group Membership Info"
     objCommand.CommandText = _
         "<LDAP://" & strDNSDomain & ">;(&(objectCategory=group)" _
         & "(sAMAccountName=" & strGroupName & "));distinguishedName;subtree"

     Set objRecordSet = objCommand.Execute

     If objRecordset.RecordCount = 0 Then
         StdOut.Write(vbTab)
         StdOut.WriteLine("Not a valid group!")
         WScript.Quit()
     Else
         Set objGroup = GetObject _
             ("LDAP://" & objRecordSet.Fields("distinguishedName"))
         objGroup.getInfo
```

```
        arrMemberOf = objGroup.GetEx("member")

        For Each Member in arrMemberOf
            dictGroup.Add Member, "Something"
        Next
    End If

    Set objGroup = Nothing
StdOut.Write(vbTab)
StdOut.WriteLine("[OK]")
```

The following code snippet steps through the arrUsers array that was created by parsing the import file:

```
'--------------------
' Get User Info
'--------------------
StatStart "Getting User Info"

For Each User In arrUsers
    Err.Clear

    objCommand.CommandText = _
        "<LDAP://" & strDNSDomain & ">;(&(objectCategory=user)" _
        & "(sAMAccountName=" & User & "));distinguishedName;subtree"

    Set objRecordSet = objCommand.Execute

    If objRecordset.RecordCount = 0 Then
        dictUsers.Add User, "Doesn't Exist"
    Else
        strUserDN = objRecordSet.Fields("distinguishedName")

        If (dictGroup.Exists(strUserDN) = True) Then
            dictUsers.Add User, "Yes"
        Else
            dictUsers.Add User, "No"
        End If
    End If

    Set objRecordset = Nothing
    strUserDN = vbNullString
Next
StatDone
```

For each user, the script performs an LDAP search in the current logon domain using the ADO object. Users who don't exist are added to the `dictUsers` object with the value `"Doesn't Exist"`. However, if a user does exist, the script takes the `distinguishedName` from the recordset returned from the LDAP search and does a comparison operation to see if that user exists in the `dictGroup` object.

To perform this comparison operation, the script uses the `Dictionary` object's `Exists()` method, which enables you to see whether a key exists in a `Dictionary` object. This is the main reason for using the `Dictionary` object instead of a VBScript array. Next, based on information returned from the `Exists()` method, the script adds the user to the `dictUsers` object with a value of `"Yes"` to indicate the user is a group member or a value of `"No"` when the user isn't a group member.

The result is a collection of user information stored in the `dictUsers` object. Based on information in this object, the script then loops through the users in the `dictUsers` object and writes the information to the console, as shown in this next code example:

```
Mess vbNullString
Mess "[Name],[IsMember]"

For Each User In dictUsers
    StdOut.Write User & ","
    StdOut.WriteLine dictUsers.Item(User)
Next
```

If the variable `exportfile` was defined when the script was executed, the script creates the export file using the `FSO` object. Then the script again loops through the `dictUsers` object and writes the user information into the export file. The following example shows the code for this process:

```
'--------------------
' Create Export File
'--------------------
Mess vbNullString
StdOut.Write "Creating Import File..."

If strExportFile <> "" Then
    Set objExportFile = FSO.OpenTextFile(strExportFile, ForWriting, TRUE)

    For Each User In dictUsers
        objExportFile.Write User & ","
        objExportFile.WriteLine dictUsers.Item(User)
    Next
```

6

```
    objExportFile.Close()
    Set objExportFile = Nothing

    StdOut.WriteLine "[DONE]"
End If
```

The last code snippet consists of the Subs and Functions that are used throughout the script and the closing XML elements for the script. Further review of the final section of the script is not needed because these Subs and Functions are either fairly self explanatory or have been previously discussed:

```
'====================================================================
' Subs
'====================================================================
'-------------------
' General Message Sub
'-------------------
Sub Mess(Message)
    ' Write to console
    StdOut.WriteLine(Message)
End Sub


'-------------------
' General Start Message Sub
'-------------------
Sub StatStart(Message)
    ' Write to console
    StdOut.Write(Message)
End Sub


'-------------------
' General Finish Message Sub
'-------------------
Sub StatDone
    ' Write to console
    StdOut.Write(vbTab & vbTab)
    StdOut.WriteLine("[OK]")
End Sub


'-------------------
' General Xerror Sub
'-------------------
```

```
Sub Xerror
    If Err.Number <> 0 Then
        ' Write to console
        StdOut.WriteLine(" Critical Error: " & CStr(Err.Number) _
            & " " & Err.Description)

        WScript.Quit()
    End If
End Sub


'====================================================================
' Functions
'====================================================================
Function ParseFile(file, arrname)
    ' This function parses a file and gives you back an array
    ' (Skips the first line!!!)
    On Error Resume Next
    count = -1

    ' Open file for reading
    Set objFile = FSO.OpenTextFile(file, ForReading)
    objFile.SkipLine 'note: This will always be the col headers
    Xerror

    ' Reads each line in the file and places it into an array
    Do While objFile.AtEndOfStream <> True
        count = count + 1
        If count > UBound(arrname) Then ReDim Preserve arrname(count)
        arrname(count) = objFile.Readline
    Loop
    Xerror

    ' Close the file because you are done with it.
    objFile.Close()
    Set objFile = Nothing
    count = 0
End Function
]]>
  </script>
</job>
</package>
```

The IsGroupMember.ps1 Script

IsGroupMember.ps1 is a PowerShell conversion of the IsGroupMember.wsf script.
A working copy is in the Scripts\Chapter 9\IsGroupMember folder and is downloadable
at www.samspublishing.com. You need to define two parameters to run this script.
The GroupName parameter should have its argument set to the sAMAccountName of the
group that user membership is verified against. The ImportFile parameter should have its
argument set to the name of the CSV import file listing users who need to be verified. An
optional parameter, ExportFile, should have its argument set to the name of the export
file where data written to the script should be stored. Here's the command to run the
IsGroupMember.ps1 script:

```
PS D:\Scripts> .\IsGroupMember.ps1 "TAO-D-RA-LS-LocalWorkstationPowerUsers"
".\users.csv" "export.csv"
```

Figure 9.2 shows the execution of the IsGroupMember.ps1 script without an export file
being specified and Figure 9.3 shows the execution of the script with an export file
having been specified:

FIGURE 9.2   The IsGroupMember.ps1 script being executed without an export file

FIGURE 9.3   The IsGroupMember.ps1 script being executed with an export file

The `IsGroupMember.ps1` script performs the following sequence of actions:

1. The script connects to the current logon domain by using the .NET `System.DirectoryServices.ActiveDirectory.Domain` class, and then retrieves the domain name, which is written to the PowerShell console. If this connection fails, the script halts.

2. The script verifies that the specified group exists in the current domain by using the `Get-ADObject` function. If the group exists, the function returns an object bound to the group object in Active Directory (`$Group`). If the group doesn't exist, the script halts.

3. The script uses the `Test-Path` cmdlet to verify that the import file is valid. If the file is invalid, the script halts.

4. The script uses the `Import-Csv` cmdlet to populate the `$Users` variable with the contents of the CSV import file.

5. The script uses the `Get-ADObject` function to verify that each user in the `$Users` collection exists in the current domain and to bind to that user's Active Directory user object.

6. If the user exists, the script compares the user's `distinguishedName` against distinguished names in the specified group's (`$Group`) member attribute. When a match is found, the user's object is extended by using the `Add-Member` cmdlet to indicate the user is a group member (`"Yes"`). If there's no match, the user's object is extended by using the `Add-Member` cmdlet to indicate the user isn't a group member (`"No"`). If the user doesn't exist in the current domain, the user's object is extended by using the `Add-Member` cmdlet to indicate that information (`"Doesn't Exist"`).

7. If an export file has been specified, the script uses the `Export-Csv` cmdlet to create a CSV file based on the `$Users` variable's contents. If no export file has been specified, the script writes the `$Users` variable's contents to the PowerShell console.

The first code snippet contains the header for the `IsGroupMember.ps1` script. In this header includes information about what the script does, when it was updated, and the script's author. Just after the header are the script's parameters:

```
###############################################
# IsGroupMember.ps1
# Used to check if users are members of a
# specified group.
#
# Created: 10/21/2006
# Author: Tyson Kopczynski
###############################################
param([string] $GroupName, [string] $ImportFile, [string] $ExportFile)
```

Next, as seen in the following code snippet, the script loads the `Get-ScriptHeader` and `Show-ScriptUsage` functions:

```
##################################################
# Functions
##################################################
#---------------------------------------------------
# Get-ScriptHeader
#---------------------------------------------------
# Usage:        Generates the script header statement.
# $Name:        The name of the script.
# $Usage:       What the script is used for.

function Get-ScriptHeader{
    param ($Name, $Usage)

    $Date = Date

    $Text = "################################### `n"
    $Text += "# Script        $Name `n"
    $Text += "# Usage:        $Usage `n"
    $Text += "# User:         $Env:username `n"
    $Text += "# Date:         $Date `n"
    $Text += "###################################"

    $Text
    }


#---------------------------------------------------
# Show-ScriptUsage
#---------------------------------------------------
# Usage:        Used to show script usage information.

function Show-ScriptUsage{
    write-host
    write-host "Usage: ISGroupMember -GroupName value" `
                "-ImportFile value -ExportFile value"
    write-host
    write-host "Options:"
    write-host
```

```
      write-host "GroupName `t: The name of the group to check."
      write-host "ImportFile `t: The import CSV file path/filename."
      write-host "ExportFile `t: [Optional] The export CSV file." `
                   "path/filename."
      write-host
      write-host "CSV Format:"
      write-host "sAMAccountName"
      write-host
      write-host "Example:"
      write-host 'ISGroupMember.ps1 "mygroup"' `
                   '"users.csv" "results.csv"'
      write-host
      }
```

These functions are used to display script usage information similar to what a WSF script displays, as shown in this example:

```
PS D:\Scripts .\IsGroupMember.ps1

Please specify the group name!

#####################################
# Script        IsGroupMember
# Usage:        Used to check if users are members of a specified group.
# User:         tyson
# Date:         12/17/2006 09:12:16
#####################################

Usage: ISGroupMember -GroupName value -ImportFile value -ExportFile value

Options:

GroupName      : The name of the group to check.
ImportFile     : The import CSV file path/filename.
ExportFile     : [Optional] The export CSV file. path/filename.

CSV Format:
sAMAccountName

Example:
ISGroupMember.ps1 "mygroup" "users.csv" "results.csv"

PS D:\Scripts
```

6

A helpful feature of a WSF file is that it can be used to give users information about the script's purpose and parameters and examples of how to use it. Users don't have to read comments or refer to external documentation to understand what a script does and how to use it. This feature improves users' experience with an automation script, thus increasing the chance that they will consider your scripts highly usable.

Unfortunately, PowerShell lacks this feature. The best you can do with PowerShell is define the required parameters and give information about their use by means of the throw keyword. The throw keyword has been used in previous scripts, but it doesn't display information in the same user-friendly format that WSF scripts do. To achieve this same level of usability, additional logic had to be added in the form of the Show-ScriptUsage and Get-ScriptHeader functions. Show-ScriptUsage defines what the script does, its parameters, and how it can be used. Although you can reuse this function's structure in other scripts, the content is static and must be changed for each script. Get-ScriptHeader is simply used to display a script title. It can be reused in other scripts with little modification because the $Name and $Usage parameters are what define the information in the output.

The end result is that the functions in the script usage information displayed in the previous example is similar to what's produced from a WSF script. Although modifying Show-ScriptUsage for reuse is a little cumbersome, the benefit of these simple, generic functions is the illusion of a script that has been written for users rather than scripters. These functions are used throughout the remainder of the book.

> **NOTE**
>
> A possible enhancement to the Show-ScriptUsage function is making it more generic so that it can be used in other scripts without modification. For example, the information returned from this function could be based on an XML string structured much like a WSF file.

After the script has loaded the usage functions, the next two functions to be loaded are used to interact with Active Directory:

```
#----------------------------------------------------
# Get-CurrentDomain
#----------------------------------------------------
# Usage:        Used to get the current domain.

function Get-CurrentDomain{
    [System.DirectoryServices.ActiveDirectory.Domain]::GetCurrentDomain()
    }


#----------------------------------------------------
# Get-ADObject
#----------------------------------------------------
```

```
# Usage:        Used to retrieve an object from Active Directory.
# $Item:        The object item type. (sAMAccountName or distinguishedName)
# $Name:        The name of the object. (sAMAccountName or distinguishedName)
# $Cat:         The object category.

function Get-ADObject{
    param ($Item, $Name, $Cat)

    trap{Continue}

    $Searcher = new-object DirectoryServices.DirectorySearcher

    $SearchItem = "$Item"
    $SearchValue = "$Name"
    $SearchCat = "$Cat"

    $Searcher.Filter = `
        "(&($($SearchItem)=$($SearchValue))(objectCategory=$($SearchCat)))"

    $Searcher.FindOne().GetDirectoryEntry()
    }
```

The first function, Get-CurrentDomain, is a basic function that binds to the current logon domain object. To do this, the function uses a .NET Framework reference to the System.DirectoryServices.ActiveDirectory.Domain class (as discussed in Chapter 3, "PowerShell: A More In-Depth Look") with the GetCurrentDomain() method. Next, the function returns the resulting domain object, which verifies a connection to the domain and provides a method to display the domain's DNS name to script users (a visual reminder that the domain information is being queried).

The second function, Get-ADObject, verifies an object's existence in Active Directory based on a unique identifier, such as the sAMAccountName or distinguishedName attributes. Then it connects to that object by using the System.DirectoryServices. DirectorySearcher class, which is a .NET method for performing Active Directory searches. When calling Get-ADObject, you must provide the object's unique identifier ($Name), the type of object ($Item) that the unique identifier is (sAMAccountName or distinguishedName), and the object's category ($Cat) type (User, Computer, or Group). Using these values, Get-ADObject creates a $Searcher object and sets its Filter property to an LDAP search string constructed from the information you've provided. Next, Get-ADObject uses the $Searcher object's FindOne() method, which performs the search and returns only the first entry found. Last, the GetDirectoryEntry() method is used on the returned search entry to bind to the referenced object in Active Directory. At this point, you have either verified that an object exists, or you can interrogate the object returned from the function for more information.

In the following code snippet, the $ScriptName and $ScriptUsage variables are defined. These variables will be used later in the script to display the script usage information:

```
##################################################
# Main
##################################################
#--------------------
# Set Config Vars
#--------------------
$ScriptName = "IsGroupMember"
$ScriptUsage = "Used to check if users are members of a specified group."
```

In addition to displaying information on the script's usage information, the Get-ScriptHeader and Show-ScriptUsage functions also provide a help scheme when users define the first argument as one of these strings: -?, -h, and -help. To do this, the script makes use of the match comparison operator defined in this statement: $args[0] -match '-(\?¦(h¦(help)))' as shown in the following code snippet:

```
#--------------------
# Verify Required Parameters
#--------------------
if ($args[0] -match '-(\?¦(h¦(help)))'){
    write-host
    Get-ScriptHeader $ScriptName $ScriptUsage
    Show-ScriptUsage
    Return
    }
```

The next two code sections are methods to check for required script parameters. Previous script examples relied on the throw keyword when defining a parameter (with the param keyword), thus controlling what parameters were required. In this script, instead of just using the throw keyword, you check for the required parameter later in the script to give script users a helpful message stating that they forgot to provide an argument for a required parameter. You can also give script users information about parameters, their use, and examples of arguments.

Last, Get-ScriptHeader is used to display a script header, which gives users visual confirmation that they're running the right script. In addition, if the script takes several hours to finish, the header displays the date and time the script started to let users know how long it has been running.

The point of these functions is to improve the script's usability, a quality that's often overlooked in scripts and CLIs. Lack of usability is one of the main reasons Windows system administrators have stayed away from using scripts and CLIs for managing their Windows environments. The PowerShell team recognized the usability problems of past CLIs and scripting languages and made an effort to create a shell and language not only for scripters, but also for IT professionals. When you develop your scripts, keep users' perceptions in mind. As discussed in Chapter 5, "PowerShell Scripting Best Practices," automation is but one part of the puzzle when developing a script.

```
if (!$GroupName){
    write-host
    write-host "Please specify the group name!" -Foregroundcolor Red
    write-host
    Get-ScriptHeader $ScriptName $ScriptUsage
    Show-ScriptUsage
    Return
    }

if (!$ImportFile){
    write-host
    write-host "Please specify the import CSV filename!" -Foregroundcolor Red
    write-host
    Get-ScriptHeader $ScriptName $ScriptUsage
    Show-ScriptUsage
    Return
    }
```

In the next code snippet, the Get-ScriptHeader function is used to indicate to the script operator that the automation portion of the script has started:

```
#-------------------
# Begin Script
#-------------------
write-host
Get-ScriptHeader $ScriptName $ScriptUsage
write-host
```

The next step is for the script to verify that there is a valid domain connection. To accomplish task, the script uses the Get-CurrentDomain. If a valid domain connection doesn't exist, the script halts and returns the script status to the operator. If a connection does exist, the script continues execution and writes the domain name to the console, as shown in the next code snippet:

```
.{
    trap{write-host `t "[ERROR]" -Foregroundcolor Red;
        throw write-host $_ -Foregroundcolor Red;
        Break}

    write-host "Domain Connection" -NoNewLine

    # You need to test for a domain connection
    $Domain = Get-CurrentDomain

    # You then return the domain's name
    write-host `t $Domain.Name -Foregroundcolor Green
}
```

In the next code snippet, the group name in the $GroupName variable is verified. To
perform the verification, the script uses Get-ADObject function. This function connects to
Active Directory and completes a search for the group by its name. If an object is returned
from the function, then the group name is valid; if no object is returned, the group name
is considered invalid and the script halts:

```
write-host "Checking Group Name" -NoNewLine

# Now get the group# Now get the group
$Group = Get-ADObject "sAMAccountName" $GroupName "Group"

if (!$Group){
    write-host `t "Is not valid!" -Foregroundcolor Red
    write-host
    Break
    }
else{
    write-host `t "[OK]" -Foregroundcolor Green
    }
```

The last verification task to verify the validity of import file name in the $ImportFile
variable by using the Test-Path cmdlet:

```
write-host "Checking Import File" -NoNewLine

if (!(test-path $ImportFile -pathType leaf)){
    write-host `t "Is not a valid file!" -Foregroundcolor Red
    write-host
    Break
    }
else{
    write-host `t "[OK]" -Foregroundcolor Green
    }
```

In the following code snippet, the script is completing the user's group membership verification. As explained previously, based on the user's validity in Active Directory and if
they are a member of the specified group ($GroupName), the script extends the user's
object in the $Users collection:

```
#--------------------
# Check Each User's Group Membership
#--------------------
$Users = import-csv $ImportFile

foreach ($User in $Users){
    &{
        $sAMAccountName = $User.sAMAccountName

        $ADUser = Get-ADObject "sAMAccountName" $sAMAccountName "User"

        if ($ADUser){
            [string]$DN = $ADUser.distinguishedName

            $IsMember = $Group.Member | `
                where {$_ -eq $DN}

            if ($IsMember){
                add-member -inputObject $User -membertype noteProperty `
                    -name "IsMember" -value "Yes"
                }
            else{
                add-member -inputObject $User -membertype noteProperty `
                    -name "IsMember" -value "No"
                }
            }
        }
```

6

```
    else{
        # What if the user doesn't exist?
        add-member -inputObject $User -membertype noteProperty `
            -name "IsMember" -value "Doesn't Exist"
    }
}
}
```

You might recall from previous chapters that the & call operator runs a script block in its own scope. When the script block finishes, its scope is destroyed along with anything defined in that scope.

In the previous code snippet example, the & call operator is used so that variable names can be recycled without having to worry about old data. For example, when you come out of the for loop, the $sAMAccountName and $ADUser variable names are still valid objects. Instead of risking the possibility of using these old objects accidentally, you just use the & call operator to make sure the object is destroyed after running the script block.

The task as shown in the following code snippet is to either write the contents of the $Users collection to the console. Or, if an export file has been specified, the contents are written to a CSV file using the Export-CSV cmdlet.

```
if (!$ExportFile){
    $Users
    }
else{
    write-host
    write-host "Exported Data To: " -NoNewLine
    $Users ¦ export-csv $ExportFile
    write-host "$ExportFile" -Foregroundcolor Green
    write-host
    }
```

Summary

In this chapter, you explored how PowerShell interacts with ADSI and how it can be used to read and modify Active Directory objects. During this exploration, you learned that PowerShell has the same access to Active Directory management interfaces, if not more with its relationship with .NET Framework, as WSH. In addition to reviewing how PowerShell can be used to manage Active Directory, you also reviewed a working script that is used to determine if a list of users are members of a group. Like WSH, this is but one of the many possible types of Active Directory management scripts that can be developed using PowerShell.

PART III

Using PowerShell to Meet Your Automation Needs

IN THIS PART

CHAPTER 10

Using PowerShell in the Real-World

This chapter shows you how powerful PowerShell can be when managing Windows environments. You review two PowerShell scripts used for systems management. The first script, PSShell.ps1, manages user interaction with the Windows desktop by creating a controlled, secure, and attractive desktop replacement. The second script, ChangeLocalAdminPassword.ps1, manages local administrator passwords on servers in an Active Directory domain.

These scripts demonstrate how to meet an organization's systems management needs. As you step through each script, you learn new PowerShell concepts and see how they can be applied to meet your automation needs.

The PSShell.ps1 Script

PSShell.ps1 can be used as a secure shell solution for kiosk workstations. A working copy is in the Scripts\ Chapter 10\PSShell folder and is downloadable at www.samspublishing.com. This script requires an understanding of Windows Shell Replacement. Make sure you read the following sections about the script components to ensure that you know how to deploy and use the script effectively. First, however, you should review why this script is needed.

companyabc.com manufactures processors for the general public and the U.S. government. Employees working on processors intended for government use must have special security clearance, and any data related to manufacturing these processors must be secured to prevent exposure to unauthorized entities, both inside and outside the company.

These security requirements pose a challenge for companyabc.com. Its IT department has to support business procedures for both the retail and government contract divisions. Also, companyabc.com's CEO has issued a directive that all computer use must take place on a centralized system, which means all users at any location must have access to data and applications, which further complicates security measures.

The IT department's solution to meet these requirements involves deploying Windows Terminal Services (WTS) server farms. Users working on the retail side would have one set of WTS farms with a lower level of security. Users working in the government contract division would have a different set of WTS farms isolated from retail users and with a high degree of security.

The IT department has decided to use thin clients for the WTS farms for quick deployment and a high degree of control over access and data security. However, although companyabc.com has the budget to build the WTS farms, funds to purchase thin clients and thin client software for all users aren't available. Further complicating matters is a recent company-wide Windows XP desktop refresh. In addition, desktop hardware that was just purchased must be used for another few years until it can be replaced.

To stay within the budget, the IT department has searched for an inexpensive way to turn the existing Windows XP desktops into thin clients. One systems administrator read a technical article about using Windows Shell Replacement to turn a Windows XP desktop into a secure kiosk, but it involves replacing Windows Explorer with Internet Explorer to create the kiosk interface. Although this method is fine for a simple Web browsing kiosk, the IT department needs complete control over the user interface shell.

To meet this need, the IT department has decided to use PowerShell and its support of .NET Windows Forms as a way to provide a customizable shell replacement for Windows Explorer. After development and testing, the final solution to companyabc.com's thin-client need is a hybrid of several different components. These components include Windows Shell Replacement, which uses cmd.exe as the base shell, and a PowerShell script that uses Windows Forms to present a secure, Windows Explorer–like desktop to logged on users. The following sections explain the components of PSShell.ps1 (named PSShell Kiosk) in more detail.

Component One: Shell Replacement

PSShell Kiosk's first component is the shell replacement. Windows, by default, uses the Windows Explorer shell (explorer.exe) as an interface for interacting with the operating system. However, this shell is not required to run Windows. Sometimes users want more functionality than Windows Explorer offers, or they want to decrease functionality as a way to improve security, as is the case with companyabc.com.

Windows users and administrators can modify explorer.exe or replace it with another shell (although it might not be supported by Microsoft). This process is called Windows Shell Replacement. Shells that can be used with Windows Shell Replacement range from

GUI-based shells, such as Internet Explorer (`iexplore.exe`), Geoshell, and LiteStep, to CLI-based shells, such as `cmd.exe`, `command.com`, and even PowerShell.

You can use two methods to replace `explorer.exe`. One is modifying the Windows Registry and specifying your replacement shell in the `Shell` value found in the `HKEY_LOCAL_MACHINE\Software\Microsoft\Windows NT\CurrentVersion\Winlogon` key.

For companyabc.com, changing the Registry on every Windows XP desktop isn't an option. Furthermore, getting rid of the shell for the entire Windows XP installation isn't wise. Suppose IT technicians need to log on to machines to perform system maintenance. If the default shell for the entire machine has been replaced by using the Registry method, the technicians are stuck with using the limited replacement shell because the shell has been changed for all users. Although there are ways to enable user-based shell replacement in the Registry, changing the Registry isn't a user-friendly or effective way to manage the deployment of replacement shells, as companyabc.com's IT department has discovered.

The second method for replacing `explorer.exe`, which requires Active Directory, is using the Group Policy Object (GPO) setting called Custom user interface. This setting allows you to specify the shell for users when they log on to a machine. The benefits of using GPOs include centralization and ease of management. In addition, you can have different shell settings based on the user, not the machine the user is logging on to. Because companyabc.com is looking for this type of control, the IT department has chosen the GPO method to manage the PSShell Kiosk. The following sections explain the steps to set up this solution.

Step One: Creating the PSShell Secure Kiosk GPO

To create the GPO for configuring the Windows Shell Replacement, follow these steps:

1. Using the Group Policy Management Console (GPMC), create a GPO called **PSShell Kiosk Desktop GPO.**

2. Next, disable the Computer Configuration settings.

3. Remove **Authenticated Users** from the security filter settings for the PSShell Kiosk Desktop GPO.

4. In the Active Directory Users and Computers console, create a Domain Local group called **PSShell Kiosk Desktop GPO - Apply** and add a test user account to the group.

5. Add the PSShell Kiosk Desktop GPO - Apply group to the security filter settings for the PSShell Kiosk Desktop GPO.

6. Finally, link the PSShell Kiosk Desktop GPO to the top-level organizational unit (OU) containing all your user accounts, and make sure the linking order of any other GPOs doesn't override the PSShell Kiosk Desktop GPO.

> **NOTE**
>
> Linking the PSShell Kiosk Desktop GPO to the top-level OU containing user accounts assumes there are no other GPOs linked to child OUs that might override this GPO. Furthermore, the GPO is applied to a group of users instead of a group of machines to prevent users with a higher security clearance from having a nonsecured desktop.

Step Two: Configuring the Windows Shell Replacement Settings

Next, you configure the Windows Shell Replacement settings by following these steps:

1. In the Group Policy Management Console (GPMC), edit the **PSShell Kiosk Desktop GPO**.

2. In the GPMC, click to expand **User Configuration**, **Administrative Templates**, and then **System**. Then click to select the **Custom user interface** setting.

3. Right-click **Custom user interface** and click **Properties**.

4. In the Custom user interface Properties dialog box, click to select the **Enabled** option, type **cmd /c "C:\PSShell\Launch.bat"** in the Interface file name text box, as shown in Figure 10.1, and then click **OK**.

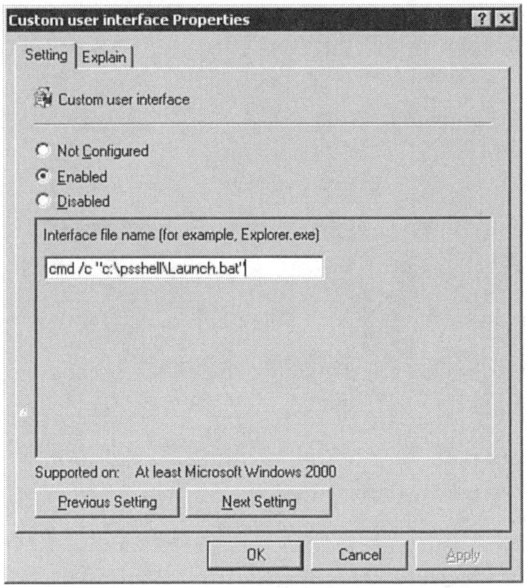

FIGURE 10.1   Custom user interface Properties dialog box

Setting the interface filename to cmd forces Windows to use cmd.exe as the replacement shell. The /c switch forces cmd to carry out the C:\PSShell\Launch.bat command and then stop, which closes the cmd window after the Launch.bat file has finished running.

> **NOTE**
>
> Using the C:\PSShell path assumes that the files for PSShell Kiosk have been copied to this location on the client's machine. However, these files don't necessarily need to be copied to this location. They can be located on clients or a Windows network share.

Component Two: PSShell.exe

You might be wondering why cmd is used as the replacement shell instead of PowerShell. Unfortunately, when you're running a PowerShell script, there's no way to do so without displaying the PowerShell console. If explorer.exe is replaced with PowerShell, the resulting desktop contains the PowerShell console.

However, companyabc.com wants users to have a desktop similar to explorer.exe, not a desktop containing the PowerShell console. The solution involves the second component, PSShell.exe. PSShell.exe is a C# Windows application that hides the PowerShell console when PSShell.ps1 runs. The following code snippet shows the source code for this application:

```
using System;
using System.Diagnostics;

namespace PSShell
{
    static class Program
    {
        static void Main()
        {
            Process Process = new Process ();

            Process.StartInfo.FileName = "powershell.exe ";
            Process.StartInfo.Arguments = "-Command \"C:\\PSShell\\PSShell.ps1\"";
            Process.StartInfo.CreateNoWindow = true;
            Process.StartInfo.WindowStyle = ProcessWindowStyle.Hidden;
            Process.Start();
        }
    }
}
```

10

To hide the PowerShell console, PSShell.exe makes use of the .NET System.Diagnostics. Process class. By using this class with the .NET ProcessWindowStyle enumeration, you can define how a process's window should appear when it starts. The style (appearance) can be Hidden, Normal, Minimized, or Maximized. For this example, you want the

PowerShell window's style to be defined as Hidden. After starting the PowerShell process by using the Start() method with the specified arguments to run PSShell.ps1, Windows doesn't draw (display) the PowerShell console.

NOTE

Again, the C:\PSShell path in the PSShell.exe source code is only a suggestion. If you change the deployment path for PSShell Kiosk, you need to update the code and build a new executable. If you're familiar with C#, however, a better solution is modifying PSShell.exe so that it can take arguments to define the path to the PSShell.ps1 script.

To understand why cmd is used as the replacement shell, remember that PSShell.exe is not a shell, but an application written to suppress the PowerShell console when running a script. It's also needed to start PowerShell and run PSShell.ps1 so that the PowerShell console is hidden. To start PSShell.exe, however, you need to call it from another shell, such as cmd. The interface filename you entered for the Custom user interface setting specified a batch file named Launch.bat, which is used to start PSShell.exe.

The result is that cmd is used to run Launch.bat, which then starts PSShell.exe. PSShell.exe, in turn, starts PowerShell, which finally runs the PSShell.ps1 script. This workaround is a bit convoluted but necessary to compensate for a feature PowerShell lacks. With this workaround, you can still use PowerShell to generate a secure desktop.

Component Three: PSShell.ps1

The last component of PSShell Kiosk is PSShell.ps1, which generates the PSShell Kiosk desktop for logged on users. This desktop is generated by a Windows Form, which is possible because of PowerShell's capability to use .NET Windows Forms. The sole purpose of this script is to give users the illusion of seeing the default Windows desktop, when they're actually using a custom desktop with limited functionality.

The PSShell Kiosk solution determines what users see and what programs they can run from the desktop. companyabc.com wants high-security users to be able to perform these tasks on a secure desktop:

▶ Starting the Microsoft Remote Desktop (RDP) client, which is configured to connect to the secure WTS farm

▶ Starting a limited instance (by GPO) of Internet Explorer that navigates to companyabc.com's Web-based e-mail site

▶ Logging off the PSShell Kiosk when they're finished using it

The first code snippet contains the header for the PSShell.ps1 script. This header includes information about what the script does, when it was updated, and the script's author:

```
##################################################
# PSShell.ps1
# Used as a shell replacement for explorer.exe.
#
# Created: 10/17/2006
# Author: Tyson Kopczynski
##################################################
```

In the next code snippet, are two long, complex statements involving the .NET
`System.Reflection.Assembly` class:

```
$Null=[System.Reflection.Assembly]::LoadWithPartialName("System.Windows.Forms")
$Null=[System.Reflection.Assembly]::LoadWithPartialName("System.Drawing")
```

These two statements are necessary because PowerShell loads only a few .NET assemblies
into its `AppDomain`. For example, if you try to create a Windows Forms object with the
`New-Object` cmdlet, you would get the following error:

```
PS C:\> $Form = new-object System.Windows.Forms.Form
New-Object : Cannot find type [System.Windows.Forms.Form]: make sure
the assembly containing this type is loaded.
At line:1 char:19
+ $Form = new-object  <<<< System.Windows.Forms.Form
PS C:\>
```

To use the `System.Windows.Forms.Form` class, you need to load the assembly into
PowerShell first by using the `LoadWithPartialName()` method. Assemblies must also be
loaded into PowerShell for .NET-based DLLs included with Microsoft SDKs, third-party
vendors, or your custom DLLs. For example, say you develop a .NET-based DLL to manage
xyz application. To use that DLL in PowerShell, you use the `LoadFrom()` or `LoadFile()`
methods from the `System.Reflection.Assembly` class, as shown in this example:

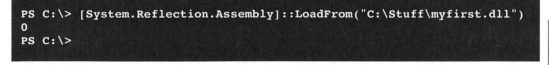

```
PS C:\> [System.Reflection.Assembly]::LoadFrom("C:\Stuff\myfirst.dll")
0
PS C:\>
```

NOTE

Microsoft has made the `LoadWithPartialName()` method obsolete. The replacement is the `Load()` method, which is meant to prevent partial binds when .NET assemblies are loaded. Using the `Load()` method requires more work. However, if you don't mind the implications of a partial bind (such as your script failing), you can continue using `LoadWithPartialName()` until it's removed from the .NET Framework.

Now that the required assemblies for Windows Forms objects have been loaded, the next task is to finish configuring the runtime environment for the script. The first step, as shown in the following code snippet, is to define a set of launch command strings that will be used to control the applications users can launch from the PSShell Kiosk desktop. These command strings are discussed in more depth later in this section:

```
# Launch command strings
$LaunchIE = {$IE = new-object -com InternetExplorer.Application; `
    $IE.navigate("webmail.companyabc.com"); $IE.visible = $True; $IE}
$LaunchRemoteDesktop = {mstsc /v:earth.companyabc.com /f}
```

Then after defining the launch command strings, the next task is to create a PowerShell Runspace, as demonstrated in the next code snippet:

```
#--------------------
# Create Runspace
#--------------------
# For more info on Runspaces see:
# http://windowssdk.msdn.microsoft.com/en-us/library/ms714459(VS.80).aspx

$Runspace =
    [System.Management.Automation.Runspaces.RunspaceFactory]::CreateRunspace()
$RunspaceInvoke =
    new-object System.Management.Automation.RunspaceInvoke($Runspace)
$Runspace.Open()
```

This code shows a PowerShell runspace, which is represented by the PowerShell `System.Management.Automation.Runspaces` namespace. A **runspace** is an abstraction of the PowerShell runtime that allows a hosting application to run PowerShell commands to perform tasks or gather information. Although `powershell.exe` is a hosting application and uses its own runspace to process commands, runspaces are most beneficial when used in applications outside PowerShell.

Runspaces are needed to support PowerShell, but they were developed mainly to create an easy way for other applications to call the PowerShell runtime and have it run PowerShell commands. In a sense, the Windows Form that PSShell.ps1 creates is an application, so it makes sense for it to interact with a PowerShell runspace to perform tasks. By taking advantage of PowerShell runspaces, you then don't have to spend time adding logic to the Windows Form to make it perform tasks for users.

Creating a runspace ($Runspace) for the Windows Form simply involves using the CreateRunspace() method from the PowerShell System.Management.Automation.Runspaces.RunspaceFactory class. Next, you create a RunspaceInvoke object that allows the Windows Form to run commands via the runspace. Last, you open the runspace by using the Open() method so that it can be used by the Windows Form.

After defining the runspace, the next task is to construct the form itself as shown in the following code snippet. The section that is titled "Define Images," a series of Drawing.Image objects are created. These objects will be used later in the form to represent such items are the PSShell Kiosk desktop start menu and application icons. Then in the code section, titled "Create Form," the form object is created using a set of predefined properties used to make the form look like the default Windows desktop.

```
#--------------------
# Define Images
#--------------------
$ImagePath = Split-Path -Parent $MyInvocation.MyCommand.Path
$ImgStart = [Drawing.Image]::FromFile("$Imagepath\Images\Start.png")
$ImgRDP = [Drawing.Image]::FromFile("$Imagepath\Images\RDP.png")
$ImgIE = [Drawing.Image]::FromFile("$Imagepath\Images\IE.png")


#--------------------
# Create Form
#--------------------
$Form = new-object System.Windows.Forms.Form
$Form.Size = new-object System.Drawing.Size @(1,1)
$Form.DesktopLocation = new-object System.Drawing.Point @(0,0)
$Form.WindowState = "Maximized"
$Form.StartPosition = "CenterScreen"
$Form.ControlBox = $False
$Form.FormBorderStyle = "FixedSingle"
$Form.BackColor = "#647258"
```

10

Having constructed the form, the final task before activating the form and showing it to the user is to add in the menu items. The following code adds several MenuItems to the ToolStripMenu that acts as the Start Menu for the PSShell Kiosk desktop:

```
#--------------------
# Build Menu
#--------------------
$MenuStrip = new-object System.Windows.Forms.MenuStrip
$MenuStrip.Dock = "Bottom"
$MenuStrip.BackColor = "#292929"


# Start Menu
$StartMenuItem = new-object System.Windows.Forms.ToolStripMenuItem("")
$StartMenuItem.Padding = 0
$StartMenuItem.Image = $ImgStart
$StartMenuItem.ImageScaling = "None"


# Menu Item 1
$MenuItem1 = new-object System.Windows.Forms.ToolStripMenuItem("&Webmail")
$MenuItem1.Image = $ImgIE
$MenuItem1.ImageScaling = "None"
$MenuItem1.add_Click({$RunspaceInvoke.Invoke($LaunchIE)})

$StartMenuItem.DropDownItems.Add($MenuItem1)


# Menu Item 2
$MenuItem2 = new-object System.Windows.Forms.ToolStripMenuItem("&Remote Desktop")
$MenuItem2.Image = $ImgRDP
$MenuItem2.ImageScaling = "None"
$MenuItem2.add_Click({$RunspaceInvoke.invoke($LaunchRemoteDesktop)})

$StartMenuItem.DropDownItems.Add($MenuItem2)


# Menu Item 3
$MenuItem3 = new-object System.Windows.Forms.ToolStripMenuItem("&Log Off")
$MenuItem3.add_Click({`
    $RunspaceInvoke.invoke({Get-WmiObject Win32_OperatingSystem | `
    foreach-object {$_.Win32Shutdown(0)}})})


$StartMenuItem.DropDownItems.Add($MenuItem3)
```

Basically, the preceding code snippet shows several MenuItems being added to the
ToolStripMenu, which is acting as the start menu for the PSShell Kiosk desktop. These
menu items are the way users start applications or log off the PSShell Kiosk desktop. Each

menu item is assigned a `click` event that uses the `$RunspaceInvoke` object and its `invoke()` method to run a specified PowerShell command. The following list describes the action each menu item performs:

- ▶ `$MenuItem1`—Uses the command specified in the `$LaunchIE` variable to start Internet Explorer

- ▶ `$MenuItem2`—Uses the command specified in the `$LaunchRemoteDesktop` variable to start `mstsc.exe` (the Microsoft RDP client)

- ▶ `$MenuItem3`—Uses the `Get-WmiObject` cmdlet to log off Windows

Last, the script needs to activate the form and show it to the user using the `ShowDialog` method. This is shown in the final code snippet:

```
#-------------------
# Show Form
#-------------------
$MenuStrip.Items.Add($StartMenuItem)
$Form.Controls.Add($MenuStrip)
$Form.Add_Shown({$Form.Activate()})
$Form.ShowDialog()
```

Putting It All Together

After the PSShell Kiosk Desktop GPO is configured and ready to be applied to users, the next step is to deploy the following PSShell Kiosk files to the desktops used as secure thin clients:

- ▶ `Launch.bat`—The batch file used to start `PSShell.exe`

- ▶ `PSShell.exe`—The C# application used to run the `PSShell.ps1` script

- ▶ `PSShell.ps1`—The PowerShell script that creates the PSShell Kiosk

- ▶ `Images` folder—The folder containing images used on the PSShell Kiosk desktop

As discussed earlier, the PSShell Kiosk solution is currently configured to reside in the `C:\PSShell` path. So after you have deployed these files to this location on each desktop, you can place users who need a secure desktop in the PSShell Kiosk Desktop GPO - Apply group. Figure 10.2 shows the PSShell Kiosk desktop with the three menu items.

10

FIGURE 10.2   The PSShell Kiosk desktop

The ChangeLocalAdminPassword.ps1 Script

The ChangeLocalAdminPassword.ps1 script was developed to address a time-consuming task for systems administrators. This task is the routine (as in scheduled) or forced (because the network was attacked) local administrator password change. Changing this password ranks as one of the biggest chores of systems management activities, and administrators often neglect this task because it's so tedious.

companyabc.com operates a Windows Server 2003 server farm of 500 servers. As part of the company's security practices, the IT department tried to change the local administrator password routinely on all 500 servers, usually every 30 days or when a systems administrator left the company. Not surprisingly, because of the time and effort to change the administrator password on 500 servers, the IT department tended to fall behind schedule in completing this task. Eventually, they stopped trying to change local administrator passwords, which soon resulted in a major security incident: An external entity took advantage of the lapse in password management practices to commandeer a number of companyabc.com's servers and demanded a ransom to return control of these systems.

This incident prompted the IT department to seek a way to change local administrator passwords quickly and en masse. They decided to use an automation script that creates a list of servers in a specified OU, and then connects to each server and changes the local administrator password. To meet this need, the ChangeLocalAdminPassword.ps1 script was developed.

A working copy is in the `Scripts\Chapter 10\ChangeLocalAdminPassword` folder and is downloadable at www.samspublishing.com. Running this script requires defining one parameter: `OUDN`. This parameter's argument should be set to the `distinguishedName` of the OU containing the servers that need to have their local administrator passwords changed. Here's the command to run the `ChangeLocalAdminPassword.ps1` script:

```
PS D:\Scripts> .\ChangeLocalAdminPassword.ps1 "OU=Servers,OU=Managed
Objects,DC=companyabc,DC=com"
```

Figures 10.3 and 10.4 show the `ChangeLocalAdminPassword.ps1` script being executed.

FIGURE 10.3   Changing the Local Admin Password

FIGURE 10.4   `ChangeLocalAdminPassword.ps1` script completion

The `ChangeLocalAdminPassword.ps1` script performs the following sequence of actions:

1. The script dot sources the `LibraryCrypto.ps1` library file, which contains a function for randomly generating passwords.

2. The script creates a new `DataTable` object (`$ServersTable`) by using the .NET `System.Data.DataSet` class. This `DataTable` object is used later in the script to store status information about machines in the specified OU.

3. In addition, the script creates an error log named `ChangeLocalAdminPassword_Errors.log` by using the `Out-File` cmdlet. This error log displays detailed error information to users.

4. The script connects to the current logon domain by using the `Get-CurrentDomain` function. Using the object returned from this function, the script then writes the domain's name to the PowerShell console. If this connection fails, the script halts.

5. Next, the script verifies that the specified OU exists in the current domain by using the `Get-ADObject` function. If the OU is not valid, the script halts.

6. The script uses the `Set-ChoiceMesssage` and `New-PromptYesNo` functions to ask users whether they want a randomly generated password or one they specify. For randomly generated passwords, the script uses the `New-RandomPassword` function from the `LibraryCrypto.ps1` library file to generate a password of a specified length that's stored as a secure string (`$Password`) and returned to the user for verification. For user-specified passwords, the script uses the `Read-Host` cmdlet with the `AsSecureString` property to collect the password and store it in a secure string (`$Password`).

7. Next, the script uses the .NET `DirectoryServices.DirectoryEntry` class to bind to the specified OU in Active Directory and then the .NET `DirectoryServices.DirectorySearcher` class to create a `$Searcher` object. The `SearchRoot` property for the `$Searcher` object is set to the bound OU object, and an LDAP search is performed to populate the `$Computers` variable with all servers in the OU.

8. Next, the script uses the `System.Net.NetworkInformation.Ping` class to ping each server that is in the `$Servers` object collection. If a server replies then a new row is added into the `$ServersTable` `DataTable` which consists of the server's name and its `"Online"` status. If a server doesn't reply, a new row is still added into the `$ServersTable` `DataTable`; however, that server's status is set to `"Offline"`.

9. The script uses the `System.Net.NetworkInformation.Ping` class to ping each server in the `$Computers` object collection. If a server replies, a new row is created in the `$ServersTable` `DataTable` consisting of the server's name and its `"Online"` status. If a server doesn't reply, a new row is created in the `$ServersTable` `DataTable` with the server's status set to `"Offline"`.

10. The listing of servers and their status information is sent to the script's error log for future reference by using the `Out-File` cmdlet.

11. Next, the script uses the .NET `System.Runtime.InteropServices.Marshal` class to convert the secure string stored in the `$Password` variable to a regular string that can be used later in the script.

12. Finally, for each server with an "Online" status in $ServersTable, the Get-WmiObject cmdlet is used to connect to the server and return a list of user accounts. The local administrator account has a security ID (SID) ending with "-500". The script binds to this account by using the ADSI WinNT provider and changes its password to the string now stored in the $Password variable.

Here's the LibraryCrypto.ps1 library file:

```
###################################################
# LibraryCrypto.ps1
# Functions within this file can be used to perform
# crypto operations.
#
# Created: 11/3/2006
# Author: Tyson Kopczynski
###################################################
#--------------------------------------------------
# New-RandomPassword
#--------------------------------------------------
# Usage:        Used to generate a random password.
# $Size:        The length of the password to generate.

function New-RandomPassword{
    param ([int] $Size)

    $Bytes = new-object System.Byte[] $Size
    $Chars = "abcdefghijklmnopqrstuvwxyz".ToCharArray()
    $Chars += "ABCDEFGHIJKLMNOPQRSTUVWXYZ".ToCharArray()
    $Chars += "0123456789``~!@#$^*()-_=+[]{}`\¦;:`'`",./".ToCharArray()

    $Crypto =
        new-object System.Security.Cryptography.RNGCryptoServiceProvider

    # Now you need to fill an array of bytes with a
    # cryptographically strong sequence of random nonzero values.
    $Crypto.GetNonZeroBytes($Bytes)

    foreach ($Byte in $Bytes){

        # For each Byte, perform a modulo operation
        $Password += $Chars[$Byte % ($Chars.Length - 1)]
    }

    # Finally, return the random password as a SecureString
    ConvertTo-SecureString "$Password" -AsPlainText -Force
}
```

10

As mentioned previously, `ChangeLocalAdminPassword.ps1` uses the `New-RandomPassword` function from the `LibraryCrypto.ps1` file to generate random passwords of a specified length based on a predetermined set of allowed characters. To do this, the function uses the .NET `System.Security.Cryptography.RNGCryptoServiceProvider` class as a cryptographically strong random number generator.

A random number generator improves the strength of passwords, even those consisting of both characters and numbers. The `New-RandomPassword` function uses the random number generator to generate random characters for passwords. To do this, the function first takes the specified length of the random password and creates a `System.Byte` array (`$Bytes`) of the same length. It then defines a character array (`$Chars`) consisting of all possible characters that can make up the random passwords.

Next, `New-RandomPassword` creates a random number generator (`$Crypto`) by using the `System.Security.Cryptography.RNGCryptoServiceProvider` class. The `GetNonZeroBytes()` method then uses `$Crypto` to populate the `$Bytes` array with a cryptographically strong sequence of random nonzero values. For each byte in the `$Bytes` array, the function performs a modulo operation (the remainder of dividing one number by another) to determine which character from the `$Chars` array is added to the `$Password` variable. The end result is a random password returned to the caller as a secure string.

The next code snippet contains the header for the `ChangeLocalAdminPassword.ps1` script. This header includes information about what the script does, when it was updated, and the script's author. Just after the header is the script's parameter `OUDN`:

```
##################################################
# ChangeLocalAdminPassword.ps1
# Used to change the local admin passwords for machine
# acounts in Active Directory.
#
# Created: 11/2/2006
# Author: Tyson Kopczynski
##################################################
param([string] $OUDN)
```

Next, the script loads the `Set-ChoiceMessage` and `New-PromptYesNo` functions, as seen in the following code snippet:

```
##################################################
# Functions
##################################################
#-------------------------------------------------
# Set-ChoiceMessage
```

```
#-----------------------------------------------------
# Usage:        Used to set yes and no choice options.
# $No:          The no message.
# $Yes:         The yes message.

function Set-ChoiceMessage{
    param ($No, $Yes)

    $N = ([System.Management.Automation.Host.ChoiceDescription]"&No")
    $N.HelpMessage = $No

    $Y = ([System.Management.Automation.Host.ChoiceDescription]"&Yes")
    $Y.HelpMessage = $Yes

    Return ($Y,$N)
    }


#-----------------------------------------------------
# New-PromptYesNo
#-----------------------------------------------------
# Usage:        Used to display a choice prompt.
# $Caption:     The prompt caption.
# $Message:     The prompt message.
# $Choices:     The object catagory.

function New-PromptYesNo{
    param ($Caption, $Message,
        [System.Management.Automation.Host.ChoiceDescription[]]$Choices)

    $Host.UI.PromptForChoice($Caption, $Message, $Choices, 0)
    }
```

In PowerShell, sometimes you're prompted to make a choice before a command continues. For example, as you learned in Chapter 4, "Code Signing," PowerShell might prompt for confirmation before running a script that isn't signed by a trusted entity, depending on your execution policy setting. Or PowerShell prompts you for confirmation before running a command when a cmdlet is used with the confirm switch parameter, as shown in this example:

10

```
PS C:\> get-process | stop-process —confirm

Confirm
Are you sure you want to perform this action?
Performing operation "Stop-Process" on Target "~e5d141.tmp (792)".
[Y] Yes  [A] Yes to All  [N] No  [L] No to All  [S] Suspend  [?] Help
(default is "Y"):
```

With the Set-ChoiceMessage and New-PromptYesNo functions, you can build a menu of
Yes or No choices to display to users in the PowerShell console. The Set-ChoiceMessage
function creates a collection of choice objects and is used with the New-PromptYesNo function to generate the choice menu. To generate this menu, New-PromptYesNo uses the
PromptForChoice() method from the $host.UI object, which is just an implementation of
the System.Management.Automation.Host.PSHostUserInterface class.

In the following code snippet, variables that will be used later in the script are defined. In
addition, there are two library files that are dot sourced into the script's scope. The first
file, LibraryGen.ps1, is a general library file that contains the script usage and Active
Directory functions that were used in Chapter 9, "PowerShell and Active Directory." The
second file is the LibraryCrypto.ps1 library, which, as mentioned previously in this
section, contains the New-RandomPassword function:

```
##################################################
# Main
##################################################
#--------------------
# Load Libraries
#--------------------
. .\LibraryGen.ps1
. .\LibraryCrypto.ps1


#--------------------
# Set Config Vars
#--------------------
$ScriptName = "ChangeLocalAdminPassword.ps1"
$ScriptUsage = "Used to change the local admin passwords on machines."
$ScriptCommand = "$ScriptName -OUDN value"
$ScriptParams = "OUDN = The distinguishedName of the OU where" `
    + "the machines are located."
$ScriptExamples = "$ScriptName ""OU=Accounts,DC=companyabc,DC=com"""
$ErrorLogName = $ScriptName + "_Errors.log"
$Date = Date
```

After defining the script's variables and the dot sourcing of any library files, the next step is to check if the user needed any usage help or if the required OUDN parameter has been defined. This step is shown in the next code snippet:

```
#--------------------
# Verify Required Parameters
#--------------------
if ($args[0] -match '-(\?¦(h¦(help)))'){
    write-host
    Get-ScriptHeader $ScriptName $ScriptUsage
    Show-ScriptUsage $ScriptCommand $ScriptParams $ScriptExamples
    Return
    }

if (!$OUDN){
    write-host
    write-host "Please specify the OU machines are located in!" `
            -Foregroundcolor Red
    write-host
    Get-ScriptHeader $ScriptName $ScriptUsage
    Show-ScriptUsage $ScriptCommand $ScriptParams $ScriptExamples
    Return
    }
```

Next, the script creates a DataTable object. This is a new concept that uses an .NET DataTable object (from the System.Data.DataTable class, part of the ADO.NET architecture):

```
#--------------------
# Define DataTable
#--------------------
$ServersTable = new-object System.Data.DataTable
$ServersTable.TableName = "Servers"
[Void]$ServersTable.Columns.Add("Name")
[Void]$ServersTable.Columns.Add("Status")
```

DataTable objects are the equivalent of a database table, except the table is located in memory. Your scripts can use this table to hold data retrieved from other sources or data you specify manually.

In this script, a DataTable is used to hold status information about the servers queried from Active Directory. The script first creates a DataTable named $ServersTable by using

10

the New-Object cmdlet and System.Data.DataTable class. When you first create a
DataTable, it's empty and lacks structure, so you must define the structure before you can
store data in it. For $ServersTable's structure, the script uses the Add() method to add
Name and Status columns to its Columns collection. Later in the script, the Add() method
is used to add rows of data to $ServersTable's Rows collection.

In the next code snippet, the Out-File cmdlet is used to create an error log and write
header information to it. Then the Get-ScriptHeader function is used to indicate to the
script operator that the automation portion of the script has started:

```
#--------------------
# Begin Script
#--------------------
# Setup ErrorLog
$ScriptName + " Ran on: " + $Date ¦ out-file $ErrorLogName


write-host
Get-ScriptHeader $ScriptName $ScriptUsage
write-host
```

The next step is for the script to verify that there is a valid domain connection. To accomplish task, the script uses the Get-CurrentDomain function. If a valid domain connection
doesn't exist, the script halts and returns the script status to the operator. If a connection
does exist, the script continues execution and writes the domain name to the console.
Then the script uses the Get-ADObject function to validate if the string in the $OUDN vari-
able is a valid distinguished name. If an object is returned from the function, then the
variable is valid; if no object is returned, the variable is considered invalid and the script
halts, as shown in the next code snippet:

```
.{
    trap{write-host `t "[ERROR]" -Foregroundcolor Red;
        throw write-host $_ -Foregroundcolor Red;
        Break}

    write-host "Domain Connection" -NoNewLine

    # You need to test for a domain connection
    $Domain = Get-CurrentDomain

    # You then return the domain's name
    write-host `t $Domain.Name -Foregroundcolor Green
}
```

```
write-host "Checking OU Name" -NoNewLine

if (!(Get-ADObject "distinguishedName" $OUDN "organizationalUnit")){
    write-host `t "Is not valid!" -Foregroundcolor Red
    write-host
    Break
    }
else{
    write-host `t "[OK]" -Foregroundcolor Green
    }
```

The following code snippet contains the logic for defining the password that will be used. First, the script asks the user if a password should be generated or specified by the user. If a password is to be generated, the script asks what the password length should be. Then based on the defined length, a password is generated using the New-RandomPassword function. If the user chooses to specify the password, then the script uses the Read-Host cmdlet with the AsSecureString switch to collect the password from the user:

```
#--------------------
# Get Password
#--------------------
$Choices = Set-ChoiceMessage "No" "Yes"
$Prompt = New-PromptYesNo "Question:" `
    "Do you want me to generate a random password?" $Choices

while(!$Password){

    trap{write-host "You need to input an integer!" `
        -Foregroundcolor Red; Continue}

    if ($Prompt -eq 0){
        write-host
        [int]$Length = read-host "Please enter the password length"

        if ($Length -gt 0){
            &{
                $Temp = New-RandomPassword $Length

                write-host
                write-host "Your new random password is:" `
                    -Foregroundcolor White
```

```
            [System.Runtime.InteropServices.Marshal]::PtrToStringAuto( `
            [System.Runtime.InteropServices.Marshal]::SecureStringToBSTR( `
                $Temp))

            $Prompt = New-PromptYesNo "Question:" `
                "Is this password ok?" $Choices

            if ($Prompt -eq 0){
                $Script:Password = $Temp
                }
        }
        }
    else{
        write-host "Password length needs to be longer then 0!" `
            -Foregroundcolor Red
        }
    }
else{
    write-host
    $Password = read-host "Then please enter a password" -AsSecureString
    }
}
```

Now that the script has the password that will be used, it must next get a list of machines that will have their passwords changed. The next code snippet contains the code that accomplishes this task. In this code, you will see usage of the DirectoryServices. DirectorySearcher class to perform search for computer objects (servers) under the defined OU. Then for each computer object that is returned from the search, the script then pings the server and adds a row to the $ServersTable DataTable that contains the server's dNSHostName and its status:

```
#-------------------
# Get computers and status
#-------------------
write-host
write-host "Getting Server Info" -NoNewLine

&{
    trap{write-host `t "[ERROR]" -Foregroundcolor Red;
        throw write-host $_ -Foregroundcolor Red;
        Break}
```

```
    $Root =
        new-object DirectoryServices.DirectoryEntry "LDAP://$OUDN"

    $Searcher = new-object DirectoryServices.DirectorySearcher
    $Searcher.SearchRoot = $Root
    $Searcher.PageSize = 1000

    $SearchItem = "CN"
    $SearchValue = "*"
    $SearchClass = "Computer"
    $SearchCat = "*"

    $Searcher.Filter =
        "(&($($SearchItem)=$($SearchValue))(objectClass=$( `
        $SearchClass))(objectCategory=$($SearchCat)))"

    $Script:Computers = $Searcher.FindAll()
}

write-host `t "[DONE]" -Foregroundcolor Green

write-host "Getting Status Info" -NoNewLine

$Computers | foreach-object -Begin {$i=0;} `
    -Process {$Ping = new-object Net.NetworkInformation.Ping;
            &{$dNSHostName = $_.GetDirectoryEntry().dNSHostName.ToString();
            trap{"Ping [ERROR]: " + $dNSHostName + " $_" | out-file `
                $ErrorLogName -Append; Continue};
            $Result = $Ping.Send($dNSHostName);
            if ($Result.Status -eq "Success"){ `
                [Void]$ServersTable.Rows.Add($dNSHostName, "Online")} `
            else{[Void]$ServersTable.Rows.Add($dNSHostName, "Offline")};
            $i = $i+1;
            write-progress -Activity "Pinging Servers - $($dNSHostName)" `
                -Status "Progress:" `
                -PercentComplete ($i / $Computers.Count * 100)}}

write-host `t "[DONE]" -Foregroundcolor Green

# Write status info to ErrorLog
$ServersTable | out-file $ErrorLogName –Append
```

10

The next task is to change the passwords on all of the online servers. First, the script converts the secure string in the $Password variable back to a regular string. Next, the script defines the $OnlineServers variable with all the server objects that have an online status using the DataTable Select() method. Then, the script uses WMI to connect to the server, figure out which account is the Administrator account, and then set its password to the string that is in the $Password variable:

```
write-host "Changing Passwords"  -NoNewLine

$Password = [System.Runtime.InteropServices.Marshal]::PtrToStringAuto( `
    [System.Runtime.InteropServices.Marshal]::SecureStringToBSTR( `
    $Password))

$OnlineServers = $ServersTable.Select("Status = 'Online'")

foreach ($Server in $OnlineServers) {
    &{
        write-progress -Activity "Getting Users - $($Server.Name)" `
            -Status "Stand by..."

        $Users = get-wmiobject -ErrorVariable Err -ErrorAction `
                SilentlyContinue Win32_UserAccount -Computer $Server.Name

        write-progress -Activity "Getting Users - $($Server.Name)" `
            -Status "Done" -completed $True

        if ($Err.Count -ne 0){
            "Getting Users [ERROR]: " + $Server.Name + " " + $Err ¦ out-file `
                $ErrorLogName -Append
            }
        else{
            foreach ($User in $Users){
                if ($User.SID.EndsWith("-500") -eq $True){
                    write-progress -Activity `
                        "Changing Password - `$($User.Name)" `
                        -Status "Stand by..."

                    trap{"Change Password [ERROR]: " + `
                        $Server.Name + " " + $_ ¦ out-file `
                        $ErrorLogName -Append; Continue}
```

```
            $WinNTUser =
                new-object System.DirectoryServices.DirectoryEntry( `
                "WinNT://" + $Server.Name + "/" + $User.Name)

            $WinNTUser.SetPassword($Password)
            $Null = $WinNTUser.SetInfo

            write-progress -Activity `
                "Changing Password - $($User.Name)" `
                -Status "Done" -completed $True
            }
        }
    }
}
}

write-host `t "[DONE]" -Foregroundcolor Green
write-host
write-host "Script is now DONE!" -Foregroundcolor Green
write-host "Check the $ErrorLogName for errors." -Foregroundcolor Yellow
```

Summary

In this chapter, you were able to review two PowerShell scripts that were developed to meet some very demanding automation needs. In the first script, you learned that PowerShell was able to act outside of its normal role as an automation tool by filling a critical security need as a Windows shell replacement. The second script gave you further insight into just how powerful of an automation tool PowerShell can be. Both scripts only scratched the surface as to what automation tasks can be tackled using PowerShell.

As it has been stressed repeatedly throughout this book, the limits to what you can accomplish with PowerShell are boundless. This chapter should only serve as a stepping stone in a continuing quest for exploring PowerShell and what it can do.

10

Using PowerShell to Manage Exchange

Introduction

This chapter explains how to use PowerShell to manage an Exchange Server 2007 environment. Exchange Server 2007 uses PowerShell to perform management and automation tasks through the Exchange Management Shell (EMS). In addition, the concept of PowerShell snap-ins is explained, and you learn that the EMS is just a PowerShell snap-in. Last, you take a look at three PowerShell scripts for managing an Exchange Server 2007 environment and see how they can be used to meet your automation needs.

The Exchange Management Shell (EMS)

For years, Exchange administrators have had two choices for performing repetitive tasks: Do them manually by using the graphical interface, or write scripts in complicated and time-consuming programming languages. Although these programming languages could be used to perform many routine tasks in an Exchange environment, they weren't developed specifically with that purpose in mind. Hence, even the simplest task could take hundreds of lines of code.

Over time, the inability to automate tasks easily has proved to be one of the most frustrating aspects of managing an Exchange environment. In fact, as pointed out throughout this book, Windows automation in general wasn't sufficient because of Microsoft's reliance on GUIs and little support for CLIs. This frustration became one of the motivations for the PowerShell team, led by Jeffrey Snover, to develop a CLI shell interface that enables administrators to do everything from the command line.

Around that time, the Exchange product team was designing the specifications for the next version of Exchange (E12, which became Exchange Server 2007). Initially, it seemed the team would develop yet another limited Microsoft Management Console (MMC) GUI as the Exchange management interface. However, the Exchange team decided to take a different course by embracing the concept of PowerShell-based management.

The result is that in Exchange Server 2007, configuration and administration are done with two new administrative tools: the EMS and the Exchange Management Console (EMC). Both utilities rely on PowerShell to access and modify information and configuration settings in an Exchange Server 2007 environment.

> **NOTE**
>
> Exchange Server 2007 is the first Microsoft product to use PowerShell exclusively to drive its management interfaces.

The EMS is a command-line management interface for performing server administration and configuration. Because it's built on a PowerShell platform, it can connect to the .NET runtime (also known as the Common Language Runtime, or CLR). So tasks that previously had to be done manually in the management application can now be scripted, giving administrators more flexibility for repetitive tasks. Furthermore, administrators can manage every aspect of Exchange Server 2007, including creating and managing e-mail accounts, configuring Simple Mail Transport Protocol (SMTP) connectors and transport agents, and setting properties for database stores. Every management task in the Exchange environment can now be accomplished from the command line. In addition, the EMS can be used to check settings, create reports, provide information on the health of Exchange servers, and, best of all, automate tasks that need to be done frequently.

The EMC is an MMC 3.0 GUI utility for viewing and modifying the configuration of Exchange Server 2007 organizations. Although similar to the Exchange System Manager (ESM) in previous Exchange versions, the EMC's interface has been redesigned to be more organized and easier to learn. The EMC is limited in the scope of modifications administrators can make, so some configuration settings can be accessed only by using the EMS.

The EMS and EMC rely on PowerShell to accomplish management tasks. The EMC is simply a graphical interface that calls the EMS to perform tasks, and the EMS is just a snap-in for PowerShell. Therefore, no matter which utility administrators use to create a report or modify a setting, they're actually using PowerShell.

It's Just a Snap-in

A snap-in is nothing more than a collection of one or more cmdlets compiled into a DLL, which is used as a way to extend PowerShell's functionality. Typically, extending functionality is done to manage an application with PowerShell and can be accomplished easily by using snap-ins, much as you add snap-ins to the MMC to increase functionality.

Like an MMC snap-in, a PowerShell snap-in must be loaded into your current PowerShell session before it can be used. For example, say you just finished creating a PowerShell snap-in in C#. You have compiled that custom snap-in into `MyFirstSnapin.dll`, and now you want to use it in PowerShell. However, you must register it with a PowerShell installation first by using the .NET Framework Installer (`installutil.exe`), as shown in this example:

```
PS C:\Dev> set-alias IntUtil
$Env:windir\Microsoft.NET\Framework\v2.0.50727\installutil.exe
PS C:\Dev> IntUtil MyFirstSnapin.dll
Microsoft (R) .NET Framework Installation utility Version 2.0.50727.42
Copyright (C) Microsoft Corporation. All rights reserved.
Running a transacted installation.
...
The transacted install has completed.
PS C:\Dev>
```

For a 64-bit version of Windows, this is the path for the .NET Framework Installer:

```
PS C:\Dev> set-alias IntUtil $Env:windir\Microsoft.NET\Framework64\
v2.0.50727\installutil.exe
```

After the snap-in has been registered, you might want to verify that it's loaded by using the `Get-PSSnapin` cmdlet with the `registered` switch parameter, as shown here:

```
PS C:\Dev> get-pssnapin —registered


Name        : MyFirstSnapin
PSVersion   : 1.0
Description : Used to take over the world.


PS C:\Dev>
```

NOTE

The list `Get-PSSnapin` returns consists of only the snap-ins registered with a PowerShell installation. This list doesn't contain any snap-ins included with the base PowerShell installation.

After verifying the snap-in registration, you load the snap-in into the current PowerShell session by using the Add-PSSnapin cmdlet, as shown in this example:

```
PS C:\Dev> add-pssnapin MyFirstSnapin
PS C:\Dev>
```

Now that the snap-in has been loaded, you use the Get-PSSnapin cmdlet to confirm its availability for the current PowerShell session, as shown here:

```
PS C:\Dev> get-pssnapin


Name        : Microsoft.PowerShell.Core
PSVersion   : 1.0
Description : This Windows PowerShell snap-in contains Windows PowerShell
              management cmdlets used to manage components of Windows PowerShell.

Name        : Microsoft.PowerShell.Host
PSVersion   : 1.0
Description : This Windows PowerShell snap-in contains cmdlets used by the
              Windows PowerShell host.

Name        : Microsoft.PowerShell.Management
PSVersion   : 1.0
Description : This Windows PowerShell snap-in contains management cmdlets used
              to manage Windows components.

Name        : Microsoft.PowerShell.Security
PSVersion   : 1.0
Description : This Windows PowerShell snap-in contains cmdlets to manage Windows
              PowerShell security.

Name        : Microsoft.PowerShell.Utility
PSVersion   : 1.0
Description : This Windows PowerShell snap-in contains utility cmdlets used to
              manipulate data.

Name        : MyFirstSnapin
PSVersion   : 1.0
Description : Used to take over the world.


PS C:\Dev>
```

You can now use the custom MyFirstSnapin in your current PowerShell session. However, if you close that session and open a new one, the snap-in must be loaded again. Like aliases, functions, and variables, a snap-in, by default, is valid only for the current

PowerShell session. To make a snap-in persistent across sessions, it must be loaded each time a PowerShell session is started.

As you learned in Chapter 2, "PowerShell Basics," one way to make aliases, functions, and variables persistent is to use a PowerShell profile. You can also use a profile to load a snap-in into your PowerShell sessions. Another method is the PowerShell console file, which is a configuration file with the .psc1 extension, consisting of XML information listing snap-ins that are loaded when the PowerShell session starts. To create a console file, you use the Export-Console cmdlet, as shown in this example that creates the MyConsole.psc1 file:

```
PS C:\Dev> export-console MyConsole
PS C:\Dev>
```

The following code snippet shows an example of a PowerShell console file:

```
<?xml version="1.0" encoding="utf-8"?>
<PSConsoleFile ConsoleSchemaVersion="1.0">
  <PSVersion>1.0</PSVersion>
  <PSSnapIns>
    <PSSnapIn Name="MyFirstSnapin" />
  </PSSnapIns>
</PSConsoleFile>
```

PowerShell can then use this XML information to load snap-ins based on a previous PowerShell console configuration. To use a console file to configure a PowerShell session at startup, you use the PSConsoleFile parameter with PowerShell.exe, as shown here:

```
C:\>powershell.exe —PSConsoleFile C:\Dev\MyConsole.psc1
```

Naturally, you don't want to type this command every time you use PowerShell. So if you're planning to use a PowerShell console file, you should create a shortcut for starting your custom configuration. This method is similar to opening the EMS from the Windows Start menu.

Because the EMS is just a PowerShell snap-in, accessing EMS cmdlets simply requires loading the EMS snap-in into your PowerShell session, as shown here:

```
PS C:\> add-pssnapin Microsoft.Exchange.Management.PowerShell.Admin
PS C:\>
```

However, there are some differences in loading the EMS snap-in and starting the EMS with the Windows Start menu shortcut. If you just load the snap-in, you don't get the customized Exchange administration console. Your PowerShell session won't look and act like the EMS because the snap-in loads only the cmdlets for managing the Exchange environment. To make your PowerShell session resemble the EMS, you need to run the same configuration script that the Start menu shortcut runs to start the EMS. This script, Exchange.ps1, is in the default Exchange Server 2007 bin directory: C:\Program Files\Microsoft\Exchange Server\Bin.

The GetDatabaseSizeReport.ps1 Script

The first Exchange Server 2007 script you examine in this chapter is the GetDatabaseSizeReport.ps1 script, which produces a report on the size of a mailbox databases in an Exchange organization. The report contains the following information:

▶ The mailbox server name

▶ The full database name, including the storage group name

▶ The drive where the database is located

▶ The free space on the drive in gigabytes

▶ The database size in gigabytes

Here's an example of the report GetDatabaseSizeReport.ps1 produces:

```
Server,Database,Drive,FreeSpace,Size
SFEX01,SG1\DB1,C:,34.67,40.453
SFEX02,SG1\DB1,F:,40.56,20.232
SFEX02,SG1\DB2,F:,40.56,30.2144
SFEX02,SG2\DB1,F:,40.56,45.333
```

Any information about your network environment is helpful. However, when you're using Exchange, an understanding of mailbox database sizes, their growth, free space on the hosting drive, and an overall picture of how mailbox databases are functioning in a network environment can help you prevent potential problems.

This script was developed for companyabc.com, a small manufacturing company with a network consisting of several hundred users and two Exchange servers. Because of budget constraints, the IT department is made up of only one person. The limited budget has also prevented companyabc.com from purchasing and installing monitoring and reporting software for IT systems. As a result, the IT employee has only manual methods for ensuring the systems' operational status and often doesn't have time to do any proactive monitoring.

As a result, the Exchange mailbox databases have grown to the point that offline maintenance can no longer be done, and database disks tend to run out of space. After several near disasters, companyabc.com's management has asked the IT employee to find a way to improve monitoring of the Exchange databases. Needing a quick, flexible, and cost-effective solution, the IT employee turned to scripting and requested the development of the `GetDatabaseSizeReport.ps1` script.

A working copy is in the `Scripts\Chapter 11\GetDatabaseSizeReport` folder and is downloadable at www.samspublishing.com. Running this script doesn't require any parameters be defined. However, an optional parameter, `ExportFile`, should have its argument set to the name of the CSV file where you want to export report data. Here's the command to run the `GetDatabaseSizeReport.ps1` script:

```
PS C:\Scripts> .\GetDatabaseSizeReport.ps1
```

Figures 11.1 and 11.2 shows the execution of the `GetDatabaseSizeReport.ps1` script.

FIGURE 11.1   The `GetDatabaseSizeReport.ps1` script being executed

FIGURE 11.2   The `GetDatabaseSizeReport.ps1` script after being executed

> **NOTE**
>
> You might notice a difference in prompts in the screenshots and some of the source documentation because the screenshots were taken when Exchange 2007 was still in beta. At the time, the EMS was using an older version of PowerShell that had the old Microsoft Shell MSH-based prompt.

The `GetDatabaseSizeReport.ps1` script performs the following sequence of actions:

1. The script creates two `DataTable` objects: `$ServersTable`, used to store status information for Exchange mailbox servers, and `$ReportTable`, used to store the Exchange database size report.

2. The script creates an error log named `GetDatabaseSizeReport_Errors.log` by using the `Out-File` cmdlet. This error log gives users detailed error information.

3. The script uses the `Get-MailboxServer` cmdlet to get a list of all Exchange mailbox servers, which is then populated into the `$MailboxServers` variable.

4. The script uses the `System.Net.NetworkInformation.Ping` class to ping each server in the `$MailboxServers` object collection. If a server responds, a new row is created in `$ServersTable` consisting of the server's name and its status as `"Online."` If a server doesn't respond, a new row is created in `$ServersTable` with the server's status set to `"Offline."`

5. The listing of servers and their status information is sent to the script's error log for future reference by using the `Out-File` cmdlet.

6. For each server with an `"Online"` status in `$ServersTable`, the script does the following:

   ▶ The `Get-MailboxDatabase` cmdlet is used to get a listing of all mailbox databases on the server. Each mailbox database's `Name`, `StorageGroupName`, and `EdbFilePath` are populated into the `$Databases` variable.

   ▶ For each mailbox database in the `$Databases` object collection, the script uses the `Get-WmiObject` cmdlet to collect information about the database size and free drive space. The script then adds a row to the `$ReportTable` containing the mailbox server name (`$Server.Name`), database name (`$DBName`), drive letter of the database's location (`$DBDriveName`), free space (`$DBDriveFreeSpace`), and database size (`$DBSize`).

7. The script exports all data from the `$ReportTable` by using the `Export-DataTable` function.

> **NOTE**
>
> This script and the remaining scripts in this chapter can be run only by using a PowerShell session that has the `Microsoft.Exchange.Management.PowerShell.Admin` snap-in loaded.

The first code snippet contains the header for the GetDatabaseSizeReport.ps1 script. This header includes information about what the script does, when it was updated, and the script's author. Just after the header is the script's only parameter ExportFile:

```
##################################################
# GetDatabaseSizeReport.ps1
# Used to generate an Exchange database size report.
#
# Created: 10/26/2006
# Author: Tyson Kopczynski
##################################################
param([string] $ExportFile)
```

For the GetDatabaseSizeReport.ps1 script, only one function (Export-DataTable) is loaded as shown in the next code snippet:

```
##################################################
# Functions
##################################################
#-------------------------------------------------
# Export-DataTable
#-------------------------------------------------
# Usage:        Used to export a DataSet to a CSV file.
# $Data:        A DataSet object.
# $FileName:    The name of the export CSV file.

function Export-DataTable{
    param ($Data, $FileName)

    $Null =
        [System.Reflection.Assembly]::LoadWithPartialName( `
            "System.Windows.Forms")

    trap{write-host "[ERROR] $_" -Foregroundcolor Red; Continue}

    if ($FileName -eq ""){
        $exFileName = new-object System.Windows.Forms.saveFileDialog
        $exFileName.DefaultExt = "csv"
        $exFileName.Filter = "CSV (Comma delimited)(*.csv)¦*.csv"
        $exFileName.ShowDialog()

        $FileName = $exFileName.FileName
        }
```

```
    if ($FileName -ne ""){
        $LogFile = new-object System.IO.StreamWriter($FileName, $False)

        for ($i=0; $i -le $Data.Columns.Count-1; $i++){
            $LogFile.Write($Data.Columns[$i].ColumnName)

            if ($i -lt $Data.Columns.Count-1){
                $LogFile.Write(",")
                }
            }

        $LogFile.WriteLine()

        foreach ($Row in $Data.Rows){
            for ($i=0; $i -le $Data.Columns.Count-1; $i++){
                $LogFile.Write($Row[$i].ToString())

                if ($i -lt $Data.Columns.Count-1){
                    $LogFile.Write(",")
                    }
                }

            $LogFile.WriteLine()
            }

        $LogFile.Close()
        }
    }
```

To perform the data export, the Export-DataTable function uses the .NET System.IO. StreamWriter class to create an object based on the .NET TextWriter class. The resulting TextWriter object ($LogFile) can be used to write an object to a string, write strings to a file, or serialize XML. In this script, $LogFile is used to dump the DataTable's contents into the CSV export file (which is created along with $LogFile). To perform this task, the Export-DataTable function writes DataTable's column names, separated with a comma (,) delimiter, to the CSV export file. Then the function loops through each value in DataTable's rows and writes these values to the CSV export file, separated with a comma (,) delimiter.

If Export-DataTable is called and a CSV export filename isn't specified, this function makes use of a .NET System.Windows.Forms.saveFileDialog class to construct a Save As dialog box for collecting the export file's name and location (see Figure 11.3).

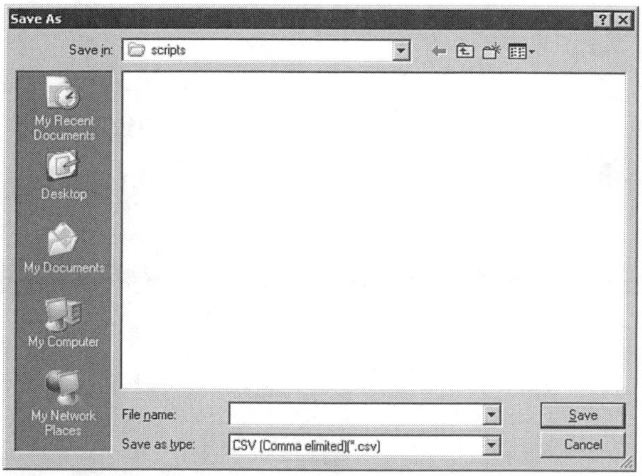

FIGURE 11.3   Windows Forms Save as dialog box

This example is only one of many that show how PowerShell can use .NET-based Windows Forms to collect or display data.

In the next code snippet, variables that will be used later in the script are defined. In addition, the library file LibraryGen.ps1, which contains the script usage functions, is being dot sourced:

```
##################################################
# Main
##################################################
#--------------------
# Load Libraries
#--------------------
. .\LibraryGen.ps1


#--------------------
# Set Config Vars
#--------------------
$ScriptName = "GetDatabaseSizeReport.ps1"
$ScriptUsage = "Used to generate an Exchange database size report."
$ScriptCommand = "$ScriptName -ExportFile value"
$ScriptParams = "ExportFile = The export CSV file path/filename."
$ScriptExamples = "$ScriptName ""report.csv"""
$ErrorLogName = "GetDatabaseSizeReport.log"
$Date = Date
```

Next, the script checks to see if the user needed any usage help, as shown in the following code snippet:

```
#--------------------
# Verify Required Parameters
#--------------------
if ($args[0] -match '-(\?¦(h¦(help)))'){
    write-host
    Get-ScriptHeader $ScriptName $ScriptUsage
    Show-ScriptUsage $ScriptCommand $ScriptParams $ScriptExamples
    Return
    }
```

Then in the next code snippet, the two DataTable objects are created. The first `DataTable` is the `$ServersTable`, which will store server information, and the second `DataTable` is the `$ReportTable`, which will store the report information:

```
#--------------------
# Define DataTables
#--------------------
$ServersTable = new-object System.Data.DataTable
$ServersTable.TableName = "Servers"
[Void]$ServersTable.Columns.Add("Name")
[Void]$ServersTable.Columns.Add("Status")

$ReportTable = new-object System.Data.DataTable
$ReportTable.TableName = "Servers"
[Void]$ReportTable.Columns.Add("Server")
[Void]$ReportTable.Columns.Add("Database")
[Void]$ReportTable.Columns.Add("Drive")
[Void]$ReportTable.Columns.Add("FreeSpace")
[Void]$ReportTable.Columns.Add("Size")
```

Next, the `Out-File` cmdlet is used to create an error log and write header information to it. Then the `Get-ScriptHeader` function is used to indicate to the script operator that the automation portion of the script has started:

```
#--------------------
# Begin Script
#--------------------
# Setup ErrorLog
```

```
$ScriptName + " Ran on: " + $Date ¦ out-file $ErrorLogName

write-host
Get-ScriptHeader $ScriptName $ScriptUsage
write-host
```

After displaying the script header to the user, the script's next task is to get a list of
mailbox servers using the Get-MailboxServer cmdlet. Then for each server object in
$MailboxServers variable, the script pings that server to determine its status. During this
task, both the resulting status and the server's name are written to a new row in the
$ServersTable DataTable, as shown in the next code snippet:

```
#-------------------
# Get Servers and Status
#-------------------
write-host "Getting Mailbox Servers" -NoNewLine
$MailboxServers = get-mailboxserver
write-host `t "[DONE]" -Foregroundcolor Green

write-host "Getting Status Info" -NoNewLine

$MailboxServers ¦ foreach-object -Begin {$i=0;} `
    -Process {&{$Ping = new-object Net.NetworkInformation.Ping;
            $MBServerName = $_.Name;
            trap{"Ping [ERROR]: " + $MBServerName + " $_" ¦ out-file `
                $ErrorLogName -Append; Continue};
            $Result = $Ping.Send($MBServerName);
            if ($Result.Status -eq "Success"){ `
                [Void]$ServersTable.Rows.Add($MBServerName, "Online")} `
            else{[Void]$ServersTable.Rows.Add($MBServerName, "Offline")};
            $i = $i+1;
            write-progress -Activity "Pinging Servers - $($MBServerName)" `
                -Status "Progress:" `
                -PercentComplete ($i / $MailboxServers.Count * 100)}}

write-host `t "[DONE]" -Foregroundcolor Green

# Write status info to ErrorLog
$ServersTable ¦ out-file $ErrorLogName –Append
```

The next task, as shown in the next code snippet, is to generate the final report. To do this, the script uses the Get-MailboxDatabase cmdlet to get the EdbFilePath for each Exchange server that is online. Then, for each mailbox database, the script uses WMI to collect the database size and free space for the drive that the database is located on. After collecting and formatting report information, the script then adds a new row to the $ReportTable DataTable that contains the database information, its size, and the drive free space:

```
#--------------------
# Get Report Info
#--------------------
write-host "Getting Report Info"  -NoNewLine

$OnlineServers = $ServersTable.Select("Status = 'Online'")

foreach ($Server in $OnlineServers) {
    &{
        trap{"Make Report [Error]: " + $Server.Name + " $_" ¦ `
            out-file $ErrorLogName -Append; Continue}

        write-progress -Activity "Getting Database Info - $($Server.Name)" `
            -Status "Stand by..."

        $Databases = get-mailboxdatabase -Server $Server.Name ¦ `
            select Name, StorageGroupName, EdbFilePath

        foreach ($Database in $Databases){
            &{
                write-progress `
                    -Activity "Getting Drive Info - $($Server.Name)" `
                    -Status "Stand by..."

                $DBDriveName = $Database.EdbFilePath.DriveName
                $DBDrive = `
                    get-wmiobject Win32_PerfRawData_PerfDisk_LogicalDisk `
                    -Computer $Server.Name -Filter "Name = '$DBDriveName'"

                write-progress -Activity `
                    "Getting Drive Size Info - $($Server.Name)" `
                    -Status "Stand by..."

                # Needed to replace \ with \\
                $DBPath = $Database.EdbFilePath.PathName.Replace("\","\\")
```

```
                    $DBFile = get-wmiobject CIM_DataFile -Computer $Server.Name `
                        -Filter "Name = '$DBPath'"

                    $DBName = $Database.StorageGroupName + "\" + $Database.Name

                    # Needed to convert from MB to GB
                    $DBDriveFreeSpace = $DBDrive.FreeMegabytes / 1000

                    # Needed to convert Bytes to GB
                    $DBSize = $DBFile.FileSize / 1073741824

                    [Void]$ReportTable.Rows.Add($Server.Name, $DBName, `
                        $DBDriveName, $DBDriveFreeSpace, $DBSize)
                }
            }

        write-progress -Activity `
            "Getting Database Info - $($Server.Name)" `
            -Status "Done" -completed $True
    }
}

write-host `t "[DONE]" -Foregroundcolor Green
```

Last, the script writes the report to the PowerShell console using the Format-Table cmdlet
and then exports the data to a CSV file using the Export-DataTable function.

```
$ReportTable ¦ format-table -groupBy Server Database, Drive, `
    FreeSpace, Size -autosize

$Null = Export-DataTable $ReportTable $ExportFile
```

The GetEvent1221Info.ps1 Script

Administrators can use the GetEvent1221Info.ps1 script to search the Application event
logs of Exchange Server 2007 mailbox servers and generate a report containing Event ID
1221 messages. Exchange administrators can use these messages to determine the amount
of whitespace present in a database over a specified time span (number of days before the
current day). Based on information gathered from Event ID 1221 messages, the report
contains the following:

▶ The mailbox server name

▶ The date and time the event was written to the Application log

▶ The full database name, including the storage group name

▶ The amount of whitespace in megabytes

Here's an example of the report `GetEvent1221Info.ps1` produces:

```
Server,TimeWritten,Database,MB
SFEX02,10/27/2006 1:00:02 AM,SG1\DB1,500
SFEX02,10/27/2006 1:00:06 AM,SG2\PF1,700
SFEX02,10/27/2006 2:00:00 AM,SG1\DB1,500
SFEX02,10/27/2006 2:00:01 AM,SG2\PF1,700
SFEX02,10/27/2006 3:00:00 AM,SG1\DB1,500
SFEX02,10/27/2006 3:00:32 AM,SG2\PF1,700
SFEX02,10/27/2006 4:00:00 AM,SG1\DB1,500
SFEX02,10/27/2006 4:00:00 AM,SG2\PF1,700
SFEX01,10/27/2006 1:00:04 AM,SG1\DB2,200
SFEX01,10/27/2006 1:00:04 AM,SG1\DB1,100
SFEX01,10/27/2006 2:00:00 AM,SG1\DB1,200
SFEX01,10/27/2006 2:00:00 AM,SG1\DB2,100
SFEX01,10/27/2006 3:15:00 AM,SG1\DB1,100
SFEX01,10/27/2006 3:15:00 AM,SG1\DB2,200
SFEX01,10/27/2006 4:00:00 AM,SG1\DB1,200
SFEX01,10/27/2006 4:00:00 AM,SG1\DB2,100
```

This script was developed for companyabc.com, a marketing firm of 50 users that has very large (4GB and up) Exchange mailboxes. It produces marketing packages consisting of digital images, which result in an average package size of more than 20MB. companyabc. com's employees are scattered among many home offices and remote locations, so they usually e-mail marketing packages to each other instead of posting them to a shared location.

Because employees have been using their mailboxes as online file systems, mailbox sizes have grown rapidly. Realizing that mailboxes of this size would be costly and difficult to maintain, companyabc.com's Exchange administrator has requested that marketing content be saved locally to users' hard drives and then deleted from their mailboxes. This practice has kept the Exchange databases from growing too quickly; however, the high deletion rate of large e-mail messages has created another problem: large areas of white-space in Exchange databases.

The amount of whitespace is important because after an Exchange database grows, its size can't be decreased until the administrator does an offline defragmentation. For example, a database has grown to 12GB, but users have deleted 3GB of messages. After an online defragmentation, Event ID 1221 logs report 3GB of whitespace. New messages written to the database use this whitespace, and the database doesn't grow until that whitespace is exhausted.

The database still takes up 12GB on the hard drive, even though it contains only 9GB of data. A larger than necessary database can increase the time needed for backup and restore jobs. By reviewing Event ID 1221 messages, administrators can determine whether an offline defragmentation is needed to shrink the database in an effort to improve overall performance. Furthermore, with periodic review of Event ID 1221 logs, administrators can track a database's average whitespace amount, which helps determine the growth patterns of actual data in a database. This information can be helpful in deciding when additional space needs to be allocated for a database.

With no budget available to purchase a suite of Exchange tools, companyabc.com requested the development of a script for monitoring the amount of whitespace in Exchange databases. The resulting script is GetEvent1221Info.ps1.

A working copy is in the Scripts\Chapter 11\GetEvent1221Info folder and is downloadable at www.samspublishing.com. Running this script requires defining one parameter. The Days parameter should have its argument set to the time period (in number of days) for querying Event ID 1221 messages from mailbox servers. An optional parameter, ExportFile, should have its argument set to the name of the CSV file where you want to export report data. Here's the command to run the GetEvent1221Info.ps1 script:

```
PS C:\Scripts> .\GetEvent1221Info.ps1 5
```

Figures 11.4 and 11.5 shows the execution of the GetEvent1221Info.ps1 script.

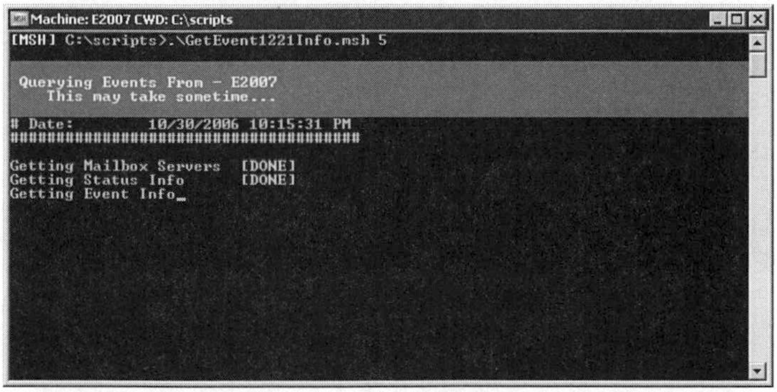

FIGURE 11.4   The GetEvent1221Info.ps1 script being executed

FIGURE 11.5   The GetEvent1221Info.ps1 script after being executed

The GetEvent1221Info.ps1 script performs the following sequence of actions:

1. The script creates two DataTable objects: $ServersTable, used to store status infor-
mation for Exchange mailbox servers, and $EventsTable, used to store the Event ID
1221 report.

2. The script creates an error log named GetEvent1221Info_Errors.log by using the
Out-File cmdlet. This error log gives users detailed error information.

3. The script uses the Get-MailboxServer cmdlet to get a list of all Exchange mailbox
servers, which is then populated to the $MailboxServers variable.

4. The script uses the System.Net.NetworkInformation.Ping class to ping each server
in the $MailboxServers object collection. If a server replies, a new row is added to
$ServersTable consisting of the server's name and its "Online" status. If a server
doesn't reply, a new row is added with the server's status set to "Offline".

5. The listing of servers and their status information is sent to the script's error log for
future reference by using the Out-File cmdlet.

6. For each server with an "Online" status in $ServersTable, the script does the
following:

   ▶ The Get-RemoteEventLog function is used to create an object ($Events) bound
   to the server's Application log. To create the object, the function uses the .NET
   System.Diagnostics.Eventlog class, which allows an application or script to
   interact with a machine's event log.

   ▶ Next, the script uses the Select-Object cmdlet to select all the 1221 events
   from the $Events object's Entries property that fall within the specified
   period ($Days). The resulting collection of events is populated to the
   $1221Events variable.

   ▶ For each $1221Event in the $1221Events object collection, the script then uses
   the get_timewritten() method of $1221Event to populate the $TimeWritten

variable with the time the event was written. Next, a regular expression is used to strip the database's free space ($MB) and name ($Database) from the event message.

▶ A row is added to $EventsTable containing the server's name ($Server.Name), time the event was written ($TimeWritten), database name ($Database), and free space in megabytes ($MB).

7. The script exports all data from $EventsTable by using the Export-DataTable function.

The first code snippet contains the header for the GetEvent1221Info.ps1 script. This header includes information about what the script does, when it was updated, and the script's author. Just after the header are the script's parameters:

```
##################################################
# GetEvent1221Info.ps1
# Used to consolidate 1221 events from mailbox servers.
#
# Created: 10/26/2006
# Author: Tyson Kopczynski
##################################################
param([int] $Days, [string] $ExportFile)
```

Next, the Get-RemoteEventLog function is loaded. This function is used to collect remote EventLog information from a machine using the System.Diagnostics.Eventlog class. Then the Export-DataTable function is loaded. This function was discussed in the previous section:

```
##################################################
# Functions
##################################################
#--------------------------------------------------
# Get-RemoteEventLog
#--------------------------------------------------
# Usage:       Used to collect remote EventLog information from a machine.
# $Machine:    The name of the machine. ("MyServer")
# $Log:        The name of the EventLog. ("Application")

function Get-RemoteEventLog{
    param ($Machine, $Log)

    trap{Continue}
```

```
    new-object System.Diagnostics.Eventlog $Log, $Machine
    }

#------------------------------------------------
# Export-DataTable
#------------------------------------------------
# Usage:        Used to export a DataSet to a CSV file.
# $Data:        A DataSet object.
# $FileName:    The name of the export CSV file.

function Export-DataTable{
    param ($Data, $FileName)

    $Null = `
        [System.Reflection.Assembly]::LoadWithPartialName( `
            "System.Windows.Forms")

    trap{write-host "[ERROR] $_" -Foregroundcolor Red; Continue}

    if ($FileName -eq ""){
        $exFileName = new-object System.Windows.Forms.saveFileDialog
        $exFileName.DefaultExt = "csv"
        $exFileName.Filter = "CSV (Comma delimited)(*.csv)|*.csv"
        $exFileName.ShowDialog()

        $FileName = $exFileName.FileName
        }

    if ($FileName -ne ""){
        $LogFile = new-object System.IO.StreamWriter($FileName, $False)

        for ($i=0; $i -le $Data.Columns.Count-1; $i++){
           $LogFile.Write($Data.Columns[$i].ColumnName)

            if ($i -lt $Data.Columns.Count-1){
                $LogFile.Write(",")
                }
            }

        $LogFile.WriteLine()

        foreach ($Row in $Data.Rows){
            for ($i=0; $i -le $Data.Columns.Count-1; $i++){
                $LogFile.Write($Row[$i].ToString())
```

```
                    if ($i -lt $Data.Columns.Count-1){
                        $LogFile.Write(",")
                        }
                    }

                $LogFile.WriteLine()
                }

        $LogFile.Close()
        }
    }
```

In the next code snippet, variables that will be used later in the script are defined. In addition, the library file `LibraryGen.ps1`, which contains the script usage functions, is being dot sourced:

```
#################################################
# Main
#################################################
#--------------------
# Load Libraries
#--------------------
. .\LibraryGen.ps1

#--------------------
# Set Config Vars
#--------------------
$ScriptName = "GetEvent1221Info.ps1"
$ScriptUsage = "Used to consolidate 1221 events from mailbox servers."
$ScriptCommand = "$ScriptName -Days value -ExportFile value"
$ScriptParams = "Days = The number of days to filter events by.", `
    "ExportFile = The export CSV file path/filename."
$ScriptExamples = "$ScriptName 5 ""report.csv"""
$ErrorLogName = "GetEvent1221Info.log"
$Date = Date
```

Next, the script checks to see if the script user needed any usage help. If no help is needed the script then checks to see if the `Days` parameter has been defined. If this parameter has not been defined, the script then informs the script operator that the parameter is required and shows the script usage information, as shown in the following code snippet:

```
#--------------------
# Verify Required Parameters
#--------------------
if ($args[0] -match '-(\?¦(h¦(help)))'){
    write-host
    Get-ScriptHeader $ScriptName $ScriptUsage
    Show-ScriptUsage $ScriptCommand $ScriptParams $ScriptExamples
    Return
    }

if (!$Days){
    write-host
    write-host "Please specify the number of days!" -Foregroundcolor Red
    write-host
    Get-ScriptHeader $ScriptName $ScriptUsage
    Show-ScriptUsage $ScriptCommand $ScriptParams $ScriptExamples
    Return
    }
```

Then in the next code snippet, the two DataTable objects are created. The first `DataTable` is the `$ServersTable`, which will store server information, and the second `DataTable` is the `$EventsTable`, which will store the report information:

```
#--------------------
# Define DataSets
#--------------------
$ServersTable = new-object System.Data.DataTable
$ServersTable.TableName = "Servers"
[Void]$ServersTable.Columns.Add("Name")
[Void]$ServersTable.Columns.Add("Status")

$EventsTable = new-object System.Data.DataTable
$EventsTable.TableName = "Servers"
[Void]$EventsTable.Columns.Add("Server")
[Void]$EventsTable.Columns.Add("TimeWritten",[DateTime])
[Void]$EventsTable.Columns.Add("Database")
[Void]$EventsTable.Columns.Add("MB")
```

Next, the `Out-File` cmdlet is used to create an error log and write header information to it. Then the `Get-ScriptHeader` function is used to indicate to the script operator that the automation portion of the script has started:

```
#- - - - - - - - - - - - - - - - - -
# Begin Script
#- - - - - - - - - - - - - - - - - -
# Setup ErrorLog
$ScriptName + " Ran on: " + $Date ¦ out-file $ErrorLogName

write-host
Get-ScriptHeader $ScriptName $ScriptUsage
write-host
```

The next task is to get a list of mailbox servers using the Get-MailboxServer cmdlet. Then
for each server object in $MailboxServers variable, the script pings that server to deter-
mine its status. During this task, both the resulting status and the server's name are
written to a new row in the $ServersTable DataTable, as shown in the next code snippet:

```
#- - - - - - - - - - - - - - - - - -
# Get Servers and Status
#- - - - - - - - - - - - - - - - - -
write-host "Getting Mailbox Servers" -NoNewLine
$MailboxServers = get-mailboxserver
write-host `t "[DONE]" -Foregroundcolor Green

write-host "Getting Status Info" -NoNewLine

$MailboxServers ¦ foreach-object -Begin {$i=0;} `
    -Process {&{$Ping = new-object Net.NetworkInformation.Ping;
            $MBServerName = $_.Name;
            trap{"Ping [ERROR]: " + $MBServerName + " $_" ¦ out-file `
                $ErrorLogName -Append; Continue};
            $Result = $Ping.Send($MBServerName);
            if ($Result.Status -eq "Success"){ `
                [Void]$ServersTable.Rows.Add($MBServerName, "Online")} `
            else{[Void]$ServersTable.Rows.Add($MBServerName, "Offline")};
            $i = $i+1;
            write-progress -Activity "Pinging Servers - $($MBServerName)" `
                -Status "Progress:" `
                -PercentComplete ($i / $MailboxServers.Count * 100)}}

write-host `t "[DONE]" -Foregroundcolor Green

# Write status info to ErrorLog
$ServersTable ¦ out-file $ErrorLogName –Append
```

In the next code snippet, the script generates the final report. To do this, the script uses the `DataTable Select()` method to create a collection of online server objects (`$OnlineServers`). Then for each server in `$OnlineServers` object collection, the script uses the `Get-RemoteEventLog` function to retrieve all of the Application event messages from that server. For each event message retrieved with an event ID of 1221, a new row is then added to the `$EventsTable` DataTable which contains formatted information from the event message and the server's name:

```
#-------------------
# Get Event Info
#-------------------
write-host "Getting Event Info"  -NoNewLine

$OnlineServers = $ServersTable.Select("Status = 'Online'")

foreach ($Server in $OnlineServers){
    &{
        trap{"Event Info [Error]: " + $Server.Name + " $_" ¦ `
            out-file $ErrorLogName -Append; Continue}

        $Events = Get-RemoteEventLog $Server.Name "Application"

        # This may take a long time depending on the number of servers
        write-progress -Activity "Querying Events From - $($Server.Name)" `
            -Status "This may take sometime..."

        $1221Events = $Events.Entries ¦ where {$_.EventID -eq "1221" -and `
            $_.TimeWritten -ge $Date.AddDays(-$Days)}

        foreach ($1221Event in $1221Events){
            &{
                $Message = $1221Event ¦ select Message
                $TimeWritten = $1221Event.get_timewritten()

                # This RegEx strips out the database name from the message
                $Database = [Regex]::Match($Message, '"[^"\r\n]*"')
                $Database = $Database.Value.Replace('"', "")

                # This RegEx strips out size of the whitespace
                $MB = [Regex]::Match($Message, '[0-9]+')

                [Void]$EventsTable.Rows.Add($Server.Name, $TimeWritten, `
                    $Database, $MB)
            }
        }
```

```
        }

      write-progress -Activity "Querying Events From - $($Server.Name)" `
        -Status "Done" -completed $True
    }
    }

write-host `t "[DONE]" -Foregroundcolor Green
```

Last, the script exports the report information from the $EventsTable DataTable using
the Export-DataTable function:

```
#-------------------
# Export Data to CSV File
#-------------------
$Null = Export-DataTable $EventsTable $ExportFile

write-host
write-host "Script is now DONE!" -Foregroundcolor Green
write-host "Check the $ErrorLogName for errors." -Foregroundcolor Yellow
```

The ProvisionExchangeUsers.ps1 Script

With the ProvisionExchangeUsers.ps1 script, Exchange administrators can provision
mail-enabled user accounts in Exchange Server 2007 environments quickly and easily
based on information in a CSV import file. This file is structured as follows:

- ▶ The user's first name
- ▶ The user's last name
- ▶ The user's e-mail alias
- ▶ The fully qualified database name

Here's an example of the import file:

```
FName,LName,Alias,Database
Stu,Gronko,sgronko,SFEX01\SG1\DB1
Caelie,Hallauer,challauer,SFEX02\SG2\DB2
Duane,Putnam,dputnam,SFEX02\SG2\DB2
Essie,Fea,efea,SFEX02\SG1\DB1
Rona,Trovato,rtrovato,SFEX01\SG1\DB2
Gottfried,Leibniz,gleibniz,SFEx01\SG1\DB1
```

With some tweaking to the code in ProvisionExchangeUsers.ps1, the format of the CSV import file and the information for provisioning mail-enabled user accounts can be tailored to fit any environment. This flexibility is important to meet ever-changing automation needs.

This script was requested by companyabc.com, a large technology company, in the process of completing several mergers resulting in the need to provision many new mail-enabled user accounts. Because of the number of accounts to create and the varying information for each merger's account-provisioning process, an automated method that could be changed to meet different needs is the best solution. To meet the flexibility requirements, companyabc.com's IT department has developed the ProvisionExchangeUsers.ps1 script.

A working copy is in the Scripts\Chapter 11\ProvisionExchangeUsers folder and is downloadable at www.samspublishing.com. Running this script requires defining three parameters. UPNSuffix should have its argument set to the UPN (universal principal name) suffix for new mail-enabled accounts. OUDN should have its argument set to the distinguishedName of the OU where new mail-enabled accounts should be stored. ImportFile should have its argument set to the name of the CSV import file containing the list of users to create. Here's the command to run the ProvisionExchangeUsers.ps1 script:

```
PS C:\Scripts> .\ProvisionExchangeUsers.ps1 "companyabc.com"
"OU=Accounts,DC=companyabc,DC=com" users.csv
```

Figures 11.6 and 11.7 shows the execution of the ProvisionExchangeUsers.ps1 script.

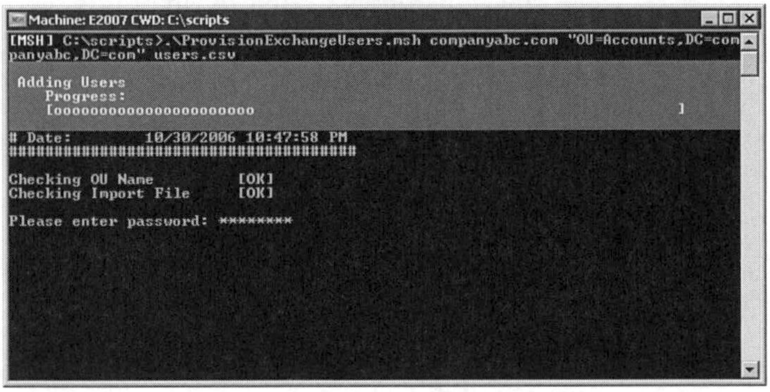

FIGURE 11.6   The ProvisionExchangeUsers.ps1 script being executed

FIGURE 11.7   The ProvisionExchangeUsers.ps1 script after being executed

The ProvisionExchangeUsers.ps1 script performs the following sequence of actions:

1. The script creates an error log named ProvisionExchangeUsers_Errors.log by using the Out-File cmdlet. This error log gives users detailed error information.

2. The script connects to the current logon domain by using Get-CurrentDomain function. Using the object returned from this function, the script writes the domain's name to the PowerShell console. If this connection fails, the script halts.

3. The script verifies that the specified OU exists in the current domain by using the Get-ADObject function. If the OU isn't valid, the script halts.

4. The script uses the Test-Path cmdlet to verify that the import file is valid. If the file is invalid, the script halts.

5. The script uses the Read-Host cmdlet and its AsSecureString parameter to request the password for all new user accounts. The resulting secure string is then populated into the $Password variable.

6. The script uses the Import-Csv cmdlet to populate the $Users variable with the CSV import file's contents.

7. For each user in the $Users object collection, the script uses the New-Mailbox cmdlet to create a mail-enabled user account based on information in the CSV file and information provided by the user. Errors generated during account creation are sent to the script's error log by using the Out-File cmdlet.

The first code snippet contains the header for the ProvisionExchangeUsers.ps1 script. This header includes information about what the script does, when it was updated, and the script's author. Just after the header are the script's parameters:

```
***Begin gray code box***
##################################################
# ProvisionExchangeUsers.ps1
# Used to provision Exchange users based on CSV import file.
#
# Created: 10/21/2006
# Author: Tyson Kopczynski
##################################################
param([string] $UPNSuffix, [string] $OUDN, [string] $ImportFile)
```

In the next code snippet, variables that will be used later in the script are defined. In addition, the library file LibraryGen.ps1, which contains the script usage functions, is being dot sourced:

```
##################################################
# Main
##################################################
#--------------------
# Load Libraries
#--------------------
. .\LibraryGen.ps1

#--------------------
# Set Config Vars
#--------------------
$ScriptName = "ProvisionExchangeUsers.ps1"
$ScriptUsage = "Used to provision Exchange users based on CSV import file."
$ScriptCommand = "$ScriptName -UPNSuffix value -OUDN value -ImportFile value"
$ScriptParams = "UPNSuffix = The new users UPN suffix.", `
    "OUDN = The distinguishedName of the OU to create users in.", `
    "ImportFile = The import CSV file path/filename."
$ScriptExamples = "$ScriptName ""companyabc.com""" `
    + " ""OU=Accounts,DC=companyabc,DC=com""" `
    + " ""users.csv"""
$ErrorLogName = "ProvisionExchangeUsers.log"
$Date = Date
```

As shown in the following code snippet, the script next checks to see if the script user needed any usage help. If no help is needed, the script then checks to see if the UPNSuffix, OUDN, and ImportFile parameters have been defined. If either of these parameters has not been defined, the script then informs the script operator that the parameter is required and shows the script usage information:

```
#-------------------
# Verify Required Parameters
#-------------------
if ($args[0] -match '-(\?¦(h¦(help)))'){
    write-host
    Get-ScriptHeader $ScriptName $ScriptUsage
    Show-ScriptUsage $ScriptCommand $ScriptParams $ScriptExamples
    Return
    }

if (!$UPNSuffix){
    write-host
    write-host "Please specify the UPN suffix!" -Foregroundcolor Red
    write-host
    Get-ScriptHeader $ScriptName $ScriptUsage
    Show-ScriptUsage $ScriptCommand $ScriptParams $ScriptExamples
    Return
    }

if (!$OUDN){
    write-host
    write-host "Please specify the OU to create users in!" `
            -Foregroundcolor Red
    write-host
    Get-ScriptHeader $ScriptName $ScriptUsage
    Show-ScriptUsage $ScriptCommand $ScriptParams $ScriptExamples
    Return
    }

if (!$ImportFile){
    write-host
    write-host "Please specify the import CSV file name!" `
            -Foregroundcolor Red
    write-host
    Get-ScriptHeader $ScriptName $ScriptUsage
    Show-ScriptUsage $ScriptCommand $ScriptParams $ScriptExamples
    Return
    }
```

Next the `Out-File` cmdlet is used to create an error log and write header information to it. Then the `Get-ScriptHeader` function is used to indicate to the script operator that the automation portion of the script has started:

```
#-------------------
# Begin Script
#-------------------
# Setup ErrorLog
$ScriptName + " Ran on: " + $Date ¦ out-file $ErrorLogName

write-host
Get-ScriptHeader $ScriptName $ScriptUsage
write-host
write-host "Domain Connection" –NoNewLine
```

The next step is for the script to verify that there is a valid domain connection. To accomplish this task, the script uses the `Get-CurrentDomain`. If a valid domain connection doesn't exist, the script halts and returns the script status to the operator. If a connection does exist, the script continues execution and writes the domain name to the console, as shown in the next code snippet:

```
.{
    trap{write-host `t "[ERROR]" -Foregroundcolor Red;
        throw write-host $_ -Foregroundcolor Red;
        Break}

    write-host "Domain Connection" -NoNewLine

    # You need to test for a domain connection
    $Domain = Get-CurrentDomain

    # You then return the domain's name
    write-host `t $Domain.Name -Foregroundcolor Green
}
```

In the next code snippet, the distinguished name in the `$OUDN` variable is verified. To perform the verification, the script uses `Get-ADObject` function. This function connects to Active Directory and completes a search for the OU by its distinguished name. If an object is returned from the function, then the OU is valid; if no object is returned, the OU is considered invalid and the script halts:

```
write-host "Checking OU Name" -NoNewLine

if (!(Get-ADObject "distinguishedName" $OUDN "organizationalUnit")){
    write-host `t "Is not valid!" -Foregroundcolor Red
    write-host
    Break
    }
else{
    write-host `t "[OK]" -Foregroundcolor Green
    }
```

Then the script verifies that the import file is a valid file using the Test-Path cmdlet:

```
write-host "Checking Import File" -NoNewLine

if (!(test-path $ImportFile -pathType Leaf)){
    throw write-host `t "Is not a valid file!" -Foregroundcolor Red
    }
else{
    write-host `t "[OK]" -Foregroundcolor Green
    }
```

Next, to collect the password from the user, the script uses the Read-Host cmdlet with the AsSecureString switch, as shown in the next code snippet:

```
#--------------------
# Get Password
#--------------------
write-host
$Password = read-host "Please enter password" –AsSecureString
```

Last, the script provisions the new user accounts using the New-Mailbox cmdlet, information from the import file, and information provided by the script user:

```
#--------------------
# Create mailboxes
#--------------------
write-host
write-progress -Activity "Adding Users" -Status "Stand by..."

$Users = import-csv $ImportFile

$Users ¦ foreach-object -Begin {$i=0;} `
        -Process {$FName = $_.FName;
            $LName = $_.LName;
            $Alias = $_.Alias;
            $Database = $_.Database;
            $UPN = $Alias + "@" + $UPNSuffix;
            $Name = $FName + " " + $LName;
            $Null = new-mailbox -Name $Name -Database $Database `
                -OrganizationalUnit $OUDN -UserPrincipalName $UPN `
                -Password $Password -ResetPasswordOnNextLogon $True `
                -Alias $Alias -DisplayName $Name -FirstName $FName `
                -LastName $LName -ErrorVariable Err -ErrorAction `
                SilentlyContinue;
            if ($Err.Count -ne 0){ `
                "Add User [ERROR]: " + $Alias + " " + $Err ¦ `
                out-file $ErrorLogName -Append};
            $i = $i+1;
            write-progress -Activity "Adding Users" -Status "Progress:" `
                -PercentComplete ($i / $Users.Count * 100)}

write-host "Script is now DONE!" -Foregroundcolor Green
write-host "Check the $ErrorLogName for errors." -Foregroundcolor Yellow
```

Summary

In this chapter, you were introduced to how PowerShell is used to manage Exchange
Server 2007 through not only a GUI using the EMC, but also the command line using the
EMS. Exchange Server 2007 is the first of what will be many applications that use
PowerShell in this fashion. To accomplish this feat, Exchange Server 2007 makes use of
PowerShell's ability to be extended through the use of snap-ins. By using a snap-in, more
cmdlets are made available to a PowerShell user, thus further increasing their ability to
manage an Exchange organization.

The scripts that were reviewed in this chapter served as a good demonstration of what can
be accomplished using the Exchange Server 2007 snap-in. Thanks to these examples, you
should now have an understanding about how to use PowerShell to gather Exchange

database size information, calculate a database's whitespace, and quickly provision mail-enabled users. But, the limits to what can be accomplished around Exchange management don't stop there. Rather, as it has been stressed throughout this book, the limits to what can be done with PowerShell should in many respects only be bounded by your own scripting talent and imagination.

Opening your mind to the concept of what scripting can accomplish is by far the first step in understanding what PowerShell can do for you. True, you need to understand what PowerShell is before you can tackle grander and more elaborate automation needs. However, by taking that first step, you have started down a journey of discovery that will ultimately lead to using PowerShell as the PowerShell development team envisioned.

Aspects of this book should have assisted you with starting this journey in two areas. First, the book allowed you to gain an understanding of what PowerShell is and how to use it. However, background information and feature explanations were kept to only several chapters by focusing on topics most important to gaining a working understanding of PowerShell. Second, this book approached PowerShell usage from an angle not normally seen. That angle was to not try and explain every single nuance of PowerShell's features and language syntax. Instead, this book zeroed in on how to apply PowerShell.

To show the application of PowerShell, there were a number of chapters that showed comparisons between Windows scripting and PowerShell. In these comparisons, both command-line examples and working scripts were analyzed using VBScript and PowerShell. By doing this, the goal was to allow you to relate your existing Windows scripting knowledge to new PowerShell concepts. The last two chapters were dedicated to showing you how PowerShell might be used to meet various automation needs and how PowerShell is used to manage Exchange Server 2007. Again like the previous chapters, the focus of these chapters was on the application of PowerShell.

Now, having reached the end of this book, your journey continues. PowerShell is one of the more amazing products to come out of Microsoft in a long time. Jeffrey Snover and the rest of the PowerShell team should be given a lot of credit for seeing a need and then developing PowerShell to meet that need. In time, as more and more Microsoft and third-party applications adopt using PowerShell, the scope to what can be accomplished will only further materialize. As a result, the depth to what you will be able to accomplish using PowerShell will only continue to grow.

Index

Symbols

A

R

Safari ®
BOOKS ONLINE
ENABLED

THIS BOOK IS SAFARI ENABLED

INCLUDES FREE 45-DAY ACCESS TO THE ONLINE EDITION

The Safari® Enabled icon on the cover of your favorite technology book means the book is available through Safari Bookshelf. When you buy this book, you get free access to the online edition for 45 days.

Safari Bookshelf is an electronic reference library that lets you easily search thousands of technical books, find code samples, download chapters, and access technical information whenever and wherever you need it.

TO GAIN 45-DAY SAFARI ENABLED ACCESS TO THIS BOOK:

● Go to **http://www.samspublishing.com/safarienabled**

● Complete the brief registration form

● Enter the coupon code found in the front of this book on the "Copyright" page

If you have difficulty registering on Safari Bookshelf or accessing the online edition, please e-mail customer-service@safaribooksonline.com.

UNLEASHED

Unleashed takes you beyond the basics, providing an exhaustive, technically sophisticated reference for professionals who need to exploit a technology to its fullest potential. It's the best resource for practical advice from the experts, and the most in-depth coverage of the latest technologies.

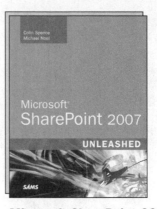

Microsoft SharePoint 2007 Unleashed
ISBN: 0672329476

OTHER UNLEASHED TITLES

ASP.NET 2.0 Unleashed
ISBN: 0672328232

Microsoft BizTalk Server 2006 Unleashed
ISBN: 0672329255

Microsoft ISA Server 2006 Unleashed
ISBN: 0672329190

Microsoft Office Project Server 2007 Unleashed
ISBN: 0672329212

Microsoft SharePoint 2007 Development Unleashed
ISBN: 0672329034

Microsoft Small Business Server 2003 Unleashed
ISBN: 0672328054

Microsoft SQL Server 2005 Unleashed
ISBN: 0672328240

Microsoft Visual C# 2005 Unleashed
ISBN: 0672327767

Microsoft Windows Server 2003 Unleashed (R2 Edition)
ISBN: 0672328984

Studio 2005 Unleashed
ISBN: 0672328194

Windows Presentation Foundation Unleashed
ISBN: 0672328917

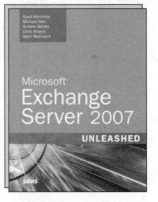

Microsoft Exchange Server 2007 Unleashed
ISBN: 0672329204

Microsoft Windows Vista Unleashed
ISBN: 0672328941

SAMS

www.samspublishing.com